Async & Performance

Kyle Simpson

Beijing · Cambridge · Farnham · Köln · Sebastopol · Tokyo

Async & Performance

by Kyle Simpson

Printed in the United States of America.

Published by O'Reilly Media, Inc., 1005 Gravenstein Highway North, Sebastopol, CA 95472.

O'Reilly books may be purchased for educational, business, or sales promotional use. Online editions are also available for most titles (*http://safaribooksonline.com*). For more information, contact our corporate/institutional sales department: 800-998-9938 or *corporate@oreilly.com*.

Editors: Simon St. Laurent and Brian MacDonald
Production Editor: Kristen Brown
Copyeditor: Jasmine Kwityn
Proofreader: Phil Dangler
Interior Designer: David Futato
Cover Designer: Ellie Volckhausen

March 2015:   First Edition

Revision History for the First Edition
2015-02-19:   First Release

See *http://oreilly.com/catalog/errata.csp?isbn=9781491904220* for release details.

978-1-491-90422-0

[LSI]

Table of Contents

Foreword

Over the years, my employer has trusted me enough to conduct interviews. If we're looking for someone with JavaScript skills, my first line of questioning...well, actually, is to check if the candidate needs the bathroom and/or a drink, because comfort is important. But once I'm past the bit about the candidate's fluid intake/output, I set about determining if the candidate knows JavaScript, or just jQuery.

Not that there's anything wrong with jQuery. It lets you do a lot without really knowing JavaScript, and that's a feature—not a bug. But if the job calls for advanced skills in JavaScript performance and maintainability, you need someone who knows how libraries such as jQuery are put together. You need to be able to harness the core of JavaScript the same way they do.

If I want to get a picture of someone's core JavaScript skill, I'm most interested in what they make of closures (you've read the *You Don't Know JS: Scope & Closures* title of this series already, right?) and how to get the most out of asynchronicity, which brings us to this book.

For starters, you'll be taken through callbacks, the bread and butter of asynchronous programming. Of course, bread and butter does not make for a particularly satisfying meal, but the next course is full of tasty, tasty Promises!

If you don't know Promises, now is the time to learn. Promises are now the official way to provide async return values in both Java-Script and the DOM. All future async DOM APIs will use them, and many already do, so be prepared! At the time of writing, Promises have shipped in most major browsers, with IE shipping soon. Once you've finished savoring Promises, I hope you left room for the next course, Generators.

Generators snuck their way into stable versions of Chrome and Firefox without too much pomp and ceremony, because, frankly, they're more complicated than they are interesting. Or, that's what I thought until I saw them combined with Promises. There, they become an important tool in readability and maintenance.

For dessert, well, I won't spoil the surprise, but prepare to gaze into the future of JavaScript! This book covers features that give you more and more control over concurrency and asynchronicity.

Well, I won't block your enjoyment of the book any longer—on with the show! If you've already read part of the book before reading this foreword, give yourself 10 asynchronous points! You deserve them!

—*Jake Archibald (http://jakearchibald.com, @jaffathecake),*
Developer Advocate at Google Chrome

Preface

I'm sure you noticed, but "JS" in the series title is not an abbreviation for words used to curse about JavaScript, though cursing at the language's quirks is something we can probably all identify with!

From the earliest days of the Web, JavaScript has been a foundational technology that drives interactive experience around the content we consume. While flickering mouse trails and annoying pop-up prompts may be where JavaScript started, nearly two decades later, the technology and capability of JavaScript has grown many orders of magnitude, and few doubt its importance at the heart of the world's most widely available software platform: the Web.

But as a language, it has perpetually been a target for a great deal of criticism, owing partly to its heritage but even more to its design philosophy. Even the name evokes, as Brendan Eich once put it, "dumb kid brother" status next to its more mature older brother Java. But the name is merely an accident of politics and marketing. The two languages are vastly different in many important ways. "JavaScript" is as related to "Java" as "Carnival" is to "Car."

Because JavaScript borrows concepts and syntax idioms from several languages, including proud C-style procedural roots as well as subtle, less obvious Scheme/Lisp-style functional roots, it is exceedingly approachable to a broad audience of developers, even those with little to no programming experience. The "Hello World" of JavaScript is so simple that the language is inviting and easy to get comfortable with in early exposure.

While JavaScript is perhaps one of the easiest languages to get up and running with, its eccentricities make solid mastery of the language a vastly less common occurrence than in many other languages. Where it takes a pretty in-depth knowledge of a language like C or C++ to write a full-scale program, full-scale production JavaScript can, and often does, barely scratch the surface of what the language can do.

Sophisticated concepts that are deeply rooted into the language tend instead to surface themselves in *seemingly* simplistic ways, such as passing around functions as callbacks, which encourages the JavaScript developer to just use the language as-is and not worry too much about what's going on under the hood.

It is simultaneously a simple, easy-to-use language that has broad appeal, and a complex and nuanced collection of language mechanics that without careful study will elude *true understanding* even for the most seasoned of JavaScript developers.

Therein lies the paradox of JavaScript, the Achilles' heel of the language, the challenge we are presently addressing. Because JavaScript *can* be used without understanding, the understanding of the language is often never attained.

Mission

If at every point that you encounter a surprise or frustration in JavaScript, your response is to add it to the blacklist (as some are accustomed to doing), you soon will be relegated to a hollow shell of the richness of JavaScript.

While this subset has been famously dubbed "The Good Parts," I would implore you, dear reader, to instead consider it the "The Easy Parts," "The Safe Parts," or even "The Incomplete Parts."

This *You Don't Know JS* series offers a contrary challenge: learn and deeply understand *all* of JavaScript, even and especially "The Tough Parts."

Here, we address head-on the tendency of JS developers to learn "just enough" to get by, without ever forcing themselves to learn exactly how and why the language behaves the way it does. Furthermore, we eschew the common advice to retreat when the road gets rough.

I am not content, nor should you be, at stopping once something just works and not really knowing *why*. I gently challenge you to journey down that bumpy "road less traveled" and embrace all that JavaScript is and can do. With that knowledge, no technique, no framework, no popular buzzword acronym of the week will be beyond your understanding.

These books each take on specific core parts of the language that are most commonly misunderstood or under-understood, and dive very deep and exhaustively into them. You should come away from reading with a firm confidence in your understanding, not just of the theoretical, but the practical "what you need to know" bits.

The JavaScript you know right now is probably parts handed down to you by others who've been burned by incomplete understanding. *That* JavaScript is but a shadow of the true language. You don't really know JavaScript *yet*, but if you dig into this series, you will. Read on, my friends. JavaScript awaits you.

Review

JavaScript is awesome. It's easy to learn partially, and much harder to learn completely (or even *sufficiently*). When developers encounter confusion, they usually blame the language instead of their lack of understanding. These books aim to fix that, inspiring a strong appreciation for the language you can now, and *should*, deeply know.

 Many of the examples in this book assume modern (and future-reaching) JavaScript engine environments, such as ES6. Some code may not work as described if run in older (pre-ES6) engines.

Conventions Used in This Book

The following typographical conventions are used in this book:

Italic
    Indicates new terms, URLs, email addresses, filenames, and file extensions.

Constant width

Used for program listings, as well as within paragraphs to refer to program elements such as variable or function names, databases, data types, environment variables, statements, and keywords.

Constant width bold

Shows commands or other text that should be typed literally by the user.

Constant width italic

Shows text that should be replaced with user-supplied values or by values determined by context.

This element signifies a tip or suggestion.

This element signifies a general note.

This element indicates a warning or caution.

Using Code Examples

Supplemental material (code examples, exercises, etc.) is available for download at *http://bit.ly/ydkjs-async-code*.

This book is here to help you get your job done. In general, if example code is offered with this book, you may use it in your programs and documentation. You do not need to contact us for permission unless you're reproducing a significant portion of the code. For example, writing a program that uses several chunks of code from this book does not require permission. Selling or distributing a CD-ROM of examples from O'Reilly books does require permission. Answering a question by citing this book and quoting example code does not require permission. Incorporating a significant amount of example code from this book into your product's documentation does require permission.

We appreciate, but do not require, attribution. An attribution usually includes the title, author, publisher, and ISBN. For example: "*You Don't Know JavaScript: Async & Performance* by Kyle Simpson (O'Reilly). Copyright 2015 Getify Solutions, Inc., 978-1-491-90422-0."

If you feel your use of code examples falls outside fair use or the permission given above, feel free to contact us at *permissions@oreilly.com*.

Safari® Books Online

 *Safari Books Online* is an on-demand digital library that delivers expert content in both book and video form from the world's leading authors in technology and business.

Technology professionals, software developers, web designers, and business and creative professionals use Safari Books Online as their primary resource for research, problem solving, learning, and certification training.

Safari Books Online offers a range of plans and pricing for enterprise, government, education, and individuals.

Members have access to thousands of books, training videos, and prepublication manuscripts in one fully searchable database from publishers like O'Reilly Media, Prentice Hall Professional, Addison-Wesley Professional, Microsoft Press, Sams, Que, Peachpit Press, Focal Press, Cisco Press, John Wiley & Sons, Syngress, Morgan Kaufmann, IBM Redbooks, Packt, Adobe Press, FT Press, Apress, Manning, New Riders, McGraw-Hill, Jones & Bartlett, Course Technology, and hundreds more. For more information about Safari Books Online, please visit us online.

How to Contact Us

Please address comments and questions concerning this book to the publisher:

O'Reilly Media, Inc.
1005 Gravenstein Highway North
Sebastopol, CA 95472
800-998-9938 (in the United States or Canada)
707-829-0515 (international or local)
707-829-0104 (fax)

We have a web page for this book, where we list errata, examples, and any additional information. You can access this page at *http://bit.ly/ydkjs-async-performance*.

To comment or ask technical questions about this book, send email to *bookquestions@oreilly.com*.

For more information about our books, courses, conferences, and news, see our website at *http://www.oreilly.com*.

Find us on Facebook: *http://facebook.com/oreilly*

Follow us on Twitter: *http://twitter.com/oreillymedia*

Watch us on YouTube: *http://www.youtube.com/oreillymedia*

CHAPTER 1

Asynchrony: Now & Later

One of the most important and yet often misunderstood parts of programming in a language like JavaScript is how to express and manipulate program behavior spread out over a period of time.

This is not just about what happens from the beginning of a for loop to the end of a for loop, which of course takes some time (microseconds to milliseconds) to complete. It's about what happens when part of your program runs *now*, and another part of your program runs *later*—there's a gap between *now* and *later* where your program isn't actively executing.

Practically all nontrivial programs ever written (especially in JS) have in some way or another had to manage this gap, whether that be in waiting for user input, requesting data from a database or file system, sending data across the network and waiting for a response, or performing a repeated task at a fixed interval of time (like animation). In all these various ways, your program has to manage state across the gap in time. As they famously say in London (of the chasm between the subway door and the platform): "mind the gap."

In fact, the relationship between the *now* and *later* parts of your program is at the heart of asynchronous programming.

Asynchronous programming has been around since the beginning of JS, for sure. But most JS developers have never really carefully considered exactly how and why it crops up in their programs, or explored various other ways to handle it. The *good enough* approach has always been the humble callback function. Many to this day will insist that callbacks are more than sufficient.

But as JS continues to grow in both scope and complexity, to meet the ever-widening demands of a first-class programming language that runs in browsers and servers and every conceivable device in between, the pains by which we manage asynchrony are becoming increasingly crippling, and they cry out for approaches that are both more capable and more reason-able.

While this all may seem rather abstract right now, I assure you we'll tackle it more completely and concretely as we go on through this book. We'll explore a variety of emerging techniques for async Java-Script programming over the next several chapters.

But before we can get there, we're going to have to understand much more deeply what asynchrony is and how it operates in JS.

A Program in Chunks

You may write your JS program in one *.js* file, but your program is almost certainly comprised of several chunks, only one of which is going to execute *now*, and the rest of which will execute *later*. The most common unit of each *chunk* is the function.

The problem most developers new to JS seem to have is that *later* doesn't happen strictly and immediately after *now*. In other words, tasks that cannot complete *now* are, by definition, going to complete asynchronously, and thus we will not have blocking behavior as you might intuitively expect or want.

Consider:

```
// ajax(..) is some arbitrary Ajax function given by a library
var data = ajax( "http://some.url.1" );

console.log( data );
// Oops! `data` generally won't have the Ajax results
```

You're probably aware that standard Ajax requests don't complete synchronously, which means the ajax(..) function does not yet have any value to return back to be assigned to the data variable. If ajax(..) could block until the response came back, then the data = .. assignment would work fine.

But that's not how we do Ajax. We make an asynchronous Ajax request *now*, and we won't get the results back until *later*.

The simplest (but definitely not only, or necessarily even best!) way of "waiting" from *now* until *later* is to use a function, commonly called a *callback function*:

```
// ajax(..) is some arbitrary Ajax function given by a library
ajax( "http://some.url.1", function myCallbackFunction(data){

    console.log( data ); // Yay, I gots me some `data`!

} );
```

 You may have heard that it's possible to make synchronous Ajax requests. While that's technically true, you should never, ever do it, under any circumstances, because it locks the browser UI (buttons, menus, scrolling, etc.) and prevents any user interaction whatsoever. This is a terrible idea, and should always be avoided.

Before you protest in disagreement, no, your desire to avoid the mess of callbacks is not justification for blocking, synchronous Ajax.

For example, consider this code:

```
function now() {
    return 21;
}

function later() {
    answer = answer * 2;
    console.log( "Meaning of life:", answer );
}

var answer = now();

setTimeout( later, 1000 ); // Meaning of life: 42
```

There are two chunks to this program: the stuff that will run *now*, and the stuff that will run *later*. It should be fairly obvious what those two chunks are, but let's be super explicit:

Now:

```
function now() {
    return 21;
}
```

```
function later() { .. }

var answer = now();

setTimeout( later, 1000 );
```
Later:
```
answer = answer * 2;
console.log( "Meaning of life:", answer );
```

The *now* chunk runs right away, as soon as you execute your program. But `setTimeout(..)` also sets up an event (a timeout) to happen *later*, so the contents of the `later()` function will be executed at a later time (1,000 milliseconds from now).

Any time you wrap a portion of code into a `function` and specify that it should be executed in response to some event (timer, mouse click, Ajax response, etc.), you are creating a *later* chunk of your code, and thus introducing asynchrony to your program.

Async Console

There is no specification or set of requirements around how the `console.*` methods work—they are not officially part of JavaScript, but are instead added to JS by the *hosting environment* (see the *Types & Grammar* title of this series).

So, different browsers and JS environments do as they please, which can sometimes lead to confusing behavior.

In particular, there are some browsers and some conditions that `console.log(..)` does not actually immediately output what it's given. The main reason this may happen is because I/O is a very slow and blocking part of many programs (not just JS). So, it may perform better (from the page/UI perspective) for a browser to handle `console` I/O asynchronously in the background, without you perhaps even knowing that occurred.

A not terribly common, but possible, scenario where this could be *observable* (not from code itself but from the outside):

```
var a = {
    index: 1
};

// later
console.log( a ); // ??

// even later
a.index++;
```

We'd normally expect to see the a object be snapshotted at the exact moment of the console.log(..) statement, printing something like { index: 1 }, such that in the next statement when a.index++ happens, it's modifying something different than, or just strictly after, the output of a.

Most of the time, the preceding code will probably produce an object representation in your developer tools' console that's what you'd expect. But it's possible this same code could run in a situation where the browser felt it needed to defer the console I/O to the background, in which case it's possible that by the time the object is represented in the browser console, the a.index++ has already happened, and it shows { index: 2 }.

It's a moving target under what conditions exactly console I/O will be deferred, or even whether it will be observable. Just be aware of this possible asynchronicity in I/O in case you ever run into issues in debugging where objects have been modified *after* a console.log(..) statement and yet you see the unexpected modifications show up.

 If you run into this rare scenario, the best option is to use breakpoints in your JS debugger instead of relying on console output. The next best option would be to force a "snapshot" of the object in question by serializing it to a string, like with JSON.stringify(..).

Event Loop

Let's make a (perhaps shocking) claim: despite your clearly being able to write asynchronous JS code (like the timeout we just looked at), up until recently (ES6), JavaScript itself has actually never had any direct notion of asynchrony built into it.

What!? That seems like a crazy claim, right? In fact, it's quite true. The JS engine itself has never done anything more than execute a single chunk of your program at any given moment, when asked to.

"Asked to." By whom? That's the important part!

The JS engine doesn't run in isolation. It runs inside a *hosting environment*, which is for most developers the typical web browser. Over the last several years (but by no means exclusively), JS has expanded beyond the browser into other environments, such as servers, via things like Node.js. In fact, JavaScript gets embedded into all kinds of devices these days, from robots to lightbulbs.

But the one common "thread" (that's a not-so-subtle asynchronous joke, for what it's worth) of all these environments is that they have a mechanism in them that handles executing multiple chunks of your program *over time*, at each moment invoking the JS engine, called the *event loop*.

In other words, the JS engine has had no innate sense of time, but has instead been an on-demand execution environment for any arbitrary snippet of JS. It's the surrounding environment that has always *scheduled* "events" (JS code executions).

So, for example, when your JS program makes an Ajax request to fetch some data from a server, you set up the response code in a function (commonly called a *callback*), and the JS engine tells the hosting environment, "Hey, I'm going to suspend execution for now, but whenever you finish with that network request, and you have some data, please call this function back."

The browser is then set up to listen for the response from the network, and when it has something to give you, it schedules the callback function to be executed by inserting it into the event loop.

So what is the event loop?

Let's conceptualize it first through some fake-ish code:

```
// `eventLoop` is an array that acts as a queue
// (first-in, first-out)
var eventLoop = [ ];
var event;

// keep going "forever"
while (true) {
    // perform a "tick"
    if (eventLoop.length > 0) {
```

```
    // get the next event in the queue
    event = eventLoop.shift();

    // now, execute the next event
    try {
        event();
    }
    catch (err) {
        reportError(err);
    }
  }
}
```

This is, of course, vastly simplified pseudocode to illustrate the concepts. But it should be enough to help get a better understanding.

As you can see, there's a continuously running loop represented by the while loop, and each iteration of this loop is called a *tick*. For each tick, if an event is waiting on the queue, it's taken off and executed. These events are your function callbacks.

It's important to note that setTimeout(..) doesn't put your callback on the event loop queue. What it does is set up a timer; when the timer expires, the environment places your callback into the event loop, such that some future tick will pick it up and execute it.

What if there are already 20 items in the event loop at that moment? Your callback waits. It gets in line behind the others—there's not normally a path for preempting the queue and skipping ahead in line. This explains why setTimeout(..) timers may not fire with perfect temporal accuracy. You're guaranteed (roughly speaking) that your callback won't fire *before* the time interval you specify, but it can happen at or after that time, depending on the state of the event queue.

So, in other words, your program is generally broken up into lots of small chunks, which happen one after the other in the event loop queue. And technically, other events not related directly to your program can be interleaved within the queue as well.

We mentioned "up until recently" in relation to ES6 changing the nature of where the event loop queue is managed. It's mostly a formal technicality, but ES6 now specifies exactly how the event loop works, which means technically it's within the purview of the JS engine, rather than just the hosting environment. One main reason for this change is the introduction of ES6 Promises, which we'll discuss in Chapter 3, because they require the ability to have direct, fine-grained control over scheduling operations on the event loop queue (see the discussion of set Timeout(..0) in "Cooperation" on page 21).

Parallel Threading

It's very common to conflate the terms "async" and "parallel," but they are actually quite different. Remember, async is about the gap between *now* and *later*. But parallel is about things being able to occur simultaneously.

The most common tools for parallel computing are *processes* and *threads*. Processes and threads execute independently and may execute simultaneously: on separate processors, or even separate computers, but multiple threads can share the memory of a single process.

An event loop, by contrast, breaks its work into tasks and executes them in serial, disallowing parallel access and changes to shared memory. Parallelism and serialism can coexist in the form of cooperating event loops in separate threads.

The interleaving of parallel threads of execution and the interleaving of asynchronous events occur at very different levels of granularity.

For example:

```
function later() {
    answer = answer * 2;
    console.log( "Meaning of life:", answer );
}
```

While the entire contents of later() would be regarded as a single event loop queue entry, when thinking about a thread this code would run on, there's actually perhaps a dozen different low-level operations. For example, answer = answer * 2 requires first loading the current value of answer, then putting 2 somewhere, then performing the multiplication, then taking the result and storing it back into answer.

In a single-threaded environment, it really doesn't matter that the items in the thread queue are low-level operations, because nothing can interrupt the thread. But if you have a parallel system, where two different threads are operating in the same program, you could very likely have unpredictable behavior.

Consider:

```
var a = 20;

function foo() {
    a = a + 1;
}

function bar() {
    a = a * 2;
}

// ajax(..) is some arbitrary Ajax function given by a library
ajax( "http://some.url.1", foo );
ajax( "http://some.url.2", bar );
```

In JavaScript's single-threaded behavior, if foo() runs before bar(), the result is that a has 42, but if bar() runs before foo() the result in a will be 41.

If JS events sharing the same data executed in parallel, though, the problems would be much more subtle. Consider these two lists of pseudocode tasks as the threads that could respectively run the code in foo() and bar(), and consider what happens if they are running at exactly the same time:

Thread 1 (X and Y are temporary memory locations):

```
foo():
    a. load value of `a` in `X`
    b. store `1` in `Y`
    c. add `X` and `Y`, store result in `X`
    d. store value of `X` in `a`
```

Thread 2 (X and Y are temporary memory locations):

```
bar():
    a. load value of `a` in `X`
    b. store `2` in `Y`
```

```
c. multiply `X` and `Y`, store result in `X`
d. store value of `X` in `a`
```

Now, let's say that the two threads are running truly in parallel. You can probably spot the problem, right? They use shared memory locations X and Y for their temporary steps.

What's the end result in a if the steps happen like this?

```
1a  (load value of `a` in `X`    ==> `20`)
2a  (load value of `a` in `X`    ==> `20`)
1b  (store `1` in `Y`   ==> `1`)
2b  (store `2` in `Y`   ==> `2`)
1c  (add `X` and `Y`, store result in `X`    ==> `22`)
1d  (store value of `X` in `a`    ==> `22`)
2c  (multiply `X` and `Y`, store result in `X`    ==> `44`)
2d  (store value of `X` in `a`    ==> `44`)
```

The result in a will be 44. But what about this ordering?

```
1a  (load value of `a` in `X`    ==> `20`)
2a  (load value of `a` in `X`    ==> `20`)
2b  (store `2` in `Y`   ==> `2`)
1b  (store `1` in `Y`   ==> `1`)
2c  (multiply `X` and `Y`, store result in `X`    ==> `20`)
1c  (add `X` and `Y`, store result in `X`    ==> `21`)
1d  (store value of `X` in `a`   ==> `21`)
2d  (store value of `X` in `a`   ==> `21`)
```

The result in a will be 21.

So, threaded programming is very tricky, because if you don't take special steps to prevent this kind of interruption/interleaving from happening, you can get very surprising, nondeterministic behavior that frequently leads to headaches.

JavaScript never shares data across threads, which means that level of nondeterminism isn't a concern. But that doesn't mean JS is always deterministic. Remember earlier, where the relative ordering of foo() and bar() produces two different results (41 or 42)?

It may not be obvious yet, but not all nondeterminism is bad. Sometimes it's irrelevant, and sometimes it's intentional. We'll see more examples of that throughout this and the next few chapters.

Run-to-Completion

Because of JavaScript's single-threading, the code inside of `foo()` (and `bar()`) is atomic, which means that once `foo()` starts running, the entirety of its code will finish before any of the code in `bar()` can run, or vice versa. This is called *run-to-completion* behavior.

In fact, the run-to-completion semantics are more obvious when `foo()` and `bar()` have more code in them, such as:

```
var a = 1;
var b = 2;

function foo() {
    a++;
    b = b * a;
    a = b + 3;
}

function bar() {
    b--;
    a = 8 + b;
    b = a * 2;
}

// ajax(..) is some arbitrary Ajax function given by a library
ajax( "http://some.url.1", foo );
ajax( "http://some.url.2", bar );
```

Because `foo()` can't be interrupted by `bar()`, and `bar()` can't be interrupted by `foo()`, this program has only two possible outcomes depending on which starts running first—if threading were present, and the individual statements in `foo()` and `bar()` could be interleaved, the number of possible outcomes would be greatly increased!

Chunk 1 is synchronous (happens *now*), but chunks 2 and 3 are asynchronous (happen *later*), which means their execution will be separated by a gap of time.

Chunk 1:

```
var a = 1;
var b = 2;
```

Chunk 2 (`foo()`):

```
a++;
b = b * a;
a = b + 3;
```

Chunk 3 (`bar()`):

```
b--;
a = 8 + b;
b = a * 2;
```

Chunks 2 and 3 may happen in either-first order, so there are two possible outcomes for this program, as illustrated here:

Outcome 1:

```
var a = 1;
var b = 2;

// foo()
a++;
b = b * a;
a = b + 3;

// bar()
b--;
a = 8 + b;
b = a * 2;

a; // 11
b; // 22
```

Outcome 2:

```
var a = 1;
var b = 2;

// bar()
b--;
a = 8 + b;
b = a * 2;

// foo()
a++;
b = b * a;
a = b + 3;

a; // 183
b; // 180
```

Two outcomes from the same code means we still have nondeterminism! But it's at the function (event) ordering level, rather than at the statement ordering level (or, in fact, the expression operation ordering level) as it is with threads. In other words, it's more deterministic than threads would have been.

As applied to JavaScript's behavior, this function-ordering nondeterminism is the common term *race condition*, as foo() and bar() are racing against each other to see which runs first. Specifically, it's a race condition because you cannot reliably predict how a and b will turn out.

If there was a function in JS that somehow did not have run-to-completion behavior, we could have many more possible outcomes, right? It turns out ES6 introduces just such a thing (see Chapter 4), but don't worry right now, we'll come back to that!

Concurrency

Let's imagine a site that displays a list of status updates (like a social network news feed) that progressively loads as the user scrolls down the list. To make such a feature work correctly, (at least) two separate "processes" will need to be executing *simultaneously* (i.e., during the same window of time, but not necessarily at the same instant).

We're using "process" in quotes here because they aren't true operating system–level processes in the computer science sense. They're virtual processes, or tasks, that represent a logically connected, sequential series of operations. We'll use "process" instead of "task" because terminology-wise, it matches the definitions of the concepts we're exploring.

The first "process" will respond to onscroll events (making Ajax requests for new content) as they fire when the user has scrolled the page further down. The second "process" will receive Ajax responses back (to render content onto the page).

Obviously, if a user scrolls fast enough, you may see two or more onscroll events fired during the time it takes to get the first response back and process, and thus you're going to have onscroll events and Ajax response events firing rapidly, interleaved with each other.

Concurrency is when two or more "processes" are executing simultaneously over the same period, regardless of whether their individual constituent operations happen *in parallel* (at the same instant on separate processors or cores). You can think of concurrency then as "process"-level (or task-level) parallelism, as opposed to operation-level parallelism (separate-processor threads).

Concurrency also introduces an optional notion of these "processes" interacting with each other. We'll come back to that later.

For a given window of time (a few seconds worth of a user scrolling), let's visualize each independent "process" as a series of events/operations:

"Process" 1 (`onscroll` events):

```
onscroll, request 1
onscroll, request 2
onscroll, request 3
onscroll, request 4
onscroll, request 5
onscroll, request 6
onscroll, request 7
```

"Process" 2 (Ajax response events):

```
response 1
response 2
response 3
response 4
response 5
response 6
response 7
```

It's quite possible that an `onscroll` event and an Ajax response event could be ready to be processed at exactly the same *moment*. For example, let's visualize these events in a timeline:

```
onscroll, request 1
onscroll, request 2        response 1
onscroll, request 3        response 2
response 3
onscroll, request 4
onscroll, request 5
onscroll, request 6        response 4
onscroll, request 7
```

```
response 6
response 5
response 7
```

But, going back to our notion of the event loop from earlier in the chapter, JS can handle only one event at a time, so either `onscroll`, `request` 2 is going to happen first or `response` 1 is going to happen first, but they cannot happen at literally the same moment. Just like kids at a school cafeteria, no matter what crowd they form outside the doors, they'll have to merge into a single line to get their lunch!

Let's visualize the interleaving of all these events onto the event loop queue:

```
onscroll, request 1    <--- Process 1 starts
onscroll, request 2
response 1             <--- Process 2 starts
onscroll, request 3
response 2
response 3
onscroll, request 4
onscroll, request 5
onscroll, request 6
response 4
onscroll, request 7    <--- Process 1 finishes
response 6
response 5
response 7             <--- Process 2 finishes
```

"Process" 1 and "Process" 2 run concurrently (task-level parallel), but their individual events run sequentially on the event loop queue.

By the way, notice how `response` 6 and `response` 5 came back out of expected order?

The single-threaded event loop is one expression of concurrency (there are certainly others, which we'll come back to later).

Noninteracting

As two or more "processes" are interleaving their steps/events concurrently within the same program, they don't necessarily need to interact with each other if the tasks are unrelated. *If they don't interact, nondeterminism is perfectly acceptable.*

For example:

```
var res = {};
```

```
function foo(results) {
    res.foo = results;
}

function bar(results) {
    res.bar = results;
}

// ajax(..) is some arbitrary Ajax function given by a library
ajax( "http://some.url.1", foo );
ajax( "http://some.url.2", bar );
```

foo() and bar() are two concurrent "processes," and it's nondeterminate which order they will be fired in. But we've constructed the program so it doesn't matter what order they fire in, because they act independently and as such don't need to interact.

This is not a race condition bug, as the code will always work correctly, regardless of the ordering.

Interaction

More commonly, concurrent "processes" will by necessity interact, indirectly through scope and/or the DOM. When such interaction will occur, you need to coordinate these interactions to prevent race conditions, as described earlier.

Here's a simple example of two concurrent "processes" that interact because of implied ordering, which is only *sometimes broken*:

```
var res = [];

function response(data) {
    res.push( data );
}

// ajax(..) is some arbitrary Ajax function given by a library
ajax( "http://some.url.1", response );
ajax( "http://some.url.2", response );
```

The concurrent "processes" are the two response() calls that will be made to handle the Ajax responses. They can happen in either-first order.

Let's assume the expected behavior is that res[0] has the results of the "http://some.url.1" call, and res[1] has the results of the "http://some.url.2" call. Sometimes that will be the case, but sometimes they'll be flipped, depending on which call finishes first.

There's a pretty good likelihood that this nondeterminism is a race condition bug.

 Be extremely wary of assumptions you might tend to make in these situations. For example, it's not uncommon for a developer to observe that "http://some.url.2" is always much slower to respond than "http://some.url.1", perhaps by virtue of what tasks they're doing (e.g., one performing a database task and the other just fetching a static file), so the observed ordering seems to always be as expected. Even if both requests go to the same server, and it intentionally responds in a certain order, there's no real guarantee of what order the responses will arrive back in the browser.

So, to address such a race condition, you can coordinate ordering interaction:

```
var res = [];

function response(data) {
    if (data.url == "http://some.url.1") {
        res[0] = data;
    }
    else if (data.url == "http://some.url.2") {
        res[1] = data;
    }
}

// ajax(..) is some arbitrary Ajax function given by a library
ajax( "http://some.url.1", response );
ajax( "http://some.url.2", response );
```

Regardless of which Ajax response comes back first, we inspect the data.url (assuming one is returned from the server, of course!) to figure out which position the response data should occupy in the res array. res[0] will always hold the "http://some.url.1" results and res[1] will always hold the "http://some.url.2" results. Through simple coordination, we eliminated the race condition nondeterminism.

The same reasoning from this scenario would apply if multiple concurrent function calls were interacting with each other through the shared DOM, like one updating the contents of a <div> and the other updating the style or attributes of the <div> (e.g., to make the DOM element visible once it has content). You probably wouldn't want to show the DOM element before it had content, so the coordination must ensure proper ordering interaction.

Some concurrency scenarios are always broken (not just sometimes) without coordinated interaction. Consider:

```
var a, b;

function foo(x) {
    a = x * 2;
    baz();
}

function bar(y) {
    b = y * 2;
    baz();
}

function baz() {
    console.log(a + b);
}

// ajax(..) is some arbitrary Ajax function given by a library
ajax( "http://some.url.1", foo );
ajax( "http://some.url.2", bar );
```

In this example, whether foo() or bar() fires first, it will always cause baz() to run too early (either a or b will still be undefined), but the second invocation of baz() will work, as both a and b will be available.

There are different ways to address such a condition. Here's one simple way:

```
var a, b;

function foo(x) {
    a = x * 2;
    if (a && b) {
        baz();
    }
}

function bar(y) {
    b = y * 2;
    if (a && b) {
        baz();
    }
}
```

```
}

function baz() {
    console.log( a + b );
}

// ajax(..) is some arbitrary Ajax function given by a library
ajax( "http://some.url.1", foo );
ajax( "http://some.url.2", bar );
```

The if (a && b) conditional around the baz() call is traditionally called a *gate*, because we're not sure what order a and b will arrive, but we wait for both of them to get there before we proceed to open the gate (call baz()).

Another concurrency interaction condition you may run into is sometimes called a race, but more correctly called a *latch*. It's characterized by "only the first one wins" behavior. Here, nondeterminism is acceptable, in that you are explicitly saying it's OK for the "race" to the finish line to have only one winner.

Consider this broken code:

```
var a;

function foo(x) {
    a = x * 2;
    baz();
}

function bar(x) {
    a = x / 2;
    baz();
}

function baz() {
    console.log( a );
}

// ajax(..) is some arbitrary Ajax function given by a library
ajax( "http://some.url.1", foo );
ajax( "http://some.url.2", bar );
```

Whichever one (foo() or bar()) fires last will not only overwrite the assigned a value from the other, but it will also duplicate the call to baz() (likely undesired).

So, we can coordinate the interaction with a simple latch, to let only the first one through:

```
var a;

function foo(x) {
    if (!a) {
        a = x * 2;
        baz();
    }
}

function bar(x) {
    if (!a) {
        a = x / 2;
        baz();
    }
}

function baz() {
    console.log( a );
}

// ajax(..) is some arbitrary Ajax function given by a library
ajax( "http://some.url.1", foo );
ajax( "http://some.url.2", bar );
```

The if (!a) conditional allows only the first of foo() or bar()
through, and the second (and indeed any subsequent) calls would
just be ignored. There's just no virtue in coming in second place!

 In all these scenarios, we've been using global
variables for simplistic illustration purposes, but
there's nothing about our reasoning here that
requires it. As long as the functions in question
can access the variables (via scope), they'll work
as intended. Relying on lexically scoped variables (see the *Scope & Closures* title of this series), and in fact global variables as in these
examples, is one obvious downside to these
forms of concurrency coordination. As we go
through the next few chapters, we'll see other
ways of coordination that are much cleaner in
that respect.

Cooperation

Another expression of concurrency coordination is called *cooperative concurrency*. Here, the focus isn't so much on interacting via value sharing in scopes (though that's obviously still allowed!). The goal is to take a long-running "process" and break it up into steps or batches so that other concurrent "processes" have a chance to interleave their operations into the event loop queue.

For example, consider an Ajax response handler that needs to run through a long list of results to transform the values. We'll use Array#map(..) to keep the code shorter:

```
var res = [];

// `response(..)` receives array of results from the Ajax call
function response(data) {
    // add onto existing `res` array
    res = res.concat(
        // make a new transformed array with all
        // `data` values doubled
        data.map( function(val){
            return val * 2;
        } )
    );
}

// ajax(..) is some arbitrary Ajax function given by a library
ajax( "http://some.url.1", response );
ajax( "http://some.url.2", response );
```

If "http://some.url.1" gets its results back first, the entire list will be mapped into res all at once. If it's a few thousand or less records, this is not generally a big deal. But if it's, say, 10 million records, that can take a while to run (several seconds on a powerful laptop, much longer on a mobile device, etc.).

While such a "process" is running, nothing else in the page can happen, including no other response(..) calls, no UI updates, not even user events like scrolling, typing, button clicking, and the like. That's pretty painful.

So, to make a more cooperatively concurrent system, one that's friendlier and doesn't hog the event loop queue, you can process these results in asynchronous batches, after each one yielding back to the event loop to let other waiting events happen.

Here's a very simple approach:

```javascript
var res = [];

// `response(..)` receives array of results from the Ajax call
function response(data) {
    // let's just do 1000 at a time
    var chunk = data.splice( 0, 1000 );

    // add onto existing `res` array
    res = res.concat(
        // make a new transformed array with all
        // `chunk` values doubled
        chunk.map( function(val){
            return val * 2;
        } )
    );

    // anything left to process?
    if (data.length > 0) {
        // async schedule next batch
        setTimeout( function(){
            response( data );
        }, 0 );
    }
}

// ajax(..) is some arbitrary Ajax function given by a library
ajax( "http://some.url.1", response );
ajax( "http://some.url.2", response );
```

We process the data set in maximum-sized chunks of 1,000 items. By doing so, we ensure a short-running "process," even if that means many more subsequent "processes," as the interleaving onto the event loop queue will give us a much more responsive (performant) site/app.

Of course, we're not interaction-coordinating the ordering of any of these "processes," so the order of results in res won't be predictable. If ordering was required, you'd need to use interaction techniques like those we discussed earlier, or ones we will cover in later chapters of this book.

We use the setTimeout(..0) (hack) for async scheduling, which basically just means "stick this function at the end of the current event loop queue."

setTimeout(..0) is not technically inserting an item directly onto the event loop queue. The timer will insert the event at its next opportunity. For example, two subsequent setTime out(..0) calls would not be strictly guaranteed to be processed in call order, so it *is* possible to see various conditions like timer drift where the ordering of such events isn't predictable. In Node.js, a similar approach is process.next Tick(..). Despite how convenient (and usually more performant) it would be, there's not a single direct way (at least yet) across all environments to ensure async event ordering. We cover this topic in more detail in the next section.

Jobs

As of ES6, there's a new concept layered on top of the event loop queue, called the *Job queue*. The most likely exposure you'll have to it is with the asynchronous behavior of Promises (see Chapter 3).

Unfortunately, at the moment it's a mechanism without an exposed API, and thus demonstrating it is a bit more convoluted. So we're going to describe it conceptually, such that when we discuss async behavior with Promises in Chapter 3, you'll understand how those actions are being scheduled and processed.

So, the best way to think about this that I've found is that the Job queue is a queue hanging off the end of every tick in the event loop queue. Certain async-implied actions that may occur during a tick of the event loop will not cause a whole new event to be added to the event loop queue, but will instead add an item (aka Job) to the end of the current tick's Job queue.

It's kinda like saying, "oh, here's this other thing I need to do *later*, but make sure it happens right away before anything else can happen."

The event loop queue is like an amusement park ride: once you finish the ride, you have to go to the back of the line to ride again. But the Job queue is like finishing the ride, cutting in line, and getting right back on.

A Job can also cause more Jobs to be added to the end of the same queue. So, it's theoretically possible that a *Job loop* (a Job that keeps adding another Job, etc.) could spin indefinitely, thus starving the program of the ability to move on to the next event loop tick. This would conceptually be almost the same as just expressing a long-running or infinite loop (like `while (true) ..`) in your code.

Jobs are kind of like the spirit of the `setTimeout(..0)` hack, but implemented in such a way as to have a much more well-defined and guaranteed ordering: later, but as soon as possible.

Let's imagine an API for scheduling Jobs (directly, without hacks), and call it `schedule(..)`. Consider:

```
console.log( "A" );

setTimeout( function(){
    console.log( "B" );
}, 0 );

// theoretical "Job API"
schedule( function(){
    console.log( "C" );

    schedule( function(){
        console.log( "D" );
    } );
} );
```

You might expect this to print out A B C D, but instead it would print out A C D B, because the Jobs happen at the end of the current event loop tick, and the timer fires to schedule for the *next* event loop tick (if available!).

In Chapter 3, we'll see that the asynchronous behavior of Promises is based on Jobs, so it's important to keep clear how that relates to event loop behavior.

Statement Ordering

The order in which we express statements in our code is not necessarily the same order as the JS engine will execute them. That may seem like quite a strange assertion to make, so we'll just briefly explore it.

But before we do, we should be crystal clear on something: the rules/grammar of the language (see the *Types & Grammar* title of this series) dictate a very predictable and reliable behavior for statement ordering from the program point of view. So what we're about to discuss are *things you should never be able to observe* in your JS program.

 If you are ever able to observe compiler statement reordering like we're about to illustrate, that'd be a clear violation of the specification, and it would unquestionably be due to a bug in the JS engine in question—one which should promptly be reported and fixed! But it's vastly more common that you suspect something crazy is happening in the JS engine, when in fact it's just a bug (probably a race condition!) in your own code—so look there first, and again and again. The JS debugger, using breakpoints and stepping through code line by line, will be your most powerful tool for sniffing out such bugs in your code.

Consider:

```
var a, b;

a = 10;
b = 30;

a = a + 1;
b = b + 1;

console.log( a + b ); // 42
```

This code has no expressed asynchrony to it (other than the rare `console` async I/O discussed earlier!), so the most likely assumption is that it would process line by line in top-down fashion.

But it's *possible* that the JS engine, after compiling this code (yes, JS is compiled—see the *Scope & Closures* title of this series!) might find opportunities to run your code faster by rearranging (safely) the order of these statements. Essentially, as long as you can't observe the reordering, anything's fair game.

For example, the engine might find it's faster to actually execute the code like this:

```
var a, b;

a = 10;
a++;
```

```
b = 30;
b++;

console.log( a + b ); // 42
```

Or this:

```
var a, b;

a = 11;
b = 31;

console.log( a + b ); // 42
```

Or even:

```
// because `a` and `b` aren't used anymore, we can
// inline and don't even need them!
console.log( 42 ); // 42
```

In all these cases, the JS engine is performing safe optimizations during its compilation, as the end *observable* result will be the same.

But here's a scenario where these specific optimizations would be unsafe and thus couldn't be allowed (of course, not to say that it's not optimized at all):

```
var a, b;

a = 10;
b = 30;

// we need `a` and `b` in their preincremented state!
console.log( a * b ); // 300

a = a + 1;
b = b + 1;

console.log( a + b ); // 42
```

Other examples where the compiler reordering could create observable side effects (and thus must be disallowed) would include things like any function call with side effects (even and especially getter functions), or ES6 Proxy objects (see the *ES6 & Beyond* title of this series).

Consider:

```
function foo() {
    console.log( b );
    return 1;
```

```
}

var a, b, c;

// ES5.1 getter literal syntax
c = {
    get bar() {
        console.log( a );
        return 1;
    }
};

a = 10;
b = 30;

a += foo();             // 30
b += c.bar;             // 11

console.log( a + b );   // 42
```

If it weren't for the console.log(..) statements in this snippet (just used as a convenient form of observable side effect for the illustration), the JS engine would likely have been free, if it wanted to (who knows if it would!?), to reorder the code to:

```
// ...

a = 10 + foo();
b = 30 + c.bar;

// ...
```

While JS semantics thankfully protect us from the *observable* nightmares that compiler statement reordering would seem to be in danger of, it's still important to understand just how tenuous a link there is between the way source code is authored (in top-down fashion) and the way it runs after compilation.

Compiler statement reordering is almost a micro-metaphor for concurrency and interaction. As a general concept, such awareness can help you understand async JS code flow issues better.

Review

A JavaScript program is (practically) always broken up into two or more chunks, where the first chunk runs *now* and the next chunk runs *later*, in response to an event. Even though the program is executed chunk-by-chunk, all of them share the same access to the program scope and state, so each modification to state is made on top of the previous state.

Whenever there are events to run, the event loop runs until the queue is empty. Each iteration of the event loop is a tick. User interaction, IO, and timers enqueue events on the event queue.

At any given moment, only one event can be processed from the queue at a time. While an event is executing, it can directly or indirectly cause one or more subsequent events.

Concurrency is when two or more chains of events interleave over time, such that from a high-level perspective, they appear to be running simultaneously (even though at any given moment only one event is being processed).

It's often necessary to do some form of interaction coordination between these concurrent "processes" (as distinct from operating system processes), for instance to ensure ordering or to prevent race conditions. These "processes" can also cooperate by breaking themselves into smaller chunks and to allow other "process" interleaving.

CHAPTER 2
Callbacks

In Chapter 1, we explored the terminology and concepts around asynchronous programming in JavaScript. Our focus is on understanding the single-threaded (one-at-a-time) event loop queue that drives all *events* (async function invocations). We also explored various ways that concurrency patterns explain the relationships (if any!) between simultaneously running chains of events, or "processes" (tasks, function calls, etc.).

All our examples in Chapter 1 used the function as the individual, indivisible unit of operations, whereby inside the function, statements run in predictable order (above the compiler level!), but at the function-ordering level, events (aka async function invocations) can happen in a variety of orders.

In all these cases, the function is acting as a *callback*, because it serves as the target for the event loop to "call back into" the program, whenever that item in the queue is processed.

As you no doubt have observed, callbacks are by far the most common way that asynchrony in JS programs is expressed and managed. Indeed, the callback is the most fundamental async pattern in the language.

Countless JS programs, even very sophisticated and complex ones, have been written upon no other async foundation than the callback (with, of course, the concurrency interaction patterns we explored in Chapter 1). The callback function is the async workhorse for JavaScript, and it does its job respectably.

Except…callbacks are not without their shortcomings. Many developers are excited by the *promise* (pun intended!) of better async patterns. But it's impossible to effectively use any abstraction if you don't understand what it's abstracting, and why.

In this chapter, we will explore a couple of those in depth, as motivation for why more sophisticated async patterns (explored in subsequent chapters of this book and Appendix B) are necessary and desired.

Continuations

Let's go back to the async callback example we started with in Chapter 1, but let me slightly modify it to illustrate a point:

```
// A
ajax( "..", function(..){
    // C
} );
// B
```

`// A` and `// B` represent the first half of the program (aka the *now*), and `// C` marks the second half of the program (aka the *later*). The first half executes right away, and then there's a pause of indeterminate length. At some future moment, if the Ajax call completes, then the program will pick up where it left off, and continue with the second half.

In other words, the callback function wraps or encapsulates the continuation of the program.

Let's make the code even simpler:

```
// A
setTimeout( function(){
    // C
}, 1000 );
// B
```

Stop for a moment and ask yourself how you'd describe (to someone else less informed about how JS works) the way that program behaves. Go ahead, try it out loud. It's a good exercise that will help my next points make more sense.

Most readers just now probably thought or said something to the effect of: "Do A, then set up a timeout to wait 1,000 milliseconds, then once that fires, do C." How close was your rendition?

You might have caught yourself and self-edited to: "Do A, set up the timeout for 1,000 milliseconds, then do B, then after the timeout fires, do C." That's more accurate than the first version. Can you spot the difference?

Even though the second version is more accurate, both versions are deficient in explaining this code in a way that matches our brains to the code, and the code to the JS engine. The disconnect is both subtle and monumental, and is at the very heart of understanding the shortcomings of callbacks as async expression and management.

As soon as we introduce a single continuation (or several dozen, as many programs do!) in the form of a callback function, we have allowed a divergence to form between how our brains work and the way the code will operate. Any time these two diverge (and this is by far not the only place that happens, as I'm sure you know!), we run into the inevitable fact that our code becomes harder to understand, reason about, debug, and maintain.

Sequential Brain

I'm pretty sure most of you have heard someone say, or made the claim yourself: "I'm a multitasker." The effects of trying to act as a multitasker range from humorous (e.g., the silly patting-head-rubbing-stomach kids' game) to mundane (chewing gum while walking) to downright dangerous (texting while driving).

But are we multitaskers? Can we really do two conscious, intentional actions at once and think/reason about both of them at exactly the same moment? Does our highest level of brain functionality have parallel multithreading going on?

The answer may surprise you: probably not.

That's just not really how our brains appear to be set up. We're much more single taskers than many of us (especially A-type personalities!) would like to admit. We can really only think about one thing at any given instant.

I'm not talking about all our involuntary, subconscious, automatic brain functions, such as heart beating, breathing, and eyelid blinking. Those are all vital tasks to our sustained life, but we don't intentionally allocate any brain power to them. Thankfully, while we obsess about checking social network feeds for the 15th time in three minutes, our brain carries on in the background (threads!) with all those important tasks.

We're instead talking about whatever task is at the forefront of our minds at the moment. For me, it's writing the text in this book right now. Am I doing any other higher level brain function at exactly this same moment? Nope, not really. I get distracted quickly and easily—a few dozen times in these last couple of paragraphs!

When we fake multitasking, such as trying to type something at the same time we're talking to a friend or family member on the phone, what we're actually most likely doing is acting as fast context switchers. In other words, we switch back and forth between two or more tasks in rapid succession, simultaneously progressing on each task in tiny, fast little chunks. We do it so fast that to the outside world it appears as if we're doing these things in parallel.

Does that sound suspiciously like async evented concurrency (like the sort that happens in JS) to you?! If not, go back and read Chapter 1 again!

In fact, one way of simplifying (i.e., abusing) the massively complex world of neurology into something I can remotely hope to discuss here is that our brains work kinda like the event loop queue.

If you think about every single letter (or word) I type as a single async event, in just this sentence alone there are several dozen opportunities for my brain to be interrupted by some other event, such as from my senses, or even just my random thoughts.

I don't get interrupted and pulled to another "process" at every opportunity that I could be (thankfully—or this book would never be written!). But it happens often enough that I feel my own brain is nearly constantly switching to various different contexts (aka "processes"). And that's an awful lot like how the JS engine would probably feel.

Doing Versus Planning

OK, so our brains can be thought of as operating in single-threaded event loop queue like ways, as can the JS engine. That sounds like a good match.

But we need to be more nuanced than that in our analysis. There's a big, observable difference between how we plan various tasks, and how our brains actually perform those tasks.

Again, back to the writing of this text as my metaphor. My rough mental outline plan here is to keep writing and writing, going sequentially through a set of points I have ordered in my thoughts. I don't plan to have any interruptions or nonlinear activity in this writing. But yet, my brain is nevertheless switching around all the time.

Even though at an operational level our brains are async evented, we seem to plan out tasks in a sequential, synchronous way. "I need to go to the store, then buy some milk, then drop off my dry cleaning."

You'll notice that this higher level thinking (planning) doesn't seem very async evented in its formulation. In fact, it's kind of rare for us to deliberately think solely in terms of events. Instead, we plan things out carefully, sequentially (A, then B, then C), and we assume to an extent a sort of temporal blocking that forces B to wait on A, and C to wait on B.

When a developer writes code, they are planning out a set of actions to occur. If they're any good at being a developer, they're carefully planning it out. "I need to set z to the value of x, and then x to the value of y," and so forth.

When we write out synchronous code, statement by statement, it works a lot like our errands to-do list:

```
// swap `x` and `y` (via temp variable `z`)
z = x;
x = y;
y = z;
```

These three assignment statements are synchronous, so x = y waits for z = x to finish, and y = z in turn waits for x = y to finish. Another way of saying it is that these three statements are temporally bound to execute in a certain order, one right after the other. Thankfully, we don't need to be bothered with any async evented details here. If we did, the code gets a lot more complex, quickly!

So if synchronous brain planning maps well to synchronous code statements, how well do our brains do at planning out asynchronous code?

It turns out that how we express asynchrony (with callbacks) in our code doesn't map very well at all to that synchronous brain planning behavior.

Can you actually imagine having a line of thinking that plans out your to-do errands like this?

> "I need to go to the store, but on the way I'm sure I'll get a phone call, so *Hi, Mom*, and while she starts talking, I'll be looking up the store address on GPS, but that'll take a second to load, so I'll turn down the radio so I can hear Mom better, then I'll realize I forgot to put on a jacket and it's cold outside, but no matter, keep driving and talking to Mom, and then the seatbelt ding reminds me to buckle up, so *yes, Mom, I am wearing my seatbelt, I always do!* Ah, finally the GPS got the directions, now…"

As ridiculous as that sounds as a formulation for how we plan our day out and think about what to do and in what order, nonetheless it's exactly how our brains operate at a functional level. Remember, that's not multitasking, it's just fast context switching.

The reason it's difficult for us as developers to write async evented code, especially when all we have is the callback to do it, is that stream of consciousness thinking/planning is unnatural for most of us.

We think in step-by-step terms, but the tools (callbacks) available to us in code are not expressed in a step-by-step fashion once we move from synchronous to asynchronous.

And *that* is why it's so hard to accurately author and reason about async JS code with callbacks: because it's not how our brain planning works.

 The only thing worse than not knowing why some code breaks is not knowing why it worked in the first place! It's the classic "house of cards" mentality: "it works, but I'm not sure why, so nobody touch it!" You may have heard, "Hell is other people" (Sartre), and the programmer meme twist, "Hell is other people's code." I believe truly: "Hell is not understanding my own code." And callbacks are one main culprit.

Nested/Chained Callbacks

Consider:

```
listen( "click", function handler(evt){
    setTimeout( function request(){
        ajax( "http://some.url.1", function response(text){
            if (text == "hello") {
                handler();
            }
            else if (text == "world") {
                request();
            }
        } );
    }, 500) ;
} );
```

There's a good chance code like that is recognizable to you. We've got a chain of three functions nested together, each one representing a step in an asynchronous series (task, "process").

This kind of code is often called *callback hell*, and sometimes also referred to as the *pyramid of doom* (for its sideways-facing triangular shape due to the nested indentation).

But callback hell actually has almost nothing to do with the nesting/indentation. It's a far deeper problem than that. We'll see how and why as we continue through the rest of this chapter.

First, we're waiting for the click event, then we're waiting for the timer to fire, then we're waiting for the Ajax response to come back, at which point it might do it all again.

At first glance, this code may seem to map its asynchrony naturally to sequential brain planning.

First (*now*), we:

```
listen( "..", function handler(..){
    // ..
} );
```

Then *later*, we:

```
setTimeout( function request(..){
    // ..
}, 500) ;
```

Then still *later*, we:

```
ajax( "..", function response(..){
    // ..
} );
```

And finally (most *later*), we:

```
if ( .. ) {
    // ..
}
else ..
```

But there's several problems with reasoning about this code linearly in such a fashion.

First, it's an accident of the example that our steps are on subsequent lines (1, 2, 3, and 4…). In real async JS programs, there's often a lot more noise cluttering things up, noise that we have to deftly maneuver past in our brains as we jump from one function to the next. Understanding the async flow in such callback-laden code is not impossible, but it's certainly not natural or easy, even with lots of practice.

But also, there's something deeper wrong, which isn't evident just in that code example. Let me make up another scenario (pseudocode-ish) to illustrate it:

```
doA( function(){
    doB();

    doC( function(){
        doD();
    } )

    doE();
} );

doF();
```

While the experienced among you will correctly identify the true order of operations here, I'm betting it is more than a little confusing at first glance, and takes some concerted mental cycles to arrive at. The operations will happen in this order:

- doA()
- doF()
- doB()

- doC()
- doE()
- doD()

Did you get that right the very first time you glanced at the code?

OK, some of you are thinking I was unfair in my function naming, to intentionally lead you astray. I swear I was just naming in top-down appearance order. But let me try again:

```
doA( function(){
    doC();

    doD( function(){
        doF();
    } )

    doE();
} );

doB();
```

Now, I've named them alphabetically in order of actual execution. But I still bet, even with experience now in this scenario, tracing through the A → B → C → D → E → F order doesn't come naturally. Certainly your eyes do an awful lot of jumping up and down the code snippet, right?

But even if that all comes naturally to you, there's still one more hazard that could wreak havoc. Can you spot what it is?

What if doA(..) or doD(..) aren't actually async, the way we obviously assumed them to be? Uh-oh, now the order is different. If they're both in sync (and maybe only sometimes, depending on the conditions of the program at the time), the order is now A → C → D → F → E → B.

That sound you just heard faintly in the background is the sighs of thousands of JS developers who just had a face-in-hands moment.

Is nesting the problem? Is that what makes it so hard to trace the async flow? That's part of it, certainly.

But let me rewrite the previous nested event/timeout/Ajax example without using nesting:

```
listen( "click", handler );
```

```
function handler() {
    setTimeout( request, 500 );
}

function request(){
    ajax( "http://some.url.1", response );
}

function response(text){
    if (text == "hello") {
        handler();
    }
    else if (text == "world") {
        request();
    }
}
```

This formulation of the code is not hardly as recognizable as having the nesting/indentation woes of its previous form, and yet it's every bit as susceptible to callback hell. Why?

As we go to linearly (sequentially) reason about this code, we have to skip from one function, to the next, to the next, and bounce all around the code base to "see" the sequence flow. And remember, this is simplified code in sort of best-case fashion. We all know that real async JS program code bases are often fantastically more jumbled, which makes such reasoning orders of magnitude more difficult.

Another thing to notice: to get steps 2, 3, and 4 linked together so they happen in succession, the only affordance callbacks alone gives us is to hardcode step 2 into step 1, step 3 into step 2, step 4 into step 3, and so on. The hardcoding isn't necessarily a bad thing, if it really is a fixed condition that step 2 should always lead to step 3.

But the hardcoding definitely makes the code a bit more brittle, as it doesn't account for anything going wrong that might cause a deviation in the progression of steps. For example, if step 2 fails, step 3 never gets reached, nor does step 2 retry, or move to an alternate error handling flow, and so on.

All of these issues are things you can manually hardcode into each step, but that code is often very repetitive and not reusable in other steps or in other async flows in your program.

Even though our brains might plan out a series of tasks in a sequential type of way (this, then this, then this), the evented nature of our brain operation makes recovery/retry/forking of flow control almost effortless. If you're out running errands, and you realize you left a shopping list at home, it doesn't end the day because you didn't plan that ahead of time. Your brain routes around this hiccup easily: you go home, get the list, then head right back out to the store.

But the brittle nature of manually hardcoded callbacks (even with hardcoded error handling) is often far less graceful. Once you end up specifying (aka pre-planning) all the various eventualities/paths, the code becomes so convoluted that it's hard to ever maintain or update it.

That is what callback hell is all about! The nesting/indentations are basically a side show, a red herring.

And as if all that's not enough, we haven't even touched what happens when two or more chains of these callback continuations are happening simultaneously, or when the third step branches out into parallel callbacks with gates or latches, or...OMG, my brain hurts, how about yours!?

Are you catching the notion here that our sequential, blocking brain planning behaviors just don't map well onto callback-oriented async code? That's the first major deficiency of callbacks: they express asynchrony in code in ways our brains have to fight just to keep in sync with (pun intended!).

Trust Issues

The mismatch between sequential brain planning and callback-driven async JS code is only part of the problem with callbacks. There's something much deeper to be concerned about.

Let's once again revisit the notion of a callback function as the continuation (aka the second half) of our program:

```
// A
ajax( "..", function(..){
    // C
} );
// B
```

`// A` and `// B` happen *now*, under the direct control of the main JS program. But `// C` gets deferred to happen *later*, and under the control of another party—in this case, the `ajax(..)` function. In a basic sense, that sort of hand-off of control doesn't regularly cause lots of problems for programs.

But don't be fooled by its infrequency and assume that this control switch isn't a big deal. In fact, it's one of the worst (and yet most subtle) problems with callback-driven design. It revolves around the idea that sometimes `ajax(..)` (i.e., the party you hand your callback continuation to) is not a function that you wrote, or that you directly control. Many times it's a utility provided by some third party.

We call this *inversion of control*, when you take part of your program and give over control of its execution to another third party. There's an unspoken contract that exists between your code and the third-party utility—a set of things you expect to be maintained.

Tale of Five Callbacks

It might not be terribly obvious why this is such a big deal. Let me construct an exaggerated scenario to illustrate the hazards of trust at play.

Imagine you're a developer tasked with building out an ecommerce checkout system for a site that sells expensive TVs. You already have all the various pages of the checkout system built out just fine. On the last page, when the user clicks "confirm" to buy the TV, you need to call a third-party function (provided, say, by some analytics tracking company) so that the sale can be tracked.

You notice that they've provided what looks like an async tracking utility, probably for the sake of performance best practices, which means you need to pass in a callback function. In this continuation that you pass in, you will have the final code that charges the customer's credit card and displays the thank you page.

This code might look like:

```
analytics.trackPurchase( purchaseData, function(){
    chargeCreditCard();
    displayThankyouPage();
} );
```

Easy enough, right? You write the code, test it, everything works, and you deploy to production. Everyone's happy!

Six months go by and no issues. You've almost forgotten you even wrote that code. One morning, you're at a coffee shop before work, casually enjoying your latte, when you get a panicked call from your boss insisting you drop the coffee and rush into work right away.

When you arrive, you find out that a high-profile customer has had his credit card charged five times for the same TV, and he's understandably upset. Customer service has already issued an apology and processed a refund. But your boss demands to know how this could possibly have happened. "Don't we have tests for stuff like this!?"

You don't even remember the code you wrote. But you dig back in and start trying to find out what could have gone awry.

After digging through some logs, you come to the conclusion that the only explanation is that the analytics utility somehow, for some reason, called your callback five times instead of once. Nothing in their documentation mentions anything about this.

Frustrated, you contact customer support, who of course is as astonished as you are. They agree to escalate it to their developers, and promise to get back to you. The next day, you receive a lengthy email explaining what they found, which you promptly forward to your boss.

Apparently, the developers at the analytics company had been working on some experimental code that, under certain conditions, would retry the provided callback once per second, for five seconds, before failing with a timeout. They had never intended to push that into production, but somehow they did, and they're totally embarrassed and apologetic. They go into plenty of detail about how they've identified the breakdown and what they'll do to ensure it never happens again. Yadda, yadda.

What's next?

You talk it over with your boss, but he's not feeling particularly comfortable with the state of things. He insists, and you reluctantly agree, that you can't trust them anymore (that's what bit you), and that you'll need to figure out how to protect the checkout code from such a vulnerability again.

After some tinkering, you implement some simple ad hoc code like the following, which the team seems happy with:

```
var tracked = false;

analytics.trackPurchase( purchaseData, function(){
    if (!tracked) {
        tracked = true;
        chargeCreditCard();
        displayThankyouPage();
    }
} );
```

 This should look familiar to you from Chapter 1, because we're essentially creating a latch to handle any multiple concurrent invocations of our callback.

But then one of your QA engineers asks, "what happens if they never call the callback?" Oops. Neither of you had thought about that.

You begin to chase down the rabbit hole, and think of all the possible things that could go wrong with them calling your callback. Here's roughly the list you come up with of ways the analytics utility could misbehave:

- Call the callback too early (before it's been tracked)
- Call the callback too late (or never)
- Call the callback too few or too many times (like the problem you encountered!)
- Fail to pass along any necessary environment/parameters to your callback
- Swallow any errors/exceptions that may happen
- ...

That should feel like a troubling list, because it is. You're probably slowly starting to realize that you're going to have to invent an awful lot of ad hoc logic *in each and every single callback* that's passed to a utility you're not positive you can trust.

Now you realize a bit more completely just how hellish callback hell is.

Not Just Others' Code

Some of you may doubt that this is as big a deal as I'm making it out to be. Perhaps you don't interact with truly third-party utilities much, if at all. Perhaps you use versioned APIs or self-host such libraries, so that its behavior can't be changed out from underneath you.

So, contemplate this: can you even *really* trust utilities that you do theoretically control (in your own code base)?

Think of it this way: most of us agree that at least to some extent we should build our own internal functions with some defensive checks on the input parameters, to reduce/prevent unexpected issues.

Overly trusting of input:

```
function addNumbers(x,y) {
    // + is overloaded with coercion to also be
    // string concatenation, so this operation
    // isn't strictly safe depending on what's
    // passed in.
    return x + y;
}

addNumbers( 21, 21 );   // 42
addNumbers( 21, "21" ); // "2121"
```

Defensive against untrusted input:

```
function addNumbers(x,y) {
    // ensure numerical input
    if (typeof x != "number" || typeof y != "number") {
        throw Error( "Bad parameters" );
    }

    // if we get here, + will safely do numeric addition
    return x + y;
}

addNumbers( 21, 21 );   // 42
addNumbers( 21, "21" ); // Error: "Bad parameters"
```

Still safe but friendlier:

```
function addNumbers(x,y) {
    // ensure numerical input
    x = Number( x );
    y = Number( y );

    // + will safely do numeric addition
```

```
    return x + y;
}

addNumbers( 21, 21 );    // 42
addNumbers( 21, "21" );  // 42
```

However you go about it, these sorts of checks/normalizations are fairly common on function inputs, even with code we theoretically entirely trust. In a crude sort of way, it's like the programming equivalent of the geopolitical principle "trust, but verify."

So, doesn't it stand to reason that we should do the same thing about composition of async function callbacks, not just with truly external code but even with code we know is generally under our own control? Of course we should.

But callbacks don't really offer anything to assist us. We have to construct all that machinery ourselves, and it often ends up being a lot of boilerplate/overhead that we repeat for every single async callback.

The most troublesome problem with callbacks is inversion of control leading to a complete breakdown along all those trust lines.

If you have code that uses callbacks, especially but not exclusively with third-party utilities, and you're not already applying some sort of mitigation logic for all these inversion of control trust issues, your code has bugs in it right now even though they may not have bitten you yet. Latent bugs are still bugs.

Hell indeed.

Trying to Save Callbacks

There are several variations of callback design that have attempted to address some (not all!) of the trust issues we've just looked at. It's a valiant, but doomed, effort to save the callback pattern from imploding on itself.

For example, regarding more graceful error handling, some API designs provide for *split callbacks* (one for the success notification, and one for the error notification):

```
function success(data) {
    console.log( data );
}
```

```
function failure(err) {
    console.error( err );
}

ajax( "http://some.url.1", success, failure );
```

In APIs of this design, often the `failure()` error handler is
optional, and if not provided it will be assumed you want the errors
swallowed. Ugh.

> This split-callback design is what the ES6
> Promise API uses. We'll cover ES6 Promises in
> much more detail in Chapter 3.

Another common callback pattern is called "error-first style" (sometimes called "Node style," as it's also the convention used across
nearly all Node.js APIs), where the first argument of a single callback is reserved for an error object (if any). If successful, this argument will be empty/falsy (and any subsequent arguments will be the
success data), but if an error result is being signaled, the first argument is set/truthy (and usually nothing else is passed):

```
function response(err,data) {
    // error?
    if (err) {
        console.error( err );
    }
    // otherwise, assume success
    else {
        console.log( data );
    }
}

ajax( "http://some.url.1", response );
```

In both of these cases, several things should be observed.

First, it has not really resolved the majority of trust issues like it may
appear. There's nothing about either callback that prevents or filters
unwanted repeated invocations. Moreover, things are worse now,
because you may get both success and error signals, or neither, and
you still have to code around either of those conditions.

Also, don't miss the fact that while it's a standard pattern you can
employ, it's definitely more verbose and boilerplate-ish without

much reuse, so you're going to get weary of typing all that out for every single callback in your application.

What about the trust issue of never being called? If this is a concern (and it probably should be!), you likely will need to set up a timeout that cancels the event. You could make a utility (proof-of-concept only shown) to help you with that:

```
function timeoutify(fn,delay) {
    var intv = setTimeout( function(){
            intv = null;
            fn( new Error( "Timeout!" ) );
        }, delay )
    ;

    return function() {
        // timeout hasn't happened yet?
        if (intv) {
            clearTimeout( intv );
            fn.apply( this, arguments );
        }
    };
}
```

Here's how you use it:

```
// using "error-first style" callback design
function foo(err,data) {
    if (err) {
        console.error( err );
    }
    else {
        console.log( data );
    }
}

ajax( "http://some.url.1", timeoutify( foo, 500 ) );
```

Another trust issue is being called too early. In application-specific terms, this may actually involve being called before some critical task is complete. But more generally, the problem is evident in utilities that can either invoke the callback you provide *now* (synchronously), or *later* (asynchronously).

This nondeterminism around the sync-or-async behavior is almost always going to lead to very difficult to track down bugs. In some circles, the fictional insanity-inducing monster named Zalgo is used to describe the sync/async nightmares. "Don't release Zalgo!" is a common cry, and it leads to very sound advice: always invoke callbacks asynchronously, even if that's right away on the next turn of the event loop, so that all callbacks are predictably async.

 For more information on Zalgo, see Oren Golan's "Don't Release Zalgo!" (*https:// github.com/oren/oren.github.io/blob/master/ posts/zalgo.md*) and Isaac Z. Schlueter's "Designing APIs for Asynchrony" (*http:// blog.izs.me/post/59142742143/designing-apis- for-asynchrony*).

Consider:

```
function result(data) {
    console.log( a );
}

var a = 0;

ajax( "..pre-cached-url..", result );
a++;
```

Will this code print 0 (sync callback invocation) or 1 (async callback invocation)? It depends on the conditions.

You can see just how quickly the unpredictability of Zalgo can threaten any JS program. So the silly-sounding "never release Zalgo" is actually incredibly common and solid advice. Always be asyncing.

What if you don't know whether the API in question will always execute async? You could invent a utility like this asyncify(..) proof-of-concept:

```
function asyncify(fn) {
    var orig_fn = fn,
        intv = setTimeout( function(){
            intv = null;
            if (fn) fn();
        }, 0 )
    ;

    fn = null;

    return function() {
        // firing too quickly, before `intv` timer has fired to
        // indicate async turn has passed?
        if (intv) {
            fn = orig_fn.bind.apply(
                orig_fn,
```

```
                    // add the wrapper's `this` to the `bind(..)`
                    // call parameters, as well as currying any
                    // passed in parameters
                    [this].concat( [].slice.call( arguments ) )
                );
        }
        // already async
        else {
            // invoke original function
            orig_fn.apply( this, arguments );
        }
    };
}
```

You use `asyncify(..)` like this:

```
function result(data) {
    console.log( a );
}

var a = 0;

ajax( "..pre-cached-url..", asyncify( result ) );
a++;
```

Whether the Ajax request is in the cache and resolves to try to call
the callback right away, or must be fetched over the wire and thus
complete later asynchronously, this code will always output 1
instead of 0—`result(..)` cannot help but be invoked asynchronously, which means the a++ has a chance to run before `result(..)`
does.

Yay, another trust issue "solved"! But it's inefficient, and yet again
more bloated boilerplate to weigh your project down.

That's just the story, over and over again, with callbacks. They can
do pretty much anything you want, but you have to be willing to
work hard to get it, and oftentimes this effort is much more than
you can or should spend on such code reasoning.

You might find yourself wishing for built-in APIs or other language
mechanics to address these issues. ES6 has finally arrived on the
scene with some great answers, so keep reading!

Review

Callbacks are the fundamental unit of asynchrony in JS. But they're not enough for the evolving landscape of async programming as JS matures.

First, our brains plan things out in sequential, blocking, single-threaded semantic ways, but callbacks express asynchronous flow in a rather nonlinear, nonsequential way, which makes reasoning properly about such code much harder. Hard-to-reason-about code is bad code that leads to bad bugs.

We need a way to express asynchrony in a more synchronous, sequential, blocking manner, just like our brains do.

Second, and more importantly, callbacks suffer from inversion of control in that they implicitly give control over to another party (often a third-party utility not in your control!) to invoke the continuation of your program. This control transfer leads us to a troubling list of trust issues, such as whether the callback is called more times than we expect.

Inventing ad hoc logic to solve these trust issues is possible, but it's more difficult than it should be, and it produces code that is clunkier, harder to maintain, and likely insufficiently protected from these hazards until you get visibly bitten by the bugs.

We need a generalized solution to all of the trust issues, one that can be reused for as many callbacks as we create without all the extra boilerplate overhead.

We need something better than callbacks. They've served us well to this point, but the future of JavaScript demands more sophisticated and capable async patterns. The subsequent chapters in this book dive into those emerging evolutions.

CHAPTER 3

Promises

In Chapter 2, we identified two major categories of deficiencies with using callbacks to express program asynchrony and manage concurrency: lack of sequentiality and lack of trustability. Now that we understand the problems more intimately, it's time we turn our attention to patterns that can address them.

The issue we want to address first is the inversion of control, the trust that is so fragilely held and so easily lost.

Recall that we wrap up the continuation of our program in a callback function, and hand that callback over to another party (potentially even external code) and just cross our fingers that it will do the right thing with the invocation of the callback.

We do this because we want to say, "here's what happens *later*, after the current step finishes."

But what if we could uninvert that inversion of control? What if, instead of handing the continuation of our program to another party, we could expect it to return us a capability to know when its task finishes, and then our code could decide what to do next?

This paradigm is called *Promises*.

Promises are starting to take the JS world by storm, as developers and specification writers alike desperately seek to untangle the insanity of callback hell in their code/design. In fact, most new async APIs being added to the JS/DOM platform are being built on

Promises. So it's probably a good idea to dig in and learn them, don't you think!?

 The word "immediately" is used frequently in this chapter, generally to refer to some Promise resolution action. However, in essentially all cases, "immediately" means in terms of the Job queue behavior (see Chapter 1), not in the strictly synchronous *now* sense.

What Is a Promise?

When developers decide to learn a new technology or pattern, usually their first step is "show me the code!" It's quite natural for us to just jump in feet first and learn as we go.

But it turns out that some abstractions get lost on the APIs alone. Promises are one of those tools where it can be painfully obvious from how someone uses it whether they understand what it's for and about versus just learning and using the API.

So before I show the Promise code, I want to fully explain what a Promise really is conceptually. I hope this will then guide you better as you explore integrating Promise theory into your own async flow.

With that in mind, let's look at two different analogies for what a Promise *is*.

Future Value

Imagine this scenario: I walk up to the counter at a fast-food restaurant, and place an order for a cheeseburger. I hand the cashier $1.47. By placing my order and paying for it, I've made a request for a *value* back (the cheeseburger). I've started a transaction.

But often, the chesseburger is not immediately available for me. The cashier hands me something in place of my cheeseburger: a receipt with an order number on it. This order number is an IOU ("I owe you") *promise* that ensures that I should eventually receive my cheeseburger.

So I hold onto my receipt and order number. I know it represents my *future cheeseburger*, so I don't need to worry about it anymore—aside from being hungry!

While I wait, I can do other things, like send a text message to a friend that says, "Hey, can you come join me for lunch? I'm going to eat a cheeseburger."

I am reasoning about my *future cheeseburger* already, even though I don't have it in my hands yet. My brain is able to do this because it's treating the order number as a placeholder for the cheeseburger. The placeholder essentially makes the value *time independent*. It's a *future value*.

Eventually, I hear, "order 113!" and I gleefully walk back up to the counter with receipt in hand. I hand my receipt to the cashier, and I take my cheeseburger in return.

In other words, once my *future value* was ready, I exchanged my value-promise for the value itself.

But there's another possible outcome. They call my order number, but when I go to retrieve my cheeseburger, the cashier regretfully informs me, "I'm sorry, but we appear to be all out of cheeseburgers." Setting aside the customer frustration of this scenario for a moment, we can see an important characteristic of *future values*: they can either indicate a success or failure.

Every time I order a cheeseburger, I know that I'll either get a cheeseburger eventually, or I'll get the sad news of the cheeseburger shortage, and I'll have to figure out something else to eat for lunch.

In code, things are not quite as simple, because metaphorically the order number may never be called, in which case we're left indefinitely in an unresolved state. We'll come back to dealing with that case later.

Values Now and Later

This all might sound too mentally abstract to apply to your code. So let's be more concrete.

However, before we can introduce how Promises work in this fashion, we're going to derive in code that we already understand—callbacks!—how to handle these *future values*.

When you write code to reason about a value, such as performing math on a number, whether you realize it or not, you've been assuming something very fundamental about that value, which is that it's a concrete *now* value already:

```
var x, y = 2;

console.log( x + y ); // NaN  <-- because `x` isn't set yet
```

The x + y operation assumes both x and y are already set. In terms we'll expound on shortly, we assume the x and y values are already *resolved*.

It would be nonsense to expect that the + operator by itself would somehow be magically capable of detecting and waiting around until both x and y are resolved (aka ready), and only then do the operation. That would cause chaos in the program if different statements finished *now* and others finished *later*, right?

How could you possibly reason about the relationships between two statements if either one (or both) of them might not be finished yet? If statement 2 relies on statement 1 being finished, there are just two outcomes: either statement 1 finished right *now* and everything proceeds fine, or statement 1 didn't finish yet, and thus statement 2 is going to fail.

If this sort of thing sounds familiar from Chapter 1, good!

Let's go back to our x + y math operation. Imagine if there was a way to say, "Add x and y, but if either of them isn't ready yet, just wait until they are. Add them as soon as you can."

Your brain might have just jumped to callbacks. OK, so…

```
function add(getX,getY,cb) {
    var x, y;
    getX( function(xVal){
        x = xVal;
        // both are ready?
        if (y != undefined) {
            cb( x + y );    // send along sum
        }
    } );
    getY( function(yVal){
        y = yVal;
        // both are ready?
        if (x != undefined) {
            cb( x + y );    // send along sum
        }
    } );
}
```

```
// `fetchX()` and `fetchY()` are sync or async
// functions
add( fetchX, fetchY, function(sum){
    console.log( sum ); // that was easy, huh?
} );
```

Take just a moment to let the beauty (or lack thereof) of that snippet sink in (whistles patiently).

While the ugliness is undeniable, there's something very important about this async pattern.

In that snippet, we treated x and y as future values, and we express an operation add(..) that (from the outside) does not care whether x or y or both are available right away. In other words, it normalizes the *now* and *later*, such that we can rely on a predictable outcome of the add(..) operation.

By using an add(..) that is temporally consistent—it behaves the same across *now* and *later* times—the async code is much easier to reason about.

To put it more plainly: to consistently handle both *now* and *later*, we make both of them *later*: all operations become async.

Of course, this rough callbacks-based approach leaves much to be desired. It's just a first tiny step toward realizing the benefits of reasoning about future values without worrying about the time aspect of when it's available or not.

Promise Value

We'll definitely go into a lot more detail about Promises later in the chapter—so don't worry if some of this is confusing—but let's just briefly glimpse at how we can express the x + y example via Promises functions:

```
function add(xPromise,yPromise) {
    // `Promise.all([ .. ])` takes an array of promises,
    // and returns a new promise that waits on them
    // all to finish
    return Promise.all( [xPromise, yPromise] )

    // when that promise is resolved, let's take the
    // received `X` and `Y` values and add them together.
    .then( function(values){
        // `values` is an array of the messages from the
```

```
        // previously resolved promises
        return values[0] + values[1];
    } );
}

// `fetchX()` and `fetchY()` return promises for
// their respective values, which may be ready
// now or later.
add( fetchX(), fetchY() )

// we get a promise back for the sum of those
// two numbers.
// now we chain-call `then(..)` to wait for the
// resolution of that returned promise.
.then( function(sum){
    console.log( sum ); // that was easier!
} );
```

There are two layers of Promises in this snippet.

fetchX() and fetchY() are called directly, and the values they return (promises!) are passed into add(..). The underlying values those promises represent may be ready *now* or *later*, but each promise normalizes the behavior to be the same regardless. We reason about X and Y values in a time-independent way. They are future values.

The second layer is the promise that add(..) creates (via Promise.all([..])) and returns, which we wait on by calling then(..). When the add(..) operation completes, our sum future value is ready and we can print it out. We hide inside of add(..) the logic for waiting on the X and Y future values.

Inside add(..), the Promise.all([..]) call creates a promise (which is waiting on promiseX and promiseY to resolve). The chained call to .then(..) creates another promise, which the return values[0] + values[1] line immediately resolves (with the result of the addition). Thus, the then(..) call we chain off the end of the add(..) call—at the end of the snippet—is actually operating on that second promise returned, rather than the first one created by Promise.all([..]). Also, though we are not chaining off the end of that second then(..), it too has created another promise, had we chosen to observe/use it. This Promise chaining stuff will be explained in much greater detail later in this chapter.

Just like with cheeseburger orders, it's possible that the resolution of a Promise is rejection instead of fulfillment. Unlike a fulfilled Promise, where the value is always programmatic, a rejection value —commonly called a *rejection reason*—can either be set directly by the program logic, or it can result implicitly from a runtime exception.

With Promises, the then(..) call can actually take two functions, the first for fulfillment (as shown earlier), and the second for rejection:

```
add( fetchX(), fetchY() )
.then(
    // fullfillment handler
    function(sum) {
        console.log( sum );
    },
    // rejection handler
    function(err) {
        console.error( err ); // bummer!
    }
);
```

If something went wrong getting X or Y, or something somehow failed during the addition, the promise that add(..) returns is rejected, and the second callback error handler passed to then(..) will receive the rejection value from the promise.

Because Promises encapsulate the time-dependent state—waiting on the fulfillment or rejection of the underlying value—from the outside, the Promise itself is time-independent, and thus Promises can be composed (combined) in predictable ways regardless of the timing or outcome underneath.

Moreover, once a Promise is resolved, it stays that way forever—it becomes an *immutable value* at that point—and can then be observed as many times as necessary.

Because a Promise is externally immutable once resolved, it's now safe to pass that value around to any party and know that it cannot be modified accidentally or maliciously. This is especially true in relation to multiple parties observing the resolution of a Promise. It is not possible for one party to affect another party's ability to observe Promise resolution. Immutability may sound like an academic topic, but it's actually one of the most fundamental and important aspects of Promise design, and shouldn't be casually passed over.

That's one of the most powerful and important concepts to understand about Promises. With a fair amount of work, you could ad hoc create the same effects with nothing but ugly callback composition, but that's not really an effective strategy, especially because you have to do it over and over again.

Promises are an easily repeatable mechanism for encapsulating and composing future values.

Completion Event

As we just saw, an individual Promise behaves as a future value. But there's another way to think of the resolution of a Promise: as a flow-control mechanism—a temporal this-then-that—for two or more steps in an asynchronous task.

Let's imagine calling a function foo(..) to perform some task. We don't know about any of its details, nor do we care. It may complete the task right away, or it may take a while.

We just simply need to know when foo(..) finishes so that we can move on to our next task. In other words, we'd like a way to be notified of foo(..)'s completion so that we can continue.

In typical JavaScript fashion, if you need to listen for a notification, you'd likely think of that in terms of events. So we could reframe our need for notification as a need to listen for a *completion event* (or *continuation event*) emitted by foo(..).

 Whether you call it a completion or a continuation event depends on your perspective. Is the focus more on what happens with foo(..), or what happens after foo(..) finishes? Both perspectives are accurate and useful. The event notification tells us that foo(..) has completed, but also that it's OK to continue with the next step. Indeed, the callback you pass to be called for the event notification is itself what we've previously called a continuation. The completion event is a bit more focused on the foo(..), which has our attention at present, so we call it a completion event for the rest of this text.

With callbacks, the notification would be our callback invoked by the task (foo(..)). But with Promises, we turn the relationship around, and expect that we can listen for an event from foo(..), and when notified, proceed accordingly.

First, consider some pseudocode:

```
foo(x) {
    // start doing something that could take a while
}

foo( 42 )

on (foo "completion") {
    // now we can do the next step!
}

on (foo "error") {
    // oops, something went wrong in `foo(..)`
}
```

We call foo(..) and then we set up two event listeners, one for "completion" and one for "error"—the two possible final outcomes of the foo(..) call. In essence, foo(..) doesn't even appear to be aware that the calling code has subscribed to these events, which makes for a very nice *separation of concerns*.

Unfortunately, such code would require some magic of the JS environment that doesn't exist (and would likely be a bit impractical). Here's the more natural way we could express that in JS:

```
function foo(x) {
    // start doing something that could take a while

    // make a `listener` event notification
    // capability to return

    return listener;
}

var evt = foo( 42 );

evt.on( "completion", function(){
    // now we can do the next step!
} );

evt.on( "failure", function(err){
    // oops, something went wrong in `foo(..)`
} );
```

foo(..) expressly creates an event subscription capability to return back, and the calling code receives and registers the two event handlers against it.

The inversion from normal callback-oriented code should be obvious, and it's intentional. Instead of passing the callbacks to foo(..), it returns an event capability we call evt, which receives the callbacks.

But if you recall from Chapter 2, callbacks themselves represent an inversion of control. So inverting the callback pattern is actually an inversion of inversion, or an *uninversion of control*—restoring control back to the calling code where we wanted it to be in the first place.

One important benefit is that multiple separate parts of the code can be given the event listening capability, and they can all independently be notified when foo(..) completes, in order to perform subsequent steps:

```
var evt = foo( 42 );

// let `bar(..)` listen to `foo(..)`'s completion
bar( evt );

// also, let `baz(..)` listen to `foo(..)`'s completion
baz( evt );
```

Uninversion of control enables a nicer separation of concerns, where bar(..) and baz(..) don't need to be involved in how foo(..) is called. Similarly, foo(..) doesn't need to know or care that bar(..) and baz(..) exist or are waiting to be notified when foo(..) completes.

Essentially, this evt object is a neutral third-party negotiation between the separate concerns.

Promise "Events"

As you may have guessed by now, the evt event listening capability is an analogy for a Promise.

In a Promise-based approach, the previous snippet would have foo(..) creating and returning a Promise instance, and that promise would then be passed to bar(..) and baz(..).

 The Promise resolution "events" we listen for aren't strictly events (though they certainly behave like events for these purposes), and they're not typically called "completion" or "error". Instead, we use then(..) to register a "then" event. Or perhaps more precisely, then(..) registers "fulfillment" and/or "rejection" event(s), though we don't see those terms used explicitly in the code.

Consider:

```
function foo(x) {
    // start doing something that could take a while

    // construct and return a promise
    return new Promise( function(resolve,reject){
        // eventually, call `resolve(..)` or `reject(..)`,
        // which are the resolution callbacks for
        // the promise.
    } );
```

```
}

var p = foo( 42 );

bar( p );

baz( p );
```

The pattern shown with `new Promise( func tion(..){ .. } )` is generally called the *revealing constructor* (*http://domenic.me/2014/02/13/ the-revealing-constructor-pattern/*). The function passed in is executed immediately (not async deferred, as callbacks to `then(..)` are), and it's provided two parameters, which in this case we've named `resolve` and `reject`. These are the resolution functions for the promise. `resolve(..)` generally signals fulfillment, and `reject(..)` signals rejection.

You can probably guess what the internals of `bar(..)` and `baz(..)` might look like:

```
function bar(fooPromise) {
    // listen for `foo(..)` to complete
    fooPromise.then(
        function(){
            // `foo(..)` has now finished, so
            // do `bar(..)`'s task
        },
        function(){
            // oops, something went wrong in `foo(..)`
        }
    );
}

// ditto for `baz(..)`
```

Promise resolution doesn't necessarily need to involve sending along a message, as it did when we were examining Promises as future values. It can just be a flow-control signal, as used in the previous snippet.

Another way to approach this is:

```
function bar() {
    // `foo(..)` has definitely finished, so
    // do `bar(..)`'s task
}

function oopsBar() {
    // oops, something went wrong in `foo(..)`,
    // so `bar(..)` didn't run
}

// ditto for `baz()` and `oopsBaz()`

var p = foo( 42 );

p.then( bar, oopsBar );

p.then( baz, oopsBaz );
```

 If you've seen Promise-based coding before, you might be tempted to believe that the last two lines of that code could be written as p.then(..).then(..), using chaining, rather than p.then(..); p.then(..). That would have an entirely different behavior, so be careful! The difference might not be clear right now, but it's actually a different async pattern than we've seen thus far: splitting/forking. Don't worry! We'll come back to this point later in this chapter.

Instead of passing the p promise to bar(..) and baz(..), we use the promise to control when bar(..) and baz(..) will get executed, if ever. The primary difference is in the error handling.

In the first snippet's approach, bar(..) is called regardless of whether foo(..) succeeds or fails, and it handles its own fallback logic if it's notified that foo(..) failed. The same is true for baz(..), obviously.

In the second snippet, bar(..) gets called only if foo(..) succeeds, and otherwise oopsBar(..) gets called. Ditto for baz(..).

Neither approach is correct per se. There will be cases where one is preferred over the other.

In either case, the promise p that comes back from foo(..) is used to control what happens next.

Moreover, the fact that both snippets end up calling then(..) twice against the same promise p illustrates the point made earlier, which is that Promises (once resolved) retain their same resolution (fulfillment or rejection) forever, and can subsequently be observed as many times as necessary.

Whenever p is resolved, the next step will always be the same, both *now* and *later*.

Thenable Duck Typing

In Promises-land, an important detail is how to know for sure if some value is a genuine Promise or not. Or more directly, is it a value that will behave like a Promise?

Given that Promises are constructed by the new Promise(..) syntax, you might think that p instanceof Promise would be an acceptable check. But unfortunately, there are a number of reasons that's not totally sufficient.

Mainly, you can receive a Promise value from another browser window (iframe, etc.), which would have its own Promise different from the one in the current window/frame, and that check would fail to identify the Promise instance.

Moreover, a library or framework may choose to vend its own Promises and not use the native ES6 Promise implementation to do so. In fact, you may very well be using Promises with libraries in older browsers that have no Promise at all.

When we discuss Promise resolution processes later in this chapter, it will become more obvious why it is still very important to be able to recognize and assimilate a Promise-like value that is not genuine. But for now, just take my word for it that it's a critical piece of the puzzle.

As such, it was decided that the way to recognize a Promise (or something that behaves like a Promise) would be to define something called a *thenable* as any object or function which has a then(..) method on it. It is assumed that any such value is a Promise-conforming thenable.

The general term for *type checks* that make assumptions about a value's *type* based on its shape (what properties are present) is called *duck typing*—"If it looks like a duck, and quacks like a duck, it must be a duck" (see the *Types & Grammar* title of this series). So the duck typing check for a thenable would roughly be:

```
if (
    p !== null &&
    (
        typeof p === "object" ||
        typeof p === "function"
    ) &&
    typeof p.then === "function"
) {
    // assume it's a thenable!
}
else {
    // not a thenable
}
```

Yuck! Setting aside the fact that this logic is a bit ugly to implement in various places, there's something deeper and more troubling going on.

If you try to fulfill a Promise with any object/function value that happens to have a then(..) function on it, but you weren't intending it to be treated as a Promise/thenable, you're out of luck, because it will automatically be recognized as thenable and treated with special rules (see later in the chapter).

This is even true if you didn't realize the value has a then(..) on it. For example:

```
var o = { then: function(){} };

// make `v` be `[[Prototype]]`-linked to `o`
var v = Object.create( o );

v.someStuff = "cool";
v.otherStuff = "not so cool";

v.hasOwnProperty( "then" );    // false
```

v doesn't look like a Promise or thenable at all. It's just a plain object with some properties on it. You're probably just intending to send that value around like any other object.

But unknown to you, v is also [[Prototype]]-linked (see the *this & Object Prototypes* title of this series) to another object o, which happens to have a then(..) on it. So the thenable duck typing checks will think and assume v is a thenable. Uh-oh.

It doesn't even need to be something as directly intentional as that:

```
Object.prototype.then = function(){};
Array.prototype.then = function(){};

var v1 = { hello: "world" };
var v2 = [ "Hello", "World" ];
```

Both v1 and v2 will be assumed to be thenables. You can't control or predict if any other code accidentally or maliciously adds then(..) to Object.prototype, Array.prototype, or any of the other native prototypes. And if what's specified is a function that doesn't call either of its parameters as callbacks, then any Promise resolved with such a value will just silently hang forever! Crazy.

Sound implausible or unlikely? Perhaps.

But keep in mind that there were several well-known non-Promise libraries preexisting in the community prior to ES6 that happened to already have a method on them called then(..). Some of those libraries chose to rename their own methods to avoid collision (that sucks!). Others have simply been relegated to the unfortunate status of "incompatible with Promise-based coding" in reward for their inability to change to get out of the way.

The standards decision to hijack the previously nonreserved—and completely general-purpose sounding—then property name means that no value (or any of its delegates), either past, present, or future, can have a then(..) function present, either on purpose or by accident, or that value will be confused for a thenable in Promises systems, which will probably create bugs that are really hard to track down.

 I do not like how we ended up with duck typing of thenables for Promise recognition. There were other options, such as "branding" or even "anti-branding"; what we got seems like a worst-case compromise. But it's not all doom and gloom. Thenable duck typing can be helpful, as we'll see later. Just beware that thenable duck typing can be hazardous if it incorrectly identifies something as a Promise that isn't.

Promise Trust

We've now seen two strong analogies that explain different aspects of what Promises can do for our async code. But if we stop there, we've missed perhaps the single most important characteristic that the Promise pattern establishes: trust.

Whereas the future values and completion events analogies play out explicitly in the code patterns we've explored, it won't be entirely obvious why or how Promises are designed to solve all of the inversion of control trust issues we laid out in "Trust Issues" on page 39 in Chapter 2. But with a little digging, we can uncover some important guarantees that restore the confidence in async coding that Chapter 2 tore down!

Let's start by reviewing the trust issues with callbacks-only coding. When you pass a callback to a utility foo(..), it might:

- Call the callback too early
- Call the callback too late (or never)
- Call the callback too few or too many times
- Fail to pass along any necessary environment/parameters
- Swallow any errors/exceptions that may happen

The characteristics of Promises are intentionally designed to provide useful, repeatable answers to all these concerns.

Calling Too Early

Primarily, this is a concern of whether code can introduce Zalgo-like effects (see Chapter 2), where sometimes a task finishes synchronously and sometimes asynchronously, which can lead to race conditions.

Promises by definition cannot be susceptible to this concern, because even an immediately fulfilled Promise (like new Promise(function(resolve){ resolve(42); })) cannot be observed synchronously.

That is, when you call then(..) on a Promise, even if that Promise was already resolved, the callback you provide to then(..) will always be called asynchronously (for more on this, refer back to "Jobs" on page 23 in Chapter 1).

No more need to insert your own `setTimeout(..,0)` hacks. Promises prevent Zalgo automatically.

Calling Too Late

Similar to the previous point, a Promise's `then(..)` registered observation callbacks are automatically scheduled when either `resolve(..)` or `reject(..)` are called by the Promise creation capability. Those scheduled callbacks will predictably be fired at the next asynchronous moment (see "Jobs" on page 23 in Chapter 1).

It's not possible for synchronous observation, so it's not possible for a synchronous chain of tasks to run in such a way to in effect delay another callback from happening as expected. That is, when a Promise is resolved, all `then(..)` registered callbacks on it will be called, in order, immediately at the next asynchronous opportunity (again, see "Jobs" on page 23 in Chapter 1), and nothing that happens inside of one of those callbacks can affect/delay the calling of the other callbacks.

For example:

```
p.then( function(){
    p.then( function(){
        console.log( "C" );
    } );
    console.log( "A" );
} );
p.then( function(){
    console.log( "B" );
} );
// A B C
```

Here, `"C"` cannot interrupt and precede `"B"`, by virtue of how Promises are defined to operate.

Promise Scheduling Quirks

It's important to note, though, that there are lots of nuances of scheduling where the relative ordering between callbacks chained off two separate Promises is not reliably predictable.

If two promises `p1` and `p2` are both already resolved, it should be true that `p1.then(..); p2.then(..)` would end up calling the callback(s) for `p1` before the ones for `p2`. But there are subtle cases where that might not be true, such as the following:

```
var p3 = new Promise( function(resolve,reject){
    resolve( "B" );
} );

var p1 = new Promise( function(resolve,reject){
    resolve( p3 );
} );

p2 = new Promise( function(resolve,reject){
    resolve( "A" );
} );

p1.then( function(v){
    console.log( v );
} );

p2.then( function(v){
    console.log( v );
} );

// A B  <-- not  B A  as you might expect
```

We'll cover this more later, but as you can see, p1 is resolved not with an immediate value, but with another promise p3, which is itself resolved with the value "B". The specified behavior is to unwrap p3 into p1, but asynchronously, so p1's callback(s) are *behind* p2's callback(s) in the asynchronus Job queue (see "Jobs" on page 23).

To avoid such nuanced nightmares, you should never rely on anything about the ordering/scheduling of callbacks across Promises. In fact, a good practice is not to code in such a way where the ordering of multiple callbacks matters at all. Avoid that if you can.

Never Calling the Callback

This is a very common concern. It's addressable in several ways with Promises.

First, nothing (not even a JS error) can prevent a Promise from notifying you of its resolution (if it's resolved). If you register both fulfillment and rejection callbacks for a Promise, and the Promise gets resolved, one of the two callbacks will always be called.

Of course, if your callbacks themselves have JS errors, you may not see the outcome you expect, but the callback will in fact have been called. We'll cover later how to be notified of an error in your call-back, because even those don't get swallowed.

But what if the Promise itself never gets resolved either way? Even that is a condition that Promises provide an answer for, using a higher level abstraction called a *race*:

```
// a utility for timing out a Promise
function timeoutPromise(delay) {
    return new Promise( function(resolve,reject){
        setTimeout( function(){
            reject( "Timeout!" );
        }, delay );
    } );
}

// setup a timeout for `foo()`
Promise.race( [
    foo(),                      // attempt `foo()`
    timeoutPromise( 3000 )   // give it 3 seconds
] )
.then(
    function(){
        // `foo(..)` fulfilled in time!
    },
    function(err){
        // either `foo()` rejected, or it just
        // didn't finish in time, so inspect
        // `err` to know which
    }
);
```

There are more details to consider with this Promise timeout pattern, but we'll come back to it later.

Importantly, we can ensure a signal as to the outcome of foo(), to prevent it from hanging our program indefinitely.

Calling Too Few or Too Many Times

By definition, *one* is the appropriate number of times for the call-back to be called. The "too few" case would be zero calls, which is the same as the "never" case we just examined.

The "too many" case is easy to explain. Promises are defined so that they can only be resolved once. If for some reason the Promise creation code tries to call resolve(..) or reject(..) multiple times, or tries to call both, the Promise will accept only the first resolution, and silently ignore any subsequent attempts.

Because a Promise can only be resolved once, any then(..) registered callbacks will only ever be called once (each).

Of course, if you register the same callback more than once, (e.g., p.then(f); p.then(f);), it'll be called as many times as it was registered. The guarantee that a response function is called only once does not prevent you from shooting yourself in the foot.

Failing to Pass Along Any Parameters/Environment

Promises can have, at most, one resolution value (fulfillment or rejection).

If you don't explicitly resolve with a value either way, the value is undefined, as is typical in JS. But whatever the value, it will always be passed to all registered (and appropriate fulfillment or rejection) callbacks, either now or in the future.

Something to be aware of: If you call resolve(..) or reject(..) with multiple parameters, all subsequent parameters beyond the first will be silently ignored. Although that might seem a violation of the guarantee we just described, it's not exactly, because it constitutes an invalid usage of the Promise mechanism. Other invalid usages of the API (such as calling resolve(..) multiple times) are similarly protected, so the Promise behavior here is consistent (if not a tiny bit frustrating).

If you want to pass along multiple values, you must wrap them in another single value that you pass, such as an array or an object.

As for environment, functions in JS always retain their closure of the scope in which they're defined (see the *Scope & Closures* title of this series), so they of course would continue to have access to whatever surrounding state you provide. Of course, the same is true of callbacks-only design, so this isn't a specific augmentation of benefit from Promises—but it's a guarantee we can rely on nonetheless.

Swallowing Any Errors/Exceptions

In the base sense, this is a restatement of the previous point. If you reject a Promise with a *reason* (aka an error message), that value is passed to the rejection callback(s).

But there's something much bigger at play here. If at any point in the creation of a Promise, or in the observation of its resolution, a JS exception error occurs, such as a `TypeError` or `ReferenceError`, that exception will be caught, and it will force the Promise in question to become rejected.

For example:

```
var p = new Promise( function(resolve,reject){
    foo.bar();  // `foo` is not defined, so error!
    resolve( 42 );  // never gets here :(
} );

p.then(
    function fulfilled(){
        // never gets here :(
    },
    function rejected(err){
        // `err` will be a `TypeError` exception object
        // from the `foo.bar()` line.
    }
);
```

The JS exception that occurs from `foo.bar()` becomes a Promise rejection that you can catch and respond to.

This is an important detail, because it effectively solves another potential Zalgo moment, which is that errors could create a synchronous reaction whereas nonerrors would be asynchronous. Promises turn even JS exceptions into asynchronous behavior, thereby reducing the race condition chances greatly.

But what happens if a Promise is fulfilled, but there's a JS exception error during the observation (in a then(..) registered callback)? Even those aren't lost, but you may find how they're handled a bit surprising, until you dig in a little deeper:

```
var p = new Promise( function(resolve,reject){
    resolve( 42 );
} );

p.then(
    function fulfilled(msg){
        foo.bar();
        console.log( msg );  // never gets here :(
    },
    function rejected(err){
        // never gets here either :(
    }
);
```

Wait, that makes it seem like the exception from foo.bar() really did get swallowed. Never fear, it didn't. But something deeper is wrong, which is that we've failed to listen for it. The p.then(..) call itself returns another promise, and it's *that* promise that will be rejected with the TypeError exception.

Why couldn't it just call the error handler we have defined there? Seems like a logical behavior on the surface. But it would violate the fundamental principle that Promises are immutable once resolved. p was already fulfilled to the value 42, so it can't later be changed to a rejection just because there's an error in observing p's resolution.

Besides the principle violation, such behavior could wreak havoc, if say there were multiple then(..) registered callbacks on the promise p, because some would get called and others wouldn't, and it would be very opaque as to why.

Trustable Promise?

There's one last detail to examine to establish trust based on the Promise pattern.

You've no doubt noticed that Promises don't get rid of callbacks at all. They just change where the callback is passed to. Instead of passing a callback to foo(..), we get something (ostensibly a genuine Promise) back from foo(..), and we pass the callback to that something instead.

But why would this be any more trustable than just callbacks alone? How can we be sure the something we get back is in fact a trustable Promise? Isn't it basically all just a house of cards where we can trust only because we already trusted?

One of the most important, but often overlooked, details of Promises is that they have a solution to this issue as well. Included with the native ES6 Promise implementation is Promise.resolve(..).

If you pass an immediate, non-Promise, non-thenable value to Promise.resolve(..), you get a promise that's fulfilled with that value. In this case, promises p1 and p2 will behave identically:

```
var p1 = new Promise( function(resolve,reject){
    resolve( 42 );
} );

var p2 = Promise.resolve( 42 );
```

But if you pass a genuine Promise to `Promise.resolve(..)`, you just get the same promise back:

```
var p1 = Promise.resolve( 42 );

var p2 = Promise.resolve( p1 );

p1 === p2; // true
```

Even more importantly, if you pass a non-Promise thenable value to `Promise.resolve(..)`, it will attempt to unwrap that value, and the unwrapping will keep going until a concrete final non-Promise-like value is extracted.

Recall our previous discussion of thenables?

Consider:

```
var p = {
    then: function(cb) {
        cb( 42 );
    }
};

// this works OK, but only by good fortune
p
.then(
    function fulfilled(val){
        console.log( val ); // 42
    },
    function rejected(err){
        // never gets here
    }
);
```

This p is a thenable, but it's not a genuine Promise. Luckily, it's reasonable, as most will be. But what if you got back instead something that looked like:

```
var p = {
    then: function(cb,errcb) {
        cb( 42 );
        errcb( "evil laugh" );
    }
};

p
.then(
    function fulfilled(val){
        console.log( val ); // 42
    },
```

```
    function rejected(err){
        // oops, shouldn't have run
        console.log( err ); // evil laugh
    }
);
```

This p is a thenable but it's not so well behaved of a promise. Is it malicious? Or is it just ignorant of how Promises should work? It doesn't really matter, to be honest. In either case, it's not trustable as is.

Nonetheless, we can pass either of these versions of p to Promise.resolve(..), and we'll get the normalized, safe result we'd expect:

```
Promise.resolve( p )
.then(
    function fulfilled(val){
        console.log( val ); // 42
    },
    function rejected(err){
        // never gets here
    }
);
```

Promise.resolve(..) will accept any thenable, and unwrap it to its non-thenable value. But you get back from Promise.resolve(..) a real, genuine Promise in its place, one that you can trust. If what you passed in is already a genuine Promise, you just get it right back, so there's no downside at all to filtering through Promise.resolve(..) to gain trust.

So let's say we're calling a foo(..) utility and we're not sure we can trust its return value to be a well-behaving Promise, but we know it's at least a thenable. Promise.resolve(..) will give us a trustable Promise wrapper to chain off of:

```
// don't just do this:
foo( 42 )
.then( function(v){
    console.log( v );
} );

// instead, do this:
Promise.resolve( foo( 42 ) )
.then( function(v){
    console.log( v );
} );
```

Another beneficial side effect of wrapping `Promise.resolve(..)` around any function's return value (thenable or not) is that it's an easy way to normalize that function call into a well-behaving async task. If `foo(42)` returns an immediate value sometimes, or a Promise other times, `Promise.resolve( foo(42) )` makes sure it's always a Promise result. And avoiding Zalgo makes for much better code.

Trust Built

Hopefully the previous discussion now fully "resolves" (pun intended) in your mind why the Promise is trustable, and more importantly, why that trust is so critical in building robust, maintainable software.

Can you write async code in JS without trust? Of course you can. We JS developers have been coding async with nothing but callbacks for nearly two decades.

But once you start questioning just how much you can trust the mechanisms you build upon to actually be predictable and reliable, you start to realize callbacks have a pretty shaky trust foundation.

Promises are a pattern that augments callbacks with trustable semantics, so that the behavior is more reason-able and more reliable. By uninverting the inversion of control of callbacks, we place the control with a trustable system (Promises) that was designed specifically to bring sanity to our async.

Chain Flow

We've hinted at this a couple of times already, but Promises are not just a mechanism for a single-step *this-then-that* sort of operation. That's the building block, of course, but it turns out we can string multiple Promises together to represent a sequence of async steps.

The key to making this work is built on two behaviors intrinsic to Promises:

- Every time you call `then(..)` on a Promise, it creates and returns a new Promise, which we can *chain* with.

- Whatever value you return from the then(..) call's fulfillment callback (the first parameter) is automatically set as the fulfillment of the chained Promise (from the first point).

Let's first illustrate what that means, and then we'll derive how that helps us create async sequences of flow control. Consider the following:

```
var p = Promise.resolve( 21 );

var p2 = p.then( function(v){
    console.log( v );   // 21

    // fulfill `p2` with value `42`
    return v * 2;
} );
// chain off `p2`
p2.then( function(v){
    console.log( v );   // 42
} );
```

By returning v * 2 (i.e., 42), we fulfill the p2 promise that the first then(..) call created and returned. When p2's then(..) call runs, it's receiving the fulfillment from the return v * 2 statement. Of course, p2.then(..) creates yet another promise, which we could have stored in a p3 variable.

But it's a little annoying to have to create an intermediate variable p2 (or p3, etc.). Thankfully, we can easily just chain these together:

```
var p = Promise.resolve( 21 );

p
.then( function(v){
    console.log( v );   // 21

    // fulfill the chained promise with value `42`
    return v * 2;
} )
// here's the chained promise
.then( function(v){
    console.log( v );   // 42
} );
```

So now the first then(..) is the first step in an async sequence, and the second then(..) is the second step. This could keep going for as long as you need it to extend. Just keep chaining off a previous then(..) with each automatically created Promise.

But there's something missing here. What if we want step 2 to wait for step 1 to do something asynchronous? We're using an immediate `return` statement, which immediately fulfills the chained promise.

The key to making a Promise sequence truly async capable at every step is to recall how `Promise.resolve(..)` operates when what you pass to it is a Promise or thenable instead of a final value. `Promise.resolve(..)` directly returns a received genuine Promise, or it unwraps the value of a received thenable—and keeps going recursively while it keeps unwrapping thenables.

The same sort of unwrapping happens if you `return` a thenable or Promise from the fulfillment (or rejection) handler. Consider:

```
var p = Promise.resolve( 21 );

p.then( function(v){
    console.log( v );    // 21

    // create a promise and return it
    return new Promise( function(resolve,reject){
        // fulfill with value `42`
        resolve( v * 2 );
    } );
} )
.then( function(v){
    console.log( v );    // 42
} );
```

Even though we wrapped 42 up in a promise that we returned, it still got unwrapped and ended up as the resolution of the chained promise, such that the second `then(..)` still received 42. If we introduce asynchrony to that wrapping promise, everything still nicely works the same:

```
var p = Promise.resolve( 21 );

p.then( function(v){
    console.log( v );    // 21

    // create a promise to return
    return new Promise( function(resolve,reject){
        // introduce asynchrony!
        setTimeout( function(){
            // fulfill with value `42`
            resolve( v * 2 );
        }, 100 );
    } );
} );
```

```
} )
.then( function(v){
    // runs after the 100ms delay in the previous step
    console.log( v );   // 42
} );
```

That's incredibly powerful! Now we can construct a sequence of however many async steps we want, and each step can delay the next step (or not!), as necessary.

Of course, the value passing from step to step in these examples is optional. If you don't return an explicit value, an implicit `undefined` is assumed, and the promises still chain together the same way. Each Promise resolution is thus just a signal to proceed to the next step.

To further the chain illustration, let's generalize a delay-Promise creation (without resolution messages) into a utility we can reuse for multiple steps:

```
function delay(time) {
    return new Promise( function(resolve,reject){
        setTimeout( resolve, time );
    } );
}

delay( 100 ) // step 1
.then( function STEP2(){
    console.log( "step 2 (after 100ms)" );
    return delay( 200 );
} )
.then( function STEP3(){
    console.log( "step 3 (after another 200ms)" );
} )
.then( function STEP4(){
    console.log( "step 4 (next Job)" );
    return delay( 50 );
} )
.then( function STEP5(){
    console.log( "step 5 (after another 50ms)" );
} )
...
```

Calling `delay(200)` creates a promise that will fulfill in 200ms, and then we return that from the first `then(..)` fulfillment callback, which causes the second `then(..)`'s promise to wait on that 200ms promise.

As described, technically there are two promises in that interchange: the 200ms-delay promise and the chained promise that the second then(..) chains from. But you may find it easier to mentally combine these two promises together, because the Promise mechanism automatically merges their states for you. In that respect, you could think of `return delay(200)` as creating a promise that replaces the earlier-returned chained promise.

To be honest, though, sequences of delays with no message passing isn't a terribly useful example of Promise flow control. Let's look at a scenario that's a little more practical.

Instead of timers, let's consider making Ajax requests:

```
// assume an `ajax( {url}, {callback} )` utility

// Promise-aware ajax
function request(url) {
    return new Promise( function(resolve,reject){
        // the `ajax(..)` callback should be our
        // promise's `resolve(..)` function
        ajax( url, resolve );
    } );
}
```

We first define a `request(..)` utility that constructs a promise to represent the completion of the `ajax(..)` call:

```
request( "http://some.url.1/" )
.then( function(response1){
    return request( "http://some.url.2/?v=" + response1 );
} )
.then( function(response2){
    console.log( response2 );
} );
```

Developers commonly encounter situations in which they want to do Promise-aware async flow control with utilities that are not themselves Promise-enabled (like `ajax(..)` here, which expects a callback). Although the native ES6 `Promise` mechanism doesn't automatically solve this pattern for us, practically all Promise libraries do. They usually call this process "lifting," "promisifying," or some variation thereof. We'll come back to this technique later.

Using the Promise-returning `request(..)`, we create the first step in our chain implicitly by calling it with the first URL, and chain off that returned promise with the first `then(..)`.

Once `response1` comes back, we use that value to construct a second URL, and make a second `request(..)` call. That second `request(..)` promise is `returned` so that the third step in our async flow control waits for that Ajax call to complete. Finally, we print `response2` once it returns.

The Promise chain we construct is not only a flow control that expresses a multistep async sequence, but it also acts as a message channel to propagate messages from step to step.

What if something went wrong in one of the steps of the Promise chain? An error/exception is on a per-Promise basis, which means it's possible to catch such an error at any point in the chain, and that catching acts to sort of "reset" the chain back to normal operation at that point:

```
// step 1:
request( "http://some.url.1/" )

// step 2:
.then( function(response1){
    foo.bar(); // undefined, error!

    // never gets here
    return request( "http://some.url.2/?v=" + response1 );
} )

// step 3:
.then(
    function fulfilled(response2){
        // never gets here
    },
```

```
    // rejection handler to catch the error
    function rejected(err){
        console.log( err );
        // `TypeError` from `foo.bar()` error
        return 42;
    }
)
// step 4:
.then( function(msg){
    console.log( msg );      // 42
} );
```

When the error occurs in step 2, the rejection handler in step 3 catches it. The return value (42 in this snippet), if any, from that rejection handler fulfills the promise for the next step (4), such that the chain is now back in a fulfillment state.

 As we discussed earlier, when returning a promise from a fulfillment handler, it's unwrapped and can delay the next step. That's also true for returning promises from rejection handlers, such that if the return 42 in step 3 instead returned a promise, that promise could delay step 4. A thrown exception inside either the fulfillment or rejection handler of a then(..) call causes the next (chained) promise to be immediately rejected with that exception.

If you call then(..) on a promise, and you only pass a fulfillment handler to it, an assumed rejection handler is substituted:

```
var p = new Promise( function(resolve,reject){
    reject( "Oops" );
} );

var p2 = p.then(
    function fulfilled(){
        // never gets here
    }
    // assumed rejection handler, if omitted or
    // any other non-function value passed
    // function(err) {
    //     throw err;
    // }
);
```

As you can see, the assumed rejection handler simply rethrows the error, which ends up forcing p2 (the chained promise) to reject with the same error reason. In essence, this allows the error to continue propagating along a Promise chain until an explicitly defined rejection handler is encountered.

 We'll cover more details of error handling with Promises a little later, because there are other nuanced details to be concerned about.

If a proper valid function is not passed as the fulfillment handler parameter to then(..), there's also a default handler substituted:

```
var p = Promise.resolve( 42 );

p.then(
    // assumed fulfillment handler, if omitted or
    // any other non-function value passed
    // function(v) {
    //     return v;
    // }
    null,
    function rejected(err){
        // never gets here
    }
);
```

As you can see, the default fulfillment handler simply passes whatever value it receives along to the next step (Promise).

 The then(null,function(err){ .. }) pattern —only handling rejections (if any) but letting fulfillments pass through—has a shortcut in the API: catch(function(err){ .. }). We'll cover catch(..) more fully in the next section.

Let's review briefly the intrinsic behaviors of Promises that enable chaining flow control:

- A then(..) call against one Promise automatically produces a new Promise to return from the call.

- Inside the fulfillment/rejection handlers, if you return a value or an exception is thrown, the new returned (chainable) Promise is resolved accordingly.

- If the fulfillment or rejection handler returns a Promise, it is unwrapped, so that whatever its resolution is will become the resolution of the chained Promise returned from the current then(..).

While chaining flow control is helpful, it's probably most accurate to think of it as a side benefit of how Promises compose (combine) together, rather than the main intent. As we've discussed in detail several times already, Promises normalize asynchrony and encapsulate time-dependent value state, and *that* is what lets us chain them together in this useful way.

Certainly, the sequential expressiveness of the chain (this-then-this-then-this...) is a big improvement over the tangled mess of callbacks as we identified in Chapter 2. But there's still a fair amount of boilerplate (then(..) and function(){ .. }) to wade through. In Chapter 4, we'll see a significantly nicer pattern for sequential flow control expressivity, with generators.

Terminology: Resolve, Fulfill, and Reject

There's some slight confusion around the terms *resolve*, *fulfill*, and *reject* that we need to clear up, before you get too much deeper into learning about Promises. Let's first consider the Promise(..) constructor:

```
var p = new Promise( function(X,Y){
    // X() for fulfillment
    // Y() for rejection
} );
```

As you can see, two callbacks (here labeled X and Y) are provided. The first is *usually* used to mark the Promise as fulfilled, and the second *always* marks the Promise as rejected. But what's the *usually* about, and what does that imply about accurately naming those parameters?

Ultimately, it's just your user code and the identifier names aren't interpreted by the engine to mean anything, so it doesn't technically matter; foo(..) and bar(..) are equally functional. But the words you use can affect not only how you are thinking about the code, but how other developers on your team will think about it. Thinking wrongly about carefully orchestrated async code is almost surely going to be worse than the spaghetti-callback alternatives.

So it actually does kind of matter what you call them.

The second parameter is easy to decide. Almost all literature uses reject(..) as its name, and because that's exactly (and only!) what it does, that's a very good choice for the name. I'd strongly recommend you always use reject(..).

But there's a little more ambiguity around the first parameter, which in Promise literature is often labeled resolve(..). That word is obviously related to "resolution," which is what's used across the literature (including this book) to describe setting a final value/state to a Promise. We've already used "resolve the Promise" several times to mean either fulfilling or rejecting the Promise.

But if this parameter seems to be used to specifically fulfill the Promise, why shouldn't we call it fulfill(..) instead of resolve(..) to be more accurate? To answer that question, let's also take a look at two of the Promise API methods:

```
var fulfilledPr = Promise.resolve( 42 );

var rejectedPr = Promise.reject( "Oops" );
```

Promise.resolve(..) creates a Promise that's resolved to the value given to it. In this example, 42 is a normal, non-Promise, non-thenable value, so the fulfilled promise fulfilledPr is created for the value 42. Promise.reject("Oops") creates the rejected promise rejectedPr for the reason "Oops".

Let's now illustrate why the word "resolve" (such as in Promise.resolve(..)) is unambiguous and indeed more accurate, if used explicitly in a context that could result in either fulfillment or rejection:

```
var rejectedTh = {
    then: function(resolved,rejected) {
        rejected( "Oops" );
    }
};

var rejectedPr = Promise.resolve( rejectedTh );
```

As we discussed earlier in this chapter, `Promise.resolve(..)` will return a received genuine Promise directly, or unwrap a received thenable. If that thenable unwrapping reveals a rejected state, the Promise returned from `Promise.resolve(..)` is in fact in that same rejected state.

So `Promise.resolve(..)` is a good, accurate name for the API method, because it can actually result in either fulfillment or rejection.

The first callback parameter of the `Promise(..)` constructor will unwrap either a thenable (identically to `Promise.resolve(..)`) or a genuine Promise:

```
var rejectedPr = new Promise( function(resolve,reject){
    // resolve this promise with a rejected promise
    resolve( Promise.reject( "Oops" ) );
} );

rejectedPr.then(
    function fulfilled(){
        // never gets here
    },
    function rejected(err){
        console.log( err ); // "Oops"
    }
);
```

It should be clear now that `resolve(..)` is the appropriate name for the first callback parameter of the `Promise(..)` constructor.

The previously mentioned `reject(..)` does *not* do the unwrapping that `resolve(..)` does. If you pass a Promise/thenable value to `reject(..)`, that untouched value will be set as the rejection reason. A subsequent rejection handler would receive the actual Promise/thenable you passed to `reject(..)`, not its underlying immediate value.

But now let's turn our attention to the callbacks provided to `then(..)`. What should they be called (both in literature and in code)? I would suggest `fulfilled(..)` and `rejected(..)`:

```
function fulfilled(msg) {
    console.log( msg );
}
```

```
function rejected(err) {
    console.error( err );
}

p.then(
    fulfilled,
    rejected
);
```

In the case of the first parameter to then(..), it's unambiguously always the fulfillment case, so there's no need for the duality of "resolve" terminology. As a side note, the ES6 specification uses onFulfilled(..) and onRejected(..) to label these two callbacks, so they are accurate terms.

Error Handling

We've already seen several examples of how Promise rejection—either intentional through calling reject(..) or accidental through JS exceptions—allows saner error handling in asynchronous programming. Let's circle back though and be explicit about some of the details that we glossed over.

The most natural form of error handling for most developers is the synchronous try..catch construct. Unfortunately, it's synchronous-only, so it fails to help in async code patterns:

```
function foo() {
    setTimeout( function(){
        baz.bar();
    }, 100 );
}

try {
    foo();
    // later throws global error from `baz.bar()`
}
catch (err) {
    // never gets here
}
```

try..catch would certainly be nice to have, but it doesn't work across async operations. That is, unless there's some additional environmental support, which we'll come back to with generators in Chapter 4.

In callbacks, some standards have emerged for patterned error handling, most notably the *error-first callback* style:

```
function foo(cb) {
    setTimeout( function(){
        try {
            var x = baz.bar();
            cb( null, x ); // success!
        }
        catch (err) {
            cb( err );
        }
    }, 100 );
}

foo( function(err,val){
    if (err) {
        console.error( err ); // bummer :(
    }
    else {
        console.log( val );
    }
} );
```

 The try..catch here works only from the perspective that the baz.bar() call will either succeed or fail immediately, synchronously. If baz.bar() was itself its own async completing function, any async errors inside it would not be catchable.

The callback we pass to foo(..) expects to receive a signal of an error by the reserved first parameter, err. If present, error is assumed. If not, success is assumed.

This sort of error handling is technically async capable, but it doesn't compose well at all. Multiple levels of error-first callbacks woven together with these ubiquitous if statement checks will inevitably lead you to the perils of callback hell (see Chapter 2).

So we come back to error handling in Promises, with the rejection handler passed to then(..). Promises don't use the popular error-first callback design style, but instead use split-callback style; there's one callback for fulfillment and one for rejection:

```
var p = Promise.reject( "Oops" );

p.then(
    function fulfilled(){
        // never gets here
    },
    function rejected(err){
        console.log( err ); // "Oops"
    }
);
```

While this pattern of error handling makes fine sense on the surface, the nuances of Promise error handling are often a fair bit more difficult to fully grasp.

Consider:

```
var p = Promise.resolve( 42 );

p.then(
    function fulfilled(msg){
        // numbers don't have string functions,
        // so will throw an error
        console.log( msg.toLowerCase() );
    },
    function rejected(err){
        // never gets here
    }
);
```

If the `msg.toLowerCase()` legitimately throws an error (it does!), why doesn't our error handler get notified? As we explained earlier, it's because *that* error handler is for the p promise, which has already been fulfilled with value 42. The p promise is immutable, so the only promise that can be notified of the error is the one returned from p.then(..), which in this case we don't capture.

That should paint a clear picture of why error handling with Promises is error-prone (pun intended). It's far too easy to have errors swallowed, as this is very rarely what you'd intend.

If you use the Promise API in an invalid way and an error occurs that prevents proper Promise construction, the result will be an immediately thrown exception, *not a rejected Promise*. Some examples of incorrect usage that fail Promise construction: new Promise(null), Promise.all(), Promise.race(42), and so on. You can't get a rejected Promise if you don't use the Promise API validly enough to actually construct a Promise in the first place!

Pit of Despair

Jeff Atwood noted years ago that programming languages are often set up in such a way that, by default, developers fall into the "pit of despair" (*http://blog.codinghorror.com/falling-into-the-pit-of-success*) —where accidents are punished—and that you have to try harder to get it right. He implored us to instead create a "pit of success," where by default you fall into expected (successful) action, and thus would have to try hard to fail.

Promise error handling is unquestionably "pit of despair" design. By default, it assumes that you want any error to be swallowed by the Promise state, and if you forget to observe that state, the error silently languishes/dies in obscurity—usually despair.

To avoid losing an error to the silence of a forgotten/discarded Promise, some developers have claimed that a best practice for Promise chains is to always end your chain with a final catch(..), like:

```
var p = Promise.resolve( 42 );

p.then(
    function fulfilled(msg){
        // numbers don't have string functions,
        // so will throw an error
        console.log( msg.toLowerCase() );
    }
)
.catch( handleErrors );
```

Because we didn't pass a rejection handler to the then(..), the default handler was substituted, which simply propagates the error to the next promise in the chain. As such, both errors that come into p, and errors that come *after* p in its resolution (like the msg.toLo werCase() one) will filter down to the final handleErrors(..).

Problem solved, right? Not so fast!

What happens if handleErrors(..) itself also has an error in it? Who catches that? There's still yet another unattended promise: the one catch(..) returns, which we don't capture and don't register a rejection handler for.

You can't just stick another catch(..) on the end of that chain, because it too could fail. The last step in any Promise chain, whatever it is, always has the possibility, even decreasingly so, of dangling with an uncaught error stuck inside an unobserved Promise.

Sound like an impossible conundrum yet?

Uncaught Handling

It's not exactly an easy problem to solve completely. There are other (many would say better) ways to approach it.

Some Promise libraries have added methods for registering something like a "global unhandled rejection" handler, which would be called instead of a globally thrown error. But their solution for how to identify an error as uncaught is to have an arbitrary-length timer, say three seconds, running from time of rejection. If a Promise is rejected but no error handler is registered before the timer fires, then it's assumed that you won't ever be registering a handler, so it's uncaught.

In practice, this has worked well for many libraries, as most usage patterns don't typically call for significant delay between Promise rejection and observation of that rejection. But this pattern is troublesome because three seconds is so arbitrary (even if empirical), and also because there are indeed some cases where you want a Promise to hold on to its rejectedness for some indefinite period of time, and you don't really want to have your uncaught handler called for all those false positives (not-yet-handled uncaught errors).

Another more common suggestion is that Promises should have a done(..) added to them, which essentially marks the Promise chain as done. done(..) doesn't create and return a Promise, so the callbacks passed to done(..) are obviously not wired up to report problems to a chained Promise that doesn't exist.

So what happens instead? It's treated as you might usually expect in uncaught error conditions: any exception inside a done(..) rejection handler would be thrown as a global uncaught error (in the developer console, basically):

```
var p = Promise.resolve( 42 );

p.then(
    function fulfilled(msg){
        // numbers don't have string functions,
        // so will throw an error
        console.log( msg.toLowerCase() );
    }
)
.done( null, handleErrors );

// if `handleErrors(..)` caused its own exception, it would
// be thrown globally here
```

This might sound more attractive than the never-ending chain or the arbitrary timeouts. But the biggest problem is that it's not part of the ES6 standard, so no matter how good it sounds, at best it's a lot longer way off from being a reliable and ubiquitous solution.

Are we just stuck, then? Not entirely.

Browsers have a unique capability that our code does not have: they can track and know for sure when any object gets thrown away and garbage collected. So, browsers can track Promise objects, and whenever they get garbage collected, if they have a rejection in them, the browser knows for sure this was a legitimate uncaught error, and can thus confidently know it should report it to the developer console.

 At the time of this writing, both Chrome and Firefox have early attempts at this sort of uncaught rejection capability, though support is incomplete at best.

However, if a Promise doesn't get garbage collected—it's exceedingly easy for that to accidentally happen through lots of different coding patterns—the browser's garbage collection sniffing won't help you know and diagnose that you have a silently rejected Promise laying around.

Is there any other alternative? Yes.

Pit of Success

The following is just theoretical, how Promises could be someday changed to behave. I believe it would be far superior to what we currently have. And I think this change would be possible even post-ES6 because I don't think it would break web compatibility with ES6 Promises. Moreover, it can be polyfilled/prollyfilled in, if you're careful. Let's take a look:

- Promises could default to reporting (to the developer console) any rejection, on the next Job or event loop tick, if at that exact moment no error handler has been registered for the Promise.

- For the cases where you want a rejected Promise to hold onto its rejected state for an indefinite amount of time before observing, you could call defer(), which suppresses automatic error reporting on that Promise.

If a Promise is rejected, it defaults to noisily reporting that fact to the developer console (instead of defaulting to silence). You can opt out of that reporting either implicitly (by registering an error handler before rejection), or explicitly (with defer()). In either case, *you* control the false positives.

Consider:

```
var p = Promise.reject( "Oops" ).defer();

// `foo(..)` is Promise-aware
foo( 42 )
.then(
    function fulfilled(){
        return p;
    },
    function rejected(err){
        // handle `foo(..)` error
    }
);
...
```

When we create p, we know we're going to wait a while to use/ observe its rejection, so we call defer()—thus no global reporting. defer() simply returns the same promise, for chaining purposes.

The promise returned from foo(..) gets an error handler attached right away, so it's implicitly opted out and no global reporting for it occurs either.

But the promise returned from the then(..) call has no defer() or error handler attached, so if it rejects (from inside either resolution handler), then *it* will be reported to the developer console as an uncaught error.

This design is a pit of success. By default, all errors are either handled or reported—what almost all developers in almost all cases would expect. You either have to register a handler or you have to intentionally opt out, and indicate you intend to defer error handling until *later*; you're opting for the extra responsibility in just that specific case.

The only real danger in this approach is if you defer() a Promise but then fail to actually ever observe/handle its rejection.

But you had to intentionally call defer() to opt into that pit of despair—the default was the pit of success—so there's not much else we could do to save you from your own mistakes.

I think there's still hope for Promise error handling (post-ES6). I hope the powers that be will rethink the situation and consider this alternative. In the meantime, you can implement this yourself (a challenging exercise for the reader!), or use a smarter Promise library that does so for you!

This exact model for error handling/reporting is implemented in my *asynquence* Promise abstraction library, which is discussed in Appendix A of this book.

Promise Patterns

We've already implicitly seen the sequence pattern with Promise chains (this-then-this-then-that flow control) but there are lots of variations on asynchronous patterns that we can build as abstractions on top of Promises. These patterns serve to simplify the expression of async flow control—which helps make our code more reason-able and more maintainable—even in the most complex parts of our programs.

Two such patterns are codified directly into the native ES6 Promise implementation, so we get them for free, to use as building blocks for other patterns.

Promise.all([..])

In an async sequence (Promise chain), only one async task is being coordinated at any given moment—step 2 strictly follows step 1, and step 3 strictly follows step 2. But what about doing two or more steps concurrently (aka "in parallel")?

In classic programming terminology, a gate is a mechanism that waits on two or more parallel/concurrent tasks to complete before continuing. It doesn't matter what order they finish in, just that all of them have to complete for the gate to open and let the flow control through.

In the Promise API, we call this pattern all([..]).

Say you wanted to make two Ajax requests at the same time, and wait for both to finish, regardless of their order, before making a third Ajax request. Consider:

```
// `request(..)` is a Promise-aware Ajax utility,
// like we defined earlier in the chapter

var p1 = request( "http://some.url.1/" );
var p2 = request( "http://some.url.2/" );

Promise.all( [p1,p2] )
.then( function(msgs){
    // both `p1` and `p2` fulfill and pass in
    // their messages here
    return request(
        "http://some.url.3/?v=" + msgs.join(",")
    );
} )
.then( function(msg){
    console.log( msg );
} );
```

Promise.all([..]) expects a single argument, an array, consisting generally of Promise instances. The promise returned from the Promise.all([..]) call will receive a fulfillment message (msgs in this snippet) that is an array of all the fulfillment messages from the passed in promises, in the same order as specified (regardless of fulfillment order).

Technically, the `array` of values passed into `Promise.all([ .. ])` can include Promises, thenables, or even immediate values. Each value in the list is essentially passed through `Promise.resolve(..)` to make sure it's a genuine Promise to be waited on, so an immediate value will just be normalized into a Promise for that value. If the `array` is empty, the main Promise is immediately fulfilled.

The main promise returned from `Promise.all([ .. ])` will only be fulfilled if and when all its constituent promises are fulfilled. If any one of those promises is instead rejected, the main `Promise.all([ .. ])` promise is immediately rejected, discarding all results from any other promises.

Remember to always attach a rejection/error handler to every promise, even and especially the one that comes back from `Promise.all([ .. ])`.

Promise.race([..])

While `Promise.all([ .. ])` coordinates multiple Promises concurrently and assumes all are needed for fulfillment, sometimes you want to respond only to the "first Promise to cross the finish line," letting the other Promises fall away.

This pattern is classically called a latch, but in Promises it's called a race.

 While the metaphor of "only the first across the finish line wins" fits the behavior well, unfortunately "race" is kind of a loaded term, because race conditions are generally taken as bugs in programs (see Chapter 1). Don't confuse `Promise.race([..])` with a race condition.

`Promise.race([ .. ])` also expects a single `array` argument, containing one or more Promises, thenables, or immediate values. It doesn't make much practical sense to have a race with immediate values, because the first one listed will obviously win—like a foot race where one runner starts at the finish line!

Similar to `Promise.all([ .. ])`, `Promise.race([ .. ])` will fulfill if and when any Promise resolution is a fulfillment, and it will reject if and when any Promise resolution is a rejection.

 A race requires at least one "runner," so if you pass an empty `array`, instead of immediately resolving, the main `race([..])` Promise will never resolve. This is a footgun! ES6 should have specified that it either fulfills, rejects, or just throws some sort of synchronous error. Unfortunately, because of precedence in Promise libraries predating ES6 `Promise`, they had to leave this gotcha in there, so be careful never to send in an empty `array`.

Let's revisit our previous concurrent Ajax example, but in the context of a race between p1 and p2:

```
// `request(..)` is a Promise-aware Ajax utility,
// like we defined earlier in the chapter

var p1 = request( "http://some.url.1/" );
var p2 = request( "http://some.url.2/" );

Promise.race( [p1,p2] )
.then( function(msg){
    // either `p1` or `p2` will win the race
    return request(
        "http://some.url.3/?v=" + msg
    );
} )
.then( function(msg){
    console.log( msg );
} );
```

Because only one promise wins, the fulfillment value is a single message, not an `array` as it was for `Promise.all([ .. ])`.

Timeout Race

We saw this example earlier, illustrating how `Promise.race([ .. ])` can be used to express the Promise timeout pattern:

```
// `foo()` is a Promise-aware function

// `timeoutPromise(..)`, defined ealier, returns
```

```
// a Promise that rejects after a specified delay

// setup a timeout for `foo()`
Promise.race( [
    foo(),                     // attempt `foo()`
    timeoutPromise( 3000 )     // give it 3 seconds
] )
.then(
    function(){
        // `foo(..)` fulfilled in time!
    },
    function(err){
        // either `foo()` rejected, or it just
        // didn't finish in time, so inspect
        // `err` to know which
    }
);
```

This timeout pattern works well in most cases. But there are some nuances to consider, and frankly they apply to both Promise.race([..]) and Promise.all([..]) equally.

"Finally"

The key question to ask is, "What happens to the promises that get discarded/ignored?" We're not asking that question from the performance perspective—they would typically end up garbage collection eligible—but from the behavioral perspective (side effects, etc.). Promises cannot be canceled—and shouldn't be as that would destroy the external immutability trust discussed in "Promise Uncancelable" on page 116—so they can only be silently ignored.

But what if foo() in the previous example is reserving some sort of resource for usage, but the timeout fires first and causes that promise to be ignored? Is there anything in this pattern that proactively frees the reserved resource after the timeout, or otherwise cancels any side effects it may have had? What if all you wanted was to log the fact that foo() timed out?

Some developers have proposed that Promises need a finally(..) callback registration, which is always called when a Promise resolves, and allows you to specify any cleanup that may be necessary. This doesn't exist in the specification at the moment, but it may come in ES7+. We'll have to wait and see.

It might look like:

```
var p = Promise.resolve( 42 );

p.then( something )
.finally( cleanup )
.then( another )
.finally( cleanup );
```

 In various Promise libraries, finally(..) still creates and returns a new Promise (to keep the chain going). If the cleanup(..) function were to return a Promise, it would be linked into the chain, which means you could still have the unhandled rejection issues we discussed earlier.

In the meantime, we could make a static helper utility that lets us observe (without interfering with) the resolution of a Promise:

```
// polyfill-safe guard check
if (!Promise.observe) {
    Promise.observe = function(pr,cb) {
        // side-observe `pr`'s resolution
        pr.then(
            function fulfilled (msg){
                // schedule callback async (as Job)
                Promise.resolve( msg ).then( cb );
            },
            function rejected(err){
                // schedule callback async (as Job)
                Promise.resolve( err ).then( cb );
            }
        );

        // return original promise
        return pr;
    };
}
```

Here's how we'd use it in the timeout example from before:

```
Promise.race( [
    Promise.observe(
        foo(),                      // attempt `foo()`
        function cleanup(msg){
            // clean up after `foo()`, even if it
            // didn't finish before the timeout
        }
    ),
    timeoutPromise( 3000 )  // give it 3 seconds
] )
```

This `Promise.observe(..)` helper is just an illustration of how you could observe the completions of Promises without interfering with them. Other Promise libraries have their own solutions. Regardless of how you do it, you'll likely have places where you want to make sure your Promises aren't just silently ignored by accident.

Variations on all([..]) and race([..])

While native ES6 Promises come with built-in `Promise.all([ .. ])` and `Promise.race([ .. ])`, there are several other commonly used patterns with variations on those semantics:

none([..])

> This pattern is like `all([ .. ])`, but fulfillments and rejections are transposed. All Promises need to be rejected—rejections become the fulfillment values and vice versa.

any([..])

> This pattern is like `all([ .. ])`, but it ignores any rejections, so only one needs to fulfill instead of *all* of them.

first([..])

> This pattern is like a race with `any([ .. ])`, which means that it ignores any rejections and fulfills as soon as the first Promise fulfills.

last([..])

> This pattern is like `first([ .. ])`, but only the latest fulfillment wins.

Some Promise abstraction libraries provide these, but you could also define them yourself using the mechanics of Promises, `race([ .. ])` and `all([ .. ])`.

For example, here's how we could define `first([ .. ])`:

```
// polyfill-safe guard check
if (!Promise.first) {
    Promise.first = function(prs) {
        return new Promise( function(resolve,reject){
            // loop through all promises
            prs.forEach( function(pr){
                // normalize the value
                Promise.resolve( pr )
                // whichever one fulfills first wins, and
```

```
            // gets to resolve the main promise
            .then( resolve );
        } );
    } );
    };
}
```

 This implementation of first(..) does not reject if all its promises reject; it simply hangs, much like a Promise.race([]) does. If desired, you could add additional logic to track each promise rejection and if all reject, call reject() on the main promise. We'll leave that as an exercise for the reader.

Concurrent Iterations

Sometimes you want to iterate over a list of Promises and perform some task against all of them, much like you can do with synchronous arrays (e.g., forEach(..), map(..), some(..), and every(..)). If the task to perform against each Promise is fundamentally synchronous, these work fine, just as we used forEach(..) in the previous snippet.

But if the tasks are fundamentally asynchronous, or can/should otherwise be performed concurrently, you can use async versions of these utilities as provided by many libraries.

For example, let's consider an asynchronous map(..) utility that takes an array of values (could be Promises or anything else), plus a function (task) to perform against each. map(..) itself returns a promise whose fulfillment value is an array that holds (in the same mapping order) the async fulfillment value from each task:

```
if (!Promise.map) {
    Promise.map = function(vals,cb) {
        // new promise that waits for all mapped promises
        return Promise.all(
            // note: regular array `map(..)`, turns
            // the array of values into an array of
            // promises
            vals.map( function(val){
                // replace `val` with a new promise that
                // resolves after `val` is async mapped
                return new Promise( function(resolve){
                    cb( val, resolve );
```

```
                } );
            } )
        );
    };
}
```

 In this implementation of map(..), you can't signal async rejection, but if a synchronous exception/error occurs inside of the mapping callback (cb(..)), the main Promise.map(..) returned promise would reject.

Let's illustrate using map(..) with a list of Promises (instead of simple values):

```
var p1 = Promise.resolve( 21 );
var p2 = Promise.resolve( 42 );
var p3 = Promise.reject( "Oops" );

// double values in list even if they're in
// Promises
Promise.map( [p1,p2,p3], function(pr,done){
    // make sure the item itself is a Promise
    Promise.resolve( pr )
    .then(
        // extract value as `v`
        function(v){
            // map fulfillment `v` to new value
            done( v * 2 );
        },
        // or, map to promise rejection message
        done
    );
} )
.then( function(vals){
    console.log( vals );    // [42,84,"Oops"]
} );
```

Promise API Recap

Let's review the ES6 Promise API that we've already seen unfold in bits and pieces throughout this chapter.

The following API is native only as of ES6, but there are specification-compliant polyfills (not just extended Promise libraries) which can define `Promise` and all its associated behavior so that you can use native Promises even in pre-ES6 browsers. One such polyfill is "Native Promise Only" (*http://github.com/getify/native-promise-only*), which I wrote!

new Promise(..) Constructor

The revealing constructor `Promise(..)` must be used with `new`, and must be provided a function callback, which is synchronously/immediately called. This function is passed two function callbacks that act as resolution capabilities for the promise. We commonly label these `resolve(..)` and `reject(..)`:

```
var p = new Promise( function(resolve,reject){
    // `resolve(..)` to resolve/fulfill the promise
    // `reject(..)` to reject the promise
} );
```

`reject(..)` simply rejects the promise, but `resolve(..)` can either fulfill the promise or reject it, depending on what it's passed. If `resolve(..)` is passed an immediate, non-Promise, non-thenable value, then the promise is fulfilled with that value.

But if `resolve(..)` is passed a genuine Promise or thenable value, that value is unwrapped recursively, and whatever its final resolution/state is will be adopted by the promise.

Promise.resolve(..) and Promise.reject(..)

A shortcut for creating an already-rejected Promise is `Promise.reject(..)`, so these two promises are equivalent:

```
var p1 = new Promise( function(resolve,reject){
    reject( "Oops" );
} );

var p2 = Promise.reject( "Oops" );
```

`Promise.resolve(..)` is usually used to create an already-fulfilled Promise in a similar way to `Promise.reject(..)`. However, `Promise.resolve(..)` also unwraps thenable values (as discusssed several times already). In that case, the Promise returned adopts the

final resolution of the thenable you passed in, which could either be
fulfillment or rejection:

```
var fulfilledTh = {
    then: function(cb) { cb( 42 ); }
};
var rejectedTh = {
    then: function(cb,errCb) {
        errCb( "Oops" );
    }
};

var p1 = Promise.resolve( fulfilledTh );
var p2 = Promise.resolve( rejectedTh );

// `p1` will be a fulfilled promise
// `p2` will be a rejected promise
```

And remember, Promise.resolve(..) doesn't do anything if what
you pass is already a genuine Promise; it just returns the value
directly. So there's no overhead to calling Promise.resolve(..) on
values that you don't know the nature of, if one happens to already
be a genuine Promise.

then(..) and catch(..)

Each Promise instance (*not* the Promise API namespace) has
then(..) and catch(..) methods, which allow registering of fulfillment and rejection handlers for the Promise. Once the Promise is
resolved, one or the other of these handlers will be called, but not
both, and it will always be called asynchronously (see "Jobs" on page
23 in Chapter 1).

then(..) takes one or two parameters, the first for the fulfillment
callback, and the second for the rejection callback. If either is omit-
ted or is otherwise passed as a non-function value, a default callback
is substituted respectively. The default fulfillment callback simply
passes the message along, while the default rejection callback simply
rethrows (propagates) the error reason it receives.

catch(..) takes only the rejection callback as a parameter, and
automatically substitutes the default fulfillment callback, as just discussed. In other words, it's equivalent to then(null,..):

```
p.then( fulfilled );

p.then( fulfilled, rejected );

p.catch( rejected ); // or `p.then( null, rejected )`
```

then(..) and catch(..) also create and return a new promise, which can be used to express Promise chain flow control. If the fulfillment or rejection callbacks have an exception thrown, the returned promise is rejected. If either callback returns an immediate, non-Promise, non-thenable value, that value is set as the fulfillment for the returned promise. If the fulfillment handler specifically returns a promise or thenable value, that value is unwrapped and becomes the resolution of the returned promise.

Promise.all([..]) and Promise.race([..])

The static helpers Promise.all([..]) and Promise.race([..]) on the ES6 Promise API both create a Promise as their return value. The resolution of that promise is controlled entirely by the array of promises that you pass in.

For Promise.all([..]), all the promises you pass in must fulfill for the returned promise to fulfill. If any promise is rejected, the main returned promise is immediately rejected, too (discarding the results of any of the other promises). For fulfillment, you receive an array of all the passed in promises' fulfillment values. For rejection, you receive just the first promise rejection reason value. This pattern is classically called a gate: all must arrive before the gate opens.

For Promise.race([..]), only the first promise to resolve (fulfillment or rejection) wins, and whatever that resolution is becomes the resolution of the returned promise. This pattern is classically called a latch: the first one to open the latch gets through. Consider:

```
var p1 = Promise.resolve( 42 );
var p2 = Promise.resolve( "Hello World" );
var p3 = Promise.reject( "Oops" );

Promise.race( [p1,p2,p3] )
.then( function(msg){
    console.log( msg );      // 42
} );

Promise.all( [p1,p2,p3] )
.catch( function(err){
    console.error( err );    // "Oops"
```

```
} );

Promise.all( [p1,p2] )
.then( function(msgs){
    console.log( msgs );    // [42,"Hello World"]
} );
```

 Be careful! If an empty array is passed to
Promise.all([..]), it will fulfill immediately, but Promise.race([..]) will hang forever and never resolve.

The ES6 Promise API is pretty simple and straightforward. It's at
least good enough to serve the most basic of async cases, and is a
good place to start when rearranging your code from callback hell to
something better.

But there's a whole lot of async sophistication that apps often
demand which Promises themselves will be limited in addressing. In
the next section, we'll dive into those limitations as motivations for
the benefit of Promise libraries.

Promise Limitations

Many of the details we'll discuss in this section have already been
alluded to in this chapter, but we'll just make sure to review these
limitations specifically.

Sequence Error Handling

We covered Promise-flavored error handling in detail earlier in this
chapter. The limitations of how Promises are designed—how they
chain, specifically—creates a very easy pitfall where an error in a
Promise chain can be silently ignored accidentally.

But there's something else to consider with Promise errors. Because
a Promise chain is nothing more than its constituent Promises
wired together, there's no entity to refer to the entire chain as a single *thing*, which means there's no external way to observe any errors
that may occur.

If you construct a Promise chain that has no error handling in it,
any error anywhere in the chain will propagate indefinitely down
the chain, until observed (by registering a rejection handler at some

step). So, in that specific case, having a reference to the last promise in the chain is enough (p in the following snippet), because you can register a rejection handler there, and it will be notified of any propagated errors:

```
// foo(..), STEP2(..) and STEP3(..) are
// all promise-aware utilities

var p = foo( 42 )
.then( STEP2 )
.then( STEP3 );
```

Although it may seem sneakily confusing, p here doesn't point to the first promise in the chain (the one from the foo(42) call), but instead from the last promise, the one that comes from the then(STEP3) call.

Also, no step in the Promise chain is observably doing its own error handling. That means that you could then register a rejection error handler on p, and it would be notified if any errors occur anywhere in the chain:

```
p.catch( handleErrors );
```

But if any step of the chain in fact does its own error handling (perhaps hidden/abstracted away from what you can see), your handle Errors(..) won't be notified. This may be what you want—it was, after all, a "handled rejection"—but it also may *not* be what you want. The complete lack of ability to be notified (of "already handled" rejection errors) is a limitation that restricts capabilities in some use cases.

It's basically the same limitation that exists with a try..catch that can catch an exception and simply swallow it. So this isn't a limitation unique to Promises, but it *is* something we might wish to have a workaround for.

Unfortunately, many times there is no reference kept for the intermediate steps in a Promise-chain sequence, so without such references, you cannot attach error handlers to reliably observe the errors.

Single Value

Promises by definition only have a single fulfillment value or a single rejection reason. In simple examples, this isn't that big of a deal, but in more sophisticated scenarios, you may find this limiting.

The typical advice is to construct a values wrapper (such as an `object` or `array`) to contain these multiple messages. This solution works, but it can be quite awkward and tedious to wrap and unwrap your messages with every single step of your Promise chain.

Splitting Values

Sometimes you can take this as a signal that you could/should decompose the problem into two or more Promises.

Imagine you have a utility `foo(..)` that produces two values (x and y) asynchronously:

```
function getY(x) {
    return new Promise( function(resolve,reject){
        setTimeout( function(){
            resolve( (3 * x) - 1 );
        }, 100 );
    } );
}

function foo(bar,baz) {
    var x = bar * baz;

    return getY( x )
    .then( function(y){
        // wrap both values into container
        return [x,y];
    } );
}

foo( 10, 20 )
.then( function(msgs){
    var x = msgs[0];
    var y = msgs[1];

    console.log( x, y );    // 200 599
} );
```

First, let's rearrange what `foo(..)` returns so that we don't have to wrap x and y into a single `array` value to transport through one promise. Instead, we can wrap each value into its own promise:

```
function foo(bar,baz) {
    var x = bar * baz;

    // return both promises
    return [
        Promise.resolve( x ),
        getY( x )
    ];
}

Promise.all(
    foo( 10, 20 )
)
.then( function(msgs){
    var x = msgs[0];
    var y = msgs[1];

    console.log( x, y );
} );
```

Is an array of promises really better than an array of values passed
through a single promise? Syntactically, it's not much of an
improvement.

But this approach more closely embraces the Promise design theory.
It's now easier in the future to refactor to split the calculation of x
and y into separate functions. It's cleaner and more flexible to let the
calling code decide how to orchestrate the two promises—using
Promise.all([..]) here, but certainly not the only option—
rather than to abstract such details away inside of foo(..).

Unwrap/Spread Arguments

The var x = .. and var y = .. assignments are still awkward
overhead. We can employ some functional trickery (hat tip to Reginald Braithwaite, @raganwald on Twitter) in a helper utility:

```
function spread(fn) {
    return Function.apply.bind( fn, null );
}

Promise.all(
    foo( 10, 20 )
)
.then(
    spread( function(x,y){
        console.log( x, y );    // 200 599
    } )
)
```

That's a bit nicer! Of course, you could inline the functional magic to avoid the extra helper:

```
Promise.all(
    foo( 10, 20 )
)
.then( Function.apply.bind(
    function(x,y){
        console.log( x, y );    // 200 599
    },
    null
) );
```

These tricks may be neat, but ES6 has an even better answer for us: destructuring. The array destructuring assignment form looks like this:

```
Promise.all(
    foo( 10, 20 )
)
.then( function(msgs){
    var [x,y] = msgs;

    console.log( x, y );    // 200 599
} );
```

But best of all, ES6 offers the array parameter destructuring form:

```
Promise.all(
    foo( 10, 20 )
)
.then( function([x,y]){
    console.log( x, y );    // 200 599
} );
```

We've now embraced the one-value-per-Promise mantra, but kept our supporting boilerplate to a minimum!

 For more information on ES6 destructuring forms, see the *ES6 & Beyond* title of this series.

Single Resolution

One of the most intrinsic behaviors of Promises is that a Promise can only be resolved once (fulfillment or rejection). For many async use cases, you're only retrieving a value once, so this works fine.

But there's also a lot of async cases that fit into a different model—one that's more akin to events and/or streams of data. It's not clear on the surface how well Promises can fit into such use cases, if at all. Without a significant abstraction on top of Promises, they will completely fall short for handling multiple value resolution.

Imagine a scenario where you might want to fire off a sequence of async steps in response to a stimulus (like an event) that can in fact happen multiple times, like a button click.

This probably won't work the way you want:

```
// `click(..)` binds the `"click"` event to a DOM element
// `request(..)` is the previously defined Promise-aware Ajax

var p = new Promise( function(resolve,reject){
    click( "#mybtn", resolve );
} );

p.then( function(evt){
    var btnID = evt.currentTarget.id;
    return request( "http://some.url.1/?id=" + btnID );
} )
.then( function(text){
    console.log( text );
} );
```

The behavior here works only if your application calls for the button to be clicked just once. If the button is clicked a second time, the p promise has already been resolved, so the second `resolve(..)` call would be ignored.

Instead, you'd probably need to invert the paradigm, creating a whole new Promise chain for each event firing:

```
click( "#mybtn", function(evt){
    var btnID = evt.currentTarget.id;

    request( "http://some.url.1/?id=" + btnID )
    .then( function(text){
        console.log( text );
    } );
} );
```

This approach will work in that a whole new Promise sequence will be fired off for each "click" event on the button.

But beyond just the ugliness of having to define the entire Promise chain inside the event handler, this design in some respects violates the idea of separation of concerns/capabilities (SoC). You might very well want to define your event handler in a different place in your code from where you define the *response* to the event (the Promise chain). That's pretty awkward to do in this pattern, without helper mechanisms.

 Another way of articulating this limitation is that it'd be nice if we could construct some sort of "observable" that we can subscribe a Promise chain to. There are libraries that have created these abstractions (such as RxJS (*http://rxjs.code plex.com*)), but the abstractions can seem so heavy that you can't even see the nature of Promises anymore. Such heavy abstraction brings important questions to mind, such as whether (sans Promises) these mechanisms are as *trustable* as Promises themselves have been designed to be. We'll revisit the "observable" pattern in Appendix B.

Inertia

One concrete barrier to starting to use Promises in your own code is all the code that currently exists that is not already Promise-aware. If you have lots of callback-based code, it's far easier to just keep coding in that same style.

"A code base in motion (with callbacks) will remain in motion (with callbacks) unless acted upon by a smart, Promises-aware developer."

Promises offer a different paradigm, and as such, the approach to the code can be anywhere from just a little different to, in some cases, radically different. You have to be intentional about it, because Promises will not just naturally shake out from the same ol' ways of doing code that have served you well thus far.

Consider a callback-based scenario like the following:

```
function foo(x,y,cb) {
    ajax(
        "http://some.url.1/?x=" + x + "&y=" + y,
        cb
    );
}

foo( 11, 31, function(err,text) {
```

```
    if (err) {
        console.error( err );
    }
    else {
        console.log( text );
    }
} );
```

Is it immediately obvious what the first steps are to convert this callback-based code to Promise-aware code? Depends on your experience. The more practice you have with it, the more natural it will feel. But certainly, Promises don't just advertise on the label exactly how to do it—there's no one-size-fits-all answer—so the responsibility is up to you.

As we've covered before, we definitely need an Ajax utility that is Promise-aware instead of callback-based, which we could call request(..). You can make your own, as we have already. But the overhead of having to manually define Promise-aware wrappers for every callback-based utility makes it less likely you'll choose to refactor to Promise-aware coding at all.

Promises offer no direct answer to that limitation. Most Promise libraries do offer a helper, however. But even without a library, imagine a helper like this:

```
// polyfill-safe guard check
if (!Promise.wrap) {
    Promise.wrap = function(fn) {
        return function() {
            var args = [].slice.call( arguments );

            return new Promise( function(resolve,reject){
                fn.apply(
                    null,
                    args.concat( function(err,v){
                        if (err) {
                            reject( err );
                        }
                        else {
                            resolve( v );
                        }
                    } )
                );
            } );
        };
    };
}
```

OK, that's more than just a tiny trivial utility. However, although it may look a bit intimidating, it's not as bad as you'd think. It takes a function that expects an error-first style callback as its last parameter, and returns a new one that automatically creates a Promise to return, and substitutes the callback for you, wired up to the Promise fulfillment/rejection.

Rather than waste too much time talking about *how* this `Promise.wrap(..)` helper works, let's just look at how we use it:

```
var request = Promise.wrap( ajax );

request( "http://some.url.1/" )
.then( .. )
..
```

Wow, that was pretty easy!

`Promise.wrap(..)` does *not* produce a Promise. It produces a function that will produce Promises. In a sense, a Promise-producing function could be seen as a Promise factory. I propose "promisory" as the name for such a thing ("Promise" + "factory").

The act of wrapping a callback-expecting function to be a Promise-aware function is sometimes referred to as "lifting" or "promisifying." But there doesn't seem to be a standard term for what to call the resultant function other than a "lifted function", so I like "promisory" better, as I think it's more descriptive.

 Promisory isn't a made-up term. It's a real word, and its definition means to contain or convey a promise. That's exactly what these functions are doing, so it turns out to be a pretty perfect terminology match!

So, `Promise.wrap(ajax)` produces an `ajax(..)` promisory we call `request(..)`, and that promisory produces Promises for Ajax responses.

If all functions were already promisories, we wouldn't need to make them ourselves, so the extra step is a tad bit of a shame. But at least the wrapping pattern is (usually) repeatable so we can put it into a `Promise.wrap(..)` helper as shown to aid our promise coding.

So back to our earlier example, we need a promisory for both `ajax(..)` and `foo(..)`:

```
// make a promisory for `ajax(..)`
var request = Promise.wrap( ajax );

// refactor `foo(..)`, but keep it externally
// callback-based for compatibility with other
// parts of the code for now--only use
// `request(..)`'s promise internally.
function foo(x,y,cb) {
    request(
        "http://some.url.1/?x=" + x + "&y=" + y
    )
    .then(
        function fulfilled(text){
            cb( null, text );
        },
        cb
    );
}

// now, for this code's purposes, make a
// promisory for `foo(..)`
var betterFoo = Promise.wrap( foo );

// and use the promisory
betterFoo( 11, 31 )
.then(
    function fulfilled(text){
        console.log( text );
    },
    function rejected(err){
        console.error( err );
    }
);
```

Of course, while we're refactoring foo(..) to use our new
request(..) promisory, we could just make foo(..) a promisory
itself, instead of remaining callback-based and needing to make and
use the subsequent betterFoo(..) promisory. This decision just
depends on whether foo(..) needs to stay callback-based compatible with other parts of the code base.

Consider:

```
`foo(..)` is now also a promisory because it
delegates to the `request(..)` promisory
function foo(x,y) {
    return request(
        "http://some.url.1/?x=" + x + "&y=" + y
    );
}
```

```
foo( 11, 31 )
.then( .. )
..
```

While ES6 Promises don't natively ship with helpers for such promisory wrapping, most libraries provide them, or you can make your own. Either way, this particular limitation of Promises is addressable without too much pain (certainly compared to the pain of callback hell!).

Promise Uncancelable

Once you create a Promise and register a fulfillment and/or rejection handler for it, there's nothing external you can do to stop that progression if something else happens to make that task moot.

Many Promise abstraction libraries provide facilities to cancel Promises, but this is a terrible idea! Many developers wish Promises had natively been designed with external cancelation capability, but the problem is that it would let one consumer/observer of a Promise affect some other consumer's ability to observe that same Promise. This violates the future-value's trustability (external immutability), but morever is the embodiment of the "action at a distance" antipattern (*http://en.wikipedia.org/wiki/ Action_at_a_distance_%28computer_program ming%29*). Regardless of how useful it seems, it will actually lead you straight back into the same nightmares as callbacks.

Consider our Promise timeout scenario from earlier:

```
var p = foo( 42 );

Promise.race( [
    p,
    timeoutPromise( 3000 )
] )
.then(
    doSomething,
    handleError
);

p.then( function(){
```

```
    // still happens even in the timeout case :(
} );
```

The "timeout" was external to the promise p, so p itself keeps going, which we probably don't want.

One option is to invasively define your resolution callbacks:

```
var OK = true;

var p = foo( 42 );

Promise.race( [
    p,
    timeoutPromise( 3000 )
    .catch( function(err){
        OK = false;
        throw err;
    } )
] )
.then(
    doSomething,
    handleError
);

p.then( function(){
    if (OK) {
        // only happens if no timeout! :)
    }
} );
```

This is ugly. It works, but it's far from ideal. Generally, you should try to avoid such scenarios.

But if you can't, the ugliness of this solution should be a clue that *cancelation* is a functionality that belongs at a higher level of abstraction on top of Promises. I'd recommend you look to Promise abstraction libraries for assistance rather than hacking it yourself.

 My *asynquence* Promise abstraction library pro-vides just such an abstraction and an abort() capability for the sequence, all of which will be discussed in Appendix A.

A single Promise is not really a flow-control mechanism (at least not in a very meaningful sense), which is exactly what *cancelation* refers to; that's why Promise cancelation would feel awkward.

By contrast, a chain of Promises taken collectively together—what I like to call a "sequence"—*is* a flow control expression, and thus it's appropriate for cancelation to be defined at that level of abstraction.

No individual Promise should be cancelable, but it's sensible for a *sequence* to be cancelable, because you don't pass around a sequence as a single immutable value like you do with a Promise.

Promise Performance

This particular limitation is both simple and complex.

Comparing how many pieces are moving with a basic callback-based async task chain versus a Promise chain, it's clear Promises have a fair bit more going on, which means they are naturally at least a tiny bit slower. Think back to just the simple list of trust guarantees that Promises offer, as compared to the ad hoc solution code you'd have to layer on top of callbacks to achieve the same protections.

More work to do, more guards to protect, means that Promises *are* slower as compared to naked, untrustable callbacks. That much is obvious, and probably simple to wrap your brain around.

But how much slower? Well...that's actually proving to be an incredibly difficult question to answer absolutely, across the board.

Frankly, it's kind of an apples-to-oranges comparison, so it's probably the wrong question to ask. You should actually compare whether an ad hoc callback system with all the same protections manually layered in is faster than a Promise implementation.

If Promises have a legitimate performance limitation, it's more that they don't really offer a line-item choice as to which trustability protections you want/need or not—you get them all, always.

Nevertheless, if we grant that a Promise is generally a *little bit slower* than its non-Promise, non-trustable callback equivalent—assuming there are places where you feel you can justify the lack of trustability —does that mean that Promises should be avoided across the board, as if your entire application is driven by nothing but must-be-utterly-the-fastest code possible?

Sanity check: if your code is legitimately like that, is JavaScript even the right language for such tasks? JavaScript can be optimized to run applications very performantly (see Chapters 5 and 6). But is obsessing over tiny performance tradeoffs with Promises, in light of all the benefits they offer, really appropriate?

Another subtle issue is that Promises make *everything* async, which means that some immediately (synchronously) complete steps still defer advancement of the next step to a Job (see Chapter 1). That means that it's possible that a sequence of Promise tasks could complete ever-so-slightly slower than the same sequence wired up with callbacks.

Of course, the question here is this: are these potential slips in tiny fractions of performance worth all the other articulated benefits of Promises we've laid out across this chapter?

My take is that in virtually all cases where you might think Promise performance is slow enough to be concerned, it's actually an anti-pattern to optimize away the benefits of Promise trustability and composability by avoiding them altogether.

Instead, you should default to using them across the code base, and then profile and analyze your application's hot (critical) paths. Are Promises really a bottleneck, or are they just a theoretical slow-down? Only then, armed with actual valid benchmarks (see Chapter 6) is it responsible and prudent to factor out the Promises in just those identified critical areas.

Promises are a little slower, but in exchange you're getting a lot of trustability, non-Zalgo predictability, and composability built in. Maybe the limitation is not actually their performance, but your lack of perception of their benefits?

Review

Promises are awesome. Use them. They solve the *inversion of control* issues that plague us with callbacks-only code.

They don't get rid of callbacks, they just redirect the orchestration of those callbacks to a trustable intermediary mechanism that sits between us and another utility.

Promise chains also begin to address (though certainly not perfectly) a better way of expressing async flow in sequential fashion, which helps our brains plan and maintain async JS code better. We'll see an even better solution to *that* problem in Chapter 4!

Generators

In Chapter 2, we identified two key drawbacks to expressing async flow control with callbacks:

- Callback-based async doesn't fit how our brain plans out steps of a task.
- Callbacks aren't trustable or composable because of inversion of control.

In Chapter 3, we detailed how Promises uninvert the inversion of control of callbacks, restoring trustability/composability.

Now we turn our attention to expressing async flow control in a sequential, synchronous-looking fashion. The "magic" that makes it possible is ES6 *generators*.

Breaking Run-to-Completion

In Chapter 1, we explained an expectation that JS developers almost universally rely on in their code: once a function starts executing, it runs until it completes, and no other code can interrupt and run in between.

As bizarre as it may seem, ES6 introduces a new type of function that does not behave with the run-to-completion behavior. This new type of function is called a generator.

To understand the implications, let's consider this example:

```
var x = 1;

function foo() {
    x++;
    bar();                   // <-- what about this line?
    console.log( "x:", x );
}

function bar() {
    x++;
}

foo();                       // x: 3
```

In this example, we know for sure that `bar()` runs in between `x++` and `console.log(x)`. But what if `bar()` wasn't there? Obviously the result would be 2 instead of 3.

Now let's twist your brain. What if `bar()` wasn't present, but it could still somehow run between the `x++` and `console.log(x)` statements? How would that be possible?

In *preemptive* multithreaded languages, it would essentially be possible for `bar()` to interrupt and run at exactly the right moment between those two statements. But JS is not preemptive, nor is it (currently) multithreaded. And yet, a *cooperative* form of this interruption (concurrency) is possible, if `foo()` itself could somehow indicate a pause at that part in the code.

 I use the word "cooperative" not only because of the connection to classical concurrency terminology (see Chapter 1), but because as you'll see in the next snippet, the ES6 syntax for indicating a pause point in code is `yield`—suggesting a politely cooperative yielding of control.

Here's the ES6 code to accomplish such cooperative concurrency:

```
var x = 1;

function *foo() {
    x++;
    yield; // pause!
    console.log( "x:", x );
}
```

```
function bar() {
    x++;
}
```

You will likely see most other JS documentation/code that will format a generator declaration as `function* foo() { .. }` instead of as I've done here with `function *foo() { .. }`—the only difference being the stylistic positioning of the `*`. The two forms are functionally/syntactically identical, as is a third `function*foo()` `{ .. }` (no space) form. There are arguments for both styles, but I basically prefer `function` `*foo..` because it then matches when I reference a generator in writing with `*foo()`. If I said only `foo()`, you wouldn't know as clearly if I was talking about a generator or a regular function. It's purely a stylistic preference.

Now, how can we run the code in that previous snippet such that `bar()` executes at the point of the `yield` inside of `*foo()`?

```
// construct an iterator `it` to control the generator
var it = foo();

// start `foo()` here!
it.next();
x;                    // 2
bar();
x;                    // 3
it.next();            // x: 3
```

OK, there's quite a bit of new and potentially confusing stuff in those two code snippets, so we've got plenty to wade through. But before we explain the different mechanics/syntax with ES6 generators, let's walk through the behavior flow:

1. The `it = foo()` operation does *not* execute the `*foo()` generator yet, but it merely constructs an *iterator* that will control its execution. More on *iterators* in a bit.

2. The first `it.next()` starts the `*foo()` generator, and runs the `x++` on the first line of `*foo()`.

3. *foo() pauses at the yield statement, at which point that first it.next() call finishes. At the moment, *foo() is still running and active, but it's in a paused state.

4. We inspect the value of x, and it's now 2.

5. We call bar(), which increments x again with x++.

6. We inspect the value of x again, and it's now 3.

7. The final it.next() call resumes the *foo() generator from where it was paused, and runs the console.log(..) statement, which uses the current value of x of 3.

Clearly, foo() started, but did *not* run-to-completion—it paused at the yield. We resumed foo() later, and let it finish, but that wasn't even required.

So, a generator is a special kind of function that can start and stop one or more times, and doesn't necessarily ever have to finish. While it won't be terribly obvious yet why that's so powerful, as we go throughout the rest of this chapter, that will be one of the fundamental building blocks we use to construct generators-as-async-flow-control as a pattern for our code.

Input and Output

A generator function is a special function with the new processing model we just alluded to. But it's still a function, which means it still has some basic tenets that haven't changed—namely, that it still accepts arguments (aka input), and that it can still return a value (aka output):

```
function *foo(x,y) {
    return x * y;
}

var it = foo( 6, 7 );

var res = it.next();

res.value;      // 42
```

We pass in the arguments 6 and 7 to *foo(..) as the parameters x and y, respectively. And *foo(..) returns the value 42 back to the calling code.

We now see a difference with how the generator is invoked compared to a normal function. foo(6,7) obviously looks familiar. But subtly, the *foo(..) generator hasn't actually run yet as it would have with a function.

Instead, we're just creating an *iterator* object, which we assign to the variable it, to control the *foo(..) generator. Then we call it.next(), which instructs the *foo(..) generator to advance from its current location, stopping either at the next yield or end of the generator.

The result of that next(..) call is an object with a value property on it holding whatever value (if anything) was returned from *foo(..). In other words, yield caused a value to be sent out from the generator during the middle of its execution, kind of like an intermediate return.

Again, it won't be obvious yet why we need this whole indirect *iterator* object to control the generator. We'll get there, I *promise*.

Iteration Messaging

In addition to generators accepting arguments and having return values, there's even more powerful and compelling input/output messaging capability built into them, via yield and next(..).

Consider:

```
function *foo(x) {
    var y = x * (yield);
    return y;
}

var it = foo( 6 );

// start `foo(..)`
it.next();

var res = it.next( 7 );

res.value;      // 42
```

First, we pass in 6 as the parameter x. Then we call it.next(), and it starts up *foo(..).

Inside *foo(..), the var y = x .. statement starts to be processed, but then it runs across a yield expression. At that point, it pauses *foo(..) (in the middle of the assignment statement!), and essentially requests the calling code to provide a result value for the yield expression. Next, we call it.next(7), which is passing the 7 value back in to *be* that result of the paused yield expression.

So, at this point, the assignment statement is essentially var y = 6 * 7. Now, return y returns that 42 value back as the result of the it.next(7) call.

Notice something very important but also easily confusing, even to seasoned JS developers: depending on your perspective, there's a mismatch between the yield and the next(..) call. In general, you're going to have one more next(..) call than you have yield statements—the preceding snippet has one yield and two next(..) calls.

Why the mismatch?

Because the first next(..) always starts a generator, and runs to the first yield. But it's the second next(..) call that fulfills the first paused yield expression, and the third next(..) would fulfill the second yield, and so on.

Tale of Two Questions

Actually, which code you're thinking about primarily will affect whether there's a perceived mismatch or not.

Consider only the generator code:

```
var y = x * (yield);
return y;
```

This *first* yield is basically asking a question: "What value should I insert here?"

Who's going to answer that question? Well, the *first* next() has already run to get the generator up to this point, so obviously *it* can't answer the question. So, the *second* next(..) call must answer the question posed by the *first* yield.

See the mismatch—second-to-first?

But let's flip our perspective. Let's look at it not from the generator's point of view, but from the iterator's point of view.

To properly illustrate this perspective, we also need to explain that messages can go in both directions—yield .. as an expression can send out messages in response to next(..) calls, and next(..) can send values to a paused yield expression. Consider this slightly adjusted code:

```
function *foo(x) {
    var y = x * (yield "Hello");    // <-- yield a value!
    return y;
}

var it = foo( 6 );

var res = it.next();    // first `next()`, don't pass anything
res.value;              // "Hello"

res = it.next( 7 );     // pass `7` to waiting `yield`
res.value;              // 42
```

yield .. and next(..) pair together as a two-way message passing system *during the execution of the generator.*

So, looking only at the *iterator* code:

```
var res = it.next();    // first `next()`, don't pass anything
res.value;              // "Hello"

res = it.next( 7 );     // pass `7` to waiting `yield`
res.value;              // 42
```

 We don't pass a value to the first next() call, and that's on purpose. Only a paused yield could accept such a value passed by a next(..), and at the beginning of the generator when we call the first next(), there is no paused yield to accept such a value. The specification and all compliant browsers just silently discard anything passed to the first next(). It's still a bad idea to pass a value, as you're just creating silently failing code that's confusing. So, always start a generator with an argument-free next().

The first next() call (with nothing passed to it) is basically *asking a question*: "What *next* value does the *foo(..) generator have to give me?" And who answers this question? The first yield "hello" expression.

See? No mismatch there.

Depending on *who* you think about asking the question, there is either a mismatch between the yield and next(..) calls, or not.

But wait! There's still an extra next() compared to the number of yield statements. So, that final it.next(7) call is again asking the question about what *next* value the generator will produce. But there's no more yield statements left to answer, is there? So who answers?

The return statement answers the question!

And if there is no return in your generator—return is certainly not any more required in generators than in regular functions—there's always an assumed/implicit return; (aka return undefined;), which serves the purpose of default answering the question *posed* by the final it.next(7) call.

These questions and answers—the two-way message passing with yield and next(..)—are quite powerful, but it's not obvious at all how these mechanisms are connected to async flow control. We're getting there!

Multiple Iterators

It may appear from the syntactic usage that when you use an *iterator* to control a generator, you're controlling the declared generator function itself. But there's a subtlety that easy to miss: each time you construct an *iterator*, you are implicitly constructing an instance of the generator which that *iterator* will control.

You can have multiple instances of the same generator running at the same time, and they can even interact:

```
function *foo() {
    var x = yield 2;
    z++;
    var y = yield (x * z);
    console.log( x, y, z );
}

var z = 1;

var it1 = foo();
var it2 = foo();
```

```
var val1 = it1.next().value;        // 2 <-- yield 2
var val2 = it2.next().value;        // 2 <-- yield 2

val1 = it1.next( val2 * 10 ).value; // 40  <-- x:20,  z:2
val2 = it2.next( val1 * 5 ).value;  // 600 <-- x:200, z:3

it1.next( val2 / 2 );               // y:300
                                    // 20 300 3
it2.next( val1 / 4 );               // y:10
                                    // 200 10 3
```

The most common usage of multiple instances of the same generator running concurrently is not such interactions, but when the generator is producing its own values without input, perhaps from some independently connected resource. We'll talk more about value production in the next section.

Let's briefly walk through the processing:

1. Both instances of *foo() are started at the same time, and both next() calls reveal a value of 2 from the yield 2 statements, respectively.

2. val2 * 10 is 2 * 10, which is sent into the first generator instance it1, so that x gets value 20. z is incremented from 1 to 2, and then 20 * 2 is yielded out, setting val1 to 40.

3. val1 * 5 is 40 * 5, which is sent into the second generator instance it2, so that x gets value 200. z is incremented again, from 2 to 3, and then 200 * 3 is yielded out, setting val2 to 600.

4. val2 / 2 is 600 / 2, which is sent into the first generator instance it1, so that y gets value 300, then printing out 20 300 3 for its x y z values, respectively.

5. val1 / 4 is 40 / 4, which is sent into the second generator instance it2, so that y gets value 10, then printing out 200 10 3 for its x y z values, respectively.

That's a fun example to run through in your mind. Did you keep it straight?

Interleaving

Recall this scenario from the "Run-to-completion" section of Chapter 1:

```
var a = 1;
var b = 2;

function foo() {
    a++;
    b = b * a;
    a = b + 3;
}

function bar() {
    b--;
    a = 8 + b;
    b = a * 2;
}
```

With normal JS functions, of course either foo() can run completely first, or bar() can run completely first, but foo() cannot interleave its individual statements with bar(). So, there are only two possible outcomes to the preceding program.

However, with generators, clearly interleaving (even in the middle of statements!) is possible:

```
var a = 1;
var b = 2;

function *foo() {
    a++;
    yield;
    b = b * a;
    a = (yield b) + 3;
}

function *bar() {
    b--;
    yield;
    a = (yield 8) + b;
    b = a * (yield 2);
}
```

Depending on what respective order the *iterators* controlling *foo() and *bar() are called, the preceding program could produce several different results. In other words, we can actually illustrate (in a sort of fake-ish way) the theoretical threaded race conditions circumstances discussed in Chapter 1, by interleaving the two generator interations over the same shared variables.

First, let's make a helper called step(..) that controls an *iterator*:

```
function step(gen) {
    var it = gen();
    var last;

    return function() {
        // whatever is `yield`ed out, just
        // send it right back in the next time!
        last = it.next( last ).value;
    };
}
```

step(..) initializes a generator to create its it *iterator*, then returns a function which, when called, advances the *iterator* by one step. Additionally, the previously yielded out value is sent right back in at the *next* step. So, yield 8 will just become 8 and yield b will just be b (whatever it was at the time of yield).

Now, just for fun, let's experiment to see the effects of interleaving these different chunks of *foo() and *bar(). We'll start with the boring base case, making sure *foo() totally finishes before *bar() (just like we did in Chapter 1):

```
// make sure to reset `a` and `b`
a = 1;
b = 2;

var s1 = step( foo );
var s2 = step( bar );

// run `*foo()` completely first
s1();
s1();
s1();

// now run `*bar()`
s2();
s2();
s2();
s2();

console.log( a, b );    // 11 22
```

The end result is 11 and 22, just as it was in the Chapter 1 version. Now let's mix up the interleaving ordering and see how it changes the final values of a and b:

```
// make sure to reset `a` and `b`
a = 1;
b = 2;

var s1 = step( foo );
var s2 = step( bar );

s2();       // b--;
s2();       // yield 8
s1();       // a++;
s2();       // a = 8 + b;
            // yield 2
s1();       // b = b * a;
            // yield b
s1();       // a = b + 3;
s2();       // b = a * 2;
```

Before I tell you the results, can you figure out what a and b are after the preceding program? No cheating!

```
console.log( a, b );     // 12 18
```

As an exercise for the reader, try to see how many other combinations of results you can get back rearranging the order of the s1() and s2() calls. Don't forget you'll always need three s1() calls and four s2() calls. Recall the discussion earlier about matching next() with yield for the reasons why.

You almost certainly won't want to intentionally create *this* level of interleaving confusion, as it creates incredibly difficult to understand code. But the exercise is interesting and instructive to understand more about how multiple generators can run concurrently in the same shared scope, because there will be places where this capability is quite useful.

We'll discuss generator concurrency in more detail in "Generator Concurrency" on page 165.

Generator-ing Values

In the previous section, we mentioned an interesting use for generators, as a way to produce values. This is *not* the main focus in this chapter, but we'd be remiss if we didn't cover the basics, especially because this use case is essentially the origin of the name: generators.

We're going to take a slight diversion into the topic of *iterators* for a bit, but we'll circle back to how they relate to generators and using a generator to *generate* values.

Producers and Iterators

Imagine you're producing a series of values where each value has a definable relationship to the previous value. To do this, you're going to need a stateful producer that remembers the last value it gave out.

You can implement something like that straightforwardly using a function closure (see the *Scope & Closures* title of this series):

```
var gimmeSomething = (function(){
    var nextVal;

    return function(){
        if (nextVal === undefined) {
            nextVal = 1;
        }
        else {
            nextVal = (3 * nextVal) + 6;
        }

        return nextVal;
    };
})();

gimmeSomething();        // 1
gimmeSomething();        // 9
gimmeSomething();        // 33
gimmeSomething();        // 105
```

The nextVal computation logic here could have been simplified, but conceptually, we don't want to calculate the *next value* (aka nextVal) until the *next* gimmeSomething() call happens, because in general that could be a resource-leaky design for producers of more persistent or resource-limited values than simple numbers.

Generating an arbitrary number series isn't a terribly realistic example. But what if you were generating records from a data source? You could imagine much the same code.

In fact, this task is a very common design pattern, usually solved by iterators. An *iterator* is a well-defined interface for stepping through a series of values from a producer. The JS interface for iterators, as it is in most languages, is to call next() each time you want the next value from the producer.

We could implement the standard *iterator* interface for our number series producer:

```
var something = (function(){
    var nextVal;

    return {
        // needed for `for..of` loops
        [Symbol.iterator]: function(){ return this; },

        // standard iterator interface method
        next: function(){
            if (nextVal === undefined) {
                nextVal = 1;
            }
            else {
                nextVal = (3 * nextVal) + 6;
            }

            return { done:false, value:nextVal };
        }
    };
})();

something.next().value;     // 1
something.next().value;     // 9
something.next().value;     // 33
something.next().value;     // 105
```

We'll explain why we need the [Symbol.itera tor]: .. part of this code snippet in "Iterables" on page 137. Syntactically though, two ES6 features are at play: First, the [..] syntax is called a *computed property name* (see the *this & Object Prototypes* title of this series). It's a way in an object literal definition to specify an expression and use the result of that expression as the name for the property. Next, Symbol.iterator is one of ES6's predefined special Symbol values (see the *ES6 & Beyond* title of this series).

The next() call returns an object with two properties: done is a boolean value signaling the *iterator*'s complete status; value holds the iteration value.

ES6 also adds the for..of loop, which means that a standard *iterator* can automatically be consumed with native loop syntax:

```
for (var v of something) {
    console.log( v );

    // don't let the loop run forever!
    if (v > 500) {
        break;
    }
}
// 1 9 33 105 321 969
```

Because our something *iterator* always returns done:false, this for..of loop would run forever, which is why we put the break conditional in. It's totally OK for iterators to be never-ending, but there are also cases where the *iterator* will run over a finite set of values and eventually return a done:true.

The for..of loop automatically calls next() for each iteration—it doesn't pass any values in to the next()—and it will automatically terminate on receiving a done:true. It's quite handy for looping over a set of data.

Of course, you could manually loop over iterators, calling next() and checking for the done:true condition to know when to stop:

```
for (
    var ret;
    (ret = something.next()) && !ret.done;
) {
    console.log( ret.value );

    // don't let the loop run forever!
    if (ret.value > 500) {
        break;
    }
}
// 1 9 33 105 321 969
```

This manual for approach is certainly uglier than the ES6 for..of loop syntax, but its advantage is that it affords you the opportunity to pass in values to the next(..) calls if necessary.

In addition to making your own *iterators*, many built-in data structures in JS (as of ES6), like arrays, also have default *iterators*:

```
var a = [1,3,5,7,9];

for (var v of a) {
    console.log( v );
}
// 1 3 5 7 9
```

The for..of loop asks a for its *iterator*, and automatically uses it to iterate over a's values.

It may seem a strange omission by ES6, but regular objects intentionally do not come with a default *iterator* the way arrays do. The reasons go deeper than we will cover here. If all you want is to iterate over the properties of an object (with no particular guarantee of ordering), Object.keys(..) returns an array, which can then be used like for (var k of Object.keys(obj)) { ... Such a for..of loop over an object's keys would be similar to a for..in loop, except that Object.keys(..) does not include properties from the [[Prototype]] chain while for..in does (see the *this & Object Prototypes* title of this series).

Iterables

The `something` object in our running example is called an *iterator*, as it has the `next()` method on its interface. But a closely related term is *iterable*, which is an `object` that contains an *iterator* that can iterate over its values.

As of ES6, the way to retrieve an *iterator* from an *iterable* is that the *iterable* must have a function on it, with the name being the special ES6 symbol value `Symbol.iterator`. When this function is called, it returns an *iterator*. Though not required, generally each call should return a fresh new *iterator*.

`a` in the previous snippet is an *iterable*. The `for..of` loop automatically calls its `Symbol.iterator` function to construct an *iterator*. But we could of course call the function manually, and use the *iterator* it returns:

```
var a = [1,3,5,7,9];

var it = a[Symbol.iterator]();

it.next().value;    // 1
it.next().value;    // 3
it.next().value;    // 5
..
```

In the previous code listing that defined `something`, you may have noticed this line:

```
[Symbol.iterator]: function(){ return this; }
```

That little bit of confusing code is making the `something` value—the interface of the `something` *iterator*—also an *iterable*; it's now both an *iterable* and an *iterator*. Then, we pass `something` to the `for..of` loop:

```
for (var v of something) {
    ..
}
```

The `for..of` loop expects `something` to be an *iterable*, so it looks for and calls its `Symbol.iterator` function. We defined that function to simply `return this`, so it just gives itself back, and the `for..of` loop is none the wiser.

Generator Iterator

Let's turn our attention back to generators, in the context of *iterators*. A generator can be treated as a producer of values that we extract one at a time through an *iterator* interface's next() calls.

So, a generator itself is not technically an *iterable*, though it's very similar—when you execute the generator, you get an *iterator* back:

```
function *foo(){ .. }

var it = foo();
```

We can implement the something infinite number series producer from earlier with a generator, like this:

```
function *something() {
    var nextVal;

    while (true) {
        if (nextVal === undefined) {
            nextVal = 1;
        }
        else {
            nextVal = (3 * nextVal) + 6;
        }

        yield nextVal;
    }
}
```

A while..true loop would normally be a very bad thing to include in a real JS program, at least if it doesn't have a break or return in it, as it would likely run forever, synchronously, and block/lock-up the browser UI. However, in a generator, such a loop is generally totally OK if it has a yield in it, as the generator will pause at each iteration, yielding back to the main program and/or to the event loop queue. To put it glibly, "generators put the while..true back in JS programming!"

That's a fair bit cleaner and simpler, right? Because the generator pauses at each yield, the state (scope) of the function *something() is kept around, meaning there's no need for the closure boilerplate to preserve variable state across calls.

Not only is it simpler code—we don't have to make our own *iterator* interface—it actually is more reason-able code, because it more clearly expresses the intent. For example, the while..true loop tells us the generator is intended to run forever—to keep generating values as long as we keep asking for them.

And now we can use our shiny new *something() generator with a for..of loop, and you'll see it works basically identically:

```
for (var v of something()) {
    console.log( v );

    // don't let the loop run forever!
    if (v > 500) {
        break;
    }
}
// 1 9 33 105 321 969
```

But don't skip over for (var v of something()) ..! We didn't just reference something as a value like in earlier examples, but instead called the *something() generator to get its *iterator* for the for..of loop to use.

If you're paying close attention, two questions may arise from this interaction between the generator and the loop:

- Why couldn't we say for (var v of something) ..? Because something here is a generator, which is not an *iterable*. We have to call something() to construct a producer for the for..of loop to iterate over.

- The something() call produces an *iterator*, but the for..of loop wants an *iterable*, right? Yep. The generator's *iterator* also has a Symbol.iterator function on it, which basically does a return this, just like the something *iterable* we defined earlier. In other words, a generator's *iterator* is also an *iterable*!

Stopping the Generator

In the previous example, it would appear the *iterator* instance for the *something() generator was basically left in a suspended state forever after the break in the loop was called.

But there's a hidden behavior that takes care of that for you. "Abnormal completion" (i.e., "early termination") of the for..of loop—generally caused by a break, return, or an uncaught exception—sends a signal to the generator's *iterator* for it to terminate.

 Technically, the for..of loop also sends this signal to the *iterator* at the normal completion of the loop. For a generator, that's essentially a moot operation, as the generator's *iterator* had to complete first so the for..of loop completed. However, custom *iterators* might desire to receive this additional signal from for..of loop consumers.

While a for..of loop will automatically send this signal, you may wish to send the signal manually to an *iterator*; you do this by calling return(..).

If you specify a try..finally clause inside the generator, it will always be run even when the generator is externally completed. This is useful if you need to clean up resources (database connections, etc.):

```
function *something() {
    try {
        var nextVal;

        while (true) {
            if (nextVal === undefined) {
                nextVal = 1;
            }
            else {
                nextVal = (3 * nextVal) + 6;
            }

            yield nextVal;
        }
    }
    // cleanup clause
    finally {
        console.log( "cleaning up!" );
    }
}
```

The earlier example with break in the for..of loop will trigger the finally clause. But you could instead manually terminate the generator's *iterator* instance from the outside with return(..):

```
var it = something();
for (var v of it) {
    console.log( v );

    // don't let the loop run forever!
    if (v > 500) {
        console.log(
            // complete the generator's iterator
            it.return( "Hello World" ).value
        );
        // no `break` needed here
    }
}
// 1 9 33 105 321 969
// cleaning up!
// Hello World
```

When we call it.return(..), it immediately terminates the generator, which of course runs the finally clause. Also, it sets the returned value to whatever you passed in to return(..), which is how "Hello World" comes right back out. We also don't need to include a break now because the generator's *iterator* is set to done:true, so the for..of loop will terminate on its next iteration.

Generators owe their namesake mostly to this *consuming produced values* use. But again, that's just one of the uses for generators, and frankly not even the main one we're concerned with in the context of this book.

But now that we more fully understand some of the mechanics of how they work, we can next turn our attention to how generators apply to async concurrency.

Iterating Generators Asynchronously

What do generators have to do with async coding patterns, fixing problems with callbacks, and the like? Let's get to answering that important question.

We should revisit one of our scenarios from Chapter 3. Let's recall the callback approach:

```
function foo(x,y,cb) {
    ajax(
        "http://some.url.1/?x=" + x + "&y=" + y,
        cb
    );
}
```

```
foo( 11, 31, function(err,text) {
    if (err) {
        console.error( err );
    }
    else {
        console.log( text );
    }
} );
```

If we wanted to express this same task flow control with a generator, we could do:

```
function foo(x,y) {
    ajax(
        "http://some.url.1/?x=" + x + "&y=" + y,
        function(err,data){
            if (err) {
                // throw an error into `*main()`
                it.throw( err );
            }
            else {
                // resume `*main()` with received `data`
                it.next( data );
            }
        }
    );
}

function *main() {
    try {
        var text = yield foo( 11, 31 );
        console.log( text );
    }
    catch (err) {
        console.error( err );
    }
}

var it = main();

// start it all up!
it.next();
```

At first glance, this snippet is longer, and perhaps a little more complex looking, than the callback snippet before it. But don't let that impression get you off track. The generator snippet is actually *much* better! But there's a lot going on for us to explain.

First, let's look at this part of the code, which is the most important:

```
var text = yield foo( 11, 31 );
console.log( text );
```

Think about how that code works for a moment. We're calling a normal function foo(..) and we're apparently able to get back the text from the Ajax call, even though it's asynchronous.

How is that possible? If you recall the beginning of Chapter 1, we had almost identical code:

```
var data = ajax( "..url 1.." );
console.log( data );
```

And that code didn't work! Can you spot the difference? It's the yield used in a generator.

That's the magic! That's what allows us to have what appears to be blocking, synchronous code, but it doesn't actually block the whole program; it only pauses/blocks the code in the generator itself.

In yield foo(11,31), first the foo(11,31) call is made, which returns nothing (aka undefined), so we're making a call to request data, but we're actually then doing yield undefined. That's OK, because the code is not currently relying on a yielded value to do anything interesting. We'll revisit this point later in the chapter.

We're not using yield in a message passing sense here, only in a flow control sense to pause/block. Actually, it will have message passing, but only in one direction, after the generator is resumed.

So, the generator pauses at the yield, essentially asking the question, "what value should I return to assign to the variable text?" Who's going to answer that question?

Look at foo(..). If the Ajax request is successful, we call:

```
it.next( data );
```

That's resuming the generator with the response data, which means that our paused yield expression receives that value directly, and then as it restarts the generator code, that value gets assigned to the local variable text.

Pretty cool, huh?

Take a step back and consider the implications. We have totally synchronous-looking code inside the generator (other than the yield keyword itself), but hidden behind the scenes, inside of foo(..), the operations can complete asynchronously.

That's huge! That's a nearly perfect solution to our previously stated problem with callbacks not being able to express asynchrony in a sequential, synchronous fashion that our brains can relate to.

In essence, we are abstracting the asynchrony away as an implementation detail, so that we can reason synchronously/sequentially about our flow control: "Make an Ajax request, and when it finishes print out the response." And of course, we just expressed two steps in the flow control, but this same capabililty extends without bounds, to let us express however many steps we need to.

 This is such an important realization, just go back and read the last three paragraphs again to let it sink in!

Synchronous Error Handling

But the preceding generator code has even more goodness to *yield* to us. Let's turn our attention to the try..catch inside the generator:

```
try {
    var text = yield foo( 11, 31 );
    console.log( text );
}
catch (err) {
    console.error( err );
}
```

How does this work? The foo(..) call is asynchronously completing, and doesn't try..catch fail to catch asynchronous errors, as we looked at in Chapter 3?

We already saw how the yield lets the assignment statement pause to wait for foo(..) to finish, so that the completed response can be assigned to text. The awesome part is that this yield pausing *also* allows the generator to catch an error. We throw that error into the generator with this part of the earlier code listing:

```
if (err) {
    // throw an error into `*main()`
```

```
        it.throw( err );
    }
```

The yield-pause nature of generators means that not only do we get synchronous-looking return values from async function calls, but we can also synchronously catch errors from those async function calls!

So we've seen we can throw errors *into* a generator, but what about throwing errors *out of* a generator? Exactly as you'd expect:

```
function *main() {
    var x = yield "Hello World";

    yield x.toLowerCase();   // cause an exception!
}

var it = main();

it.next().value;             // Hello World

try {
    it.next( 42 );
}
catch (err) {
    console.error( err );    // TypeError
}
```

Of course, we could have manually thrown an error with throw .. instead of causing an exception.

We can even catch the same error that we throw(..) into the generator, essentially giving the generator a chance to handle it but if it doesn't, the *iterator* code must handle it:

```
function *main() {
    var x = yield "Hello World";

    // never gets here
    console.log( x );
}

var it = main();

it.next();

try {
    // will `*main()` handle this error? we'll see!
    it.throw( "Oops" );
}
catch (err) {
```

```
        // nope, didn't handle it!
        console.error( err );            // Oops
    }
```

Synchronous-looking error handling (via try..catch) with async code is a huge win for readability and reason-ability.

Generators + Promises

In our previous discussion, we showed how generators can be iterated asynchronously, which is a huge step forward in sequential reason-ability over the spaghetti mess of callbacks. But we lost something very important: the trustability and composability of Promises (see Chapter 3)!

Don't worry—we can get that back. The best of all worlds in ES6 is to combine generators (synchronous-looking async code) with Promises (trustable and composable).

But how?

Recall from Chapter 3 the Promise-based approach to our running Ajax example:

```
function foo(x,y) {
    return request(
        "http://some.url.1/?x=" + x + "&y=" + y
    );
}

foo( 11, 31 )
.then(
    function(text){
        console.log( text );
    },
    function(err){
        console.error( err );
    }
);
```

In our earlier generator code for the running Ajax example, foo(..) returned nothing (undefined), and our *iterator* control code didn't care about that yielded value.

But here the Promise-aware foo(..) returns a promise after making the Ajax call. That suggests that we could construct a promise with foo(..) and then yield it from the generator, and then the *iterator* control code would receive that promise.

But what should the *iterator* do with the promise?

It should listen for the promise to resolve (fulfillment or rejection), and then either resume the generator with the fulfillment message or throw an error into the generator with the rejection reason.

Let me repeat that, because it's so important. The natural way to get the most out of Promises and generators is to `yield` a Promise, and wire that Promise to control the generator's *iterator*.

Let's give it a try! First, we'll put the Promise-aware `foo(..)` together with the generator `*main()`:

```
function foo(x,y) {
    return request(
        "http://some.url.1/?x=" + x + "&y=" + y
    );
}

function *main() {
    try {
        var text = yield foo( 11, 31 );
        console.log( text );
    }
    catch (err) {
        console.error( err );
    }
}
```

The most powerful revelation in this refactor is that the code inside `*main()` did not have to change at all! Inside the generator, whatever values are `yield`ed out is just an opaque implementation detail, so we're not even aware it's happening, nor do we need to worry about it.

But how are we going to run `*main()` now? We still have some of the implementation plumbing work to do, to receive and wire up the `yield`ed promise so that it resumes the generator upon resolution. We'll start by trying that manually:

```
var it = main();

var p = it.next().value;

// wait for the `p` promise to resolve
p.then(
    function(text){
        it.next( text );
    },
```

```
    function(err){
        it.throw( err );
    }
);
```

Actually, that wasn't so painful at all, was it?

This snippet should look very similar to what we did earlier with the manually wired generator controlled by the error-first callback. Instead of an `if (err) { it.throw..`, the promise already splits fulfillment (success) and rejection (failure) for us, but otherwise the *iterator* control is identical.

Now, we've glossed over some important details.

Most importantly, we took advantage of the fact that we knew that `*main()` only had one Promise-aware step in it. What if we wanted to be able to Promise-drive a generator no matter how many steps it has? We certainly don't want to manually write out the Promise chain differently for each generator! What would be much nicer is if there was a way to repeat (aka loop over) the iteration control, and each time a Promise comes out, wait on its resolution before continuing.

Also, what if the generator throws out an error (intentionally or accidentally) during the `it.next(..)` call? Should we quit, or should we `catch` it and send it right back in? Similarly, what if we `it.throw(..)` a Promise rejection into the generator, but it's not handled, and comes right back out?

Promise-Aware Generator Runner

The more you start to explore this path, the more you realize, "wow, it'd be great if there was just some utility to do it for me." And you're absolutely correct. This is such an important pattern, and you don't want to get it wrong (or exhaust yourself repeating it over and over), so your best bet is to use a utility that is specifically designed to *run* Promise-yielding generators in the manner we've illustrated.

Several Promise abstraction libraries provide just such a utility, including my *asynquence* library and its `runner(..)`, which are discussed in Appendix A of this book.

But for the sake of learning and illustration, let's just define our own standalone utility that we'll call `run(..)`:

```
// thanks to Benjamin Gruenbaum (@benjamingr on GitHub) for
// big improvements here!
function run(gen) {
    var args = [].slice.call( arguments, 1), it;

    // initialize the generator in the current context
    it = gen.apply( this, args );

    // return a promise for the generator completing
    return Promise.resolve()
        .then( function handleNext(value){
            // run to the next yielded value
            var next = it.next( value );

            return (function handleResult(next){
                // generator has completed running?
                if (next.done) {
                    return next.value;
                }
                // otherwise keep going
                else {
                    return Promise.resolve( next.value )
                        .then(
                            // resume the async loop on
                            // success, sending the resolved
                            // value back into the generator
                            handleNext,

                            // if `value` is a rejected
                            // promise, propagate error back
                            // into the generator for its own
                            // error handling
                            function handleErr(err) {
                                return Promise.resolve(
                                    it.throw( err )
                                )
                                .then( handleResult );
                            }
                        );
                }
            })(next);
        } );
}
```

As you can see, it's a quite a bit more complex than you'd probably want to author yourself, and you especially wouldn't want to repeat this code for each generator you use. So, a utility/library helper is definitely the way to go. Nevertheless, I encourage you to spend a few minutes studying that code listing to get a better sense of how to manage the generator + Promise negotiation.

How would you use `run(..)` with `*main()` in our *running* Ajax example?

```
function *main() {
    // ..
}

run( main );
```

That's it! The way we wired `run(..)`, it will automatically advance the generator you pass to it, asynchronously until completion.

The `run(..)` we defined returns a promise which is wired to resolve once the generator is complete, or receive an uncaught exception if the generator doesn't handle it. We don't show that capability here, but we'll come back to it later in the chapter.

ES7: async and await?

The preceding pattern—generators `yield`ing Promises that then control the generator's *iterator* to advance it to completion—is such a powerful and useful approach, it would be nicer if we could do it without the clutter of the library utility helper (aka `run(..)`).

There's probably good news on that front. At the time of this writing, there's early but strong support for a proposal for more syntactic addition in this realm for the post-ES6, ES7-ish timeframe. Obviously, it's too early to guarantee the details, but there's a pretty decent chance it will shake out similar to the following:

```
function foo(x,y) {
    return request(
        "http://some.url.1/?x=" + x + "&y=" + y
    );
}

async function main() {
    try {
        var text = await foo( 11, 31 );
        console.log( text );
    }
    catch (err) {
        console.error( err );
    }
}
```

```
main();
```

As you can see, there's no `run(..)` call (meaning no need for a library utility!) to invoke and drive `main()`—it's just called as a normal function. Also, `main()` isn't declared as a generator function anymore; it's a new kind of function: `async function`. And finally, instead of `yield`ing a Promise, we `await` for it to resolve.

The `async function` automatically knows what to do if you `await` a Promise—it will pause the function (just like with generators) until the Promise resolves. We didn't illustrate it in this snippet, but calling an async function like `main()` automatically returns a promise that's resolved whenever the function finishes completely.

 The `async` / `await` syntax should look very familiar to readers with experience in C#, because it's basically identical.

The proposal essentially codifies support for the pattern we've already derived, into a syntactic mechanism: combining Promises with sync-looking flow control code. That's the best of both worlds combined, to effectively address practically all of the major concerns we outlined with callbacks.

The mere fact that such a ES7-ish proposal already exists and has early support and enthusiasm is a major vote of confidence in the future importance of this async pattern.

Promise Concurrency in Generators

So far, all we've demonstrated is a single-step async flow with Promises + generators. But real-world code will often have many async steps.

If you're not careful, the sync-looking style of generators may lull you into complacency with how you structure your async concurrency, leading to suboptimal performance patterns. So we want to spend a little time exploring the options.

Imagine a scenario where you need to fetch data from two different sources, then combine those responses to make a third request, and finally print out the last response. We explored a similar scenario with Promises in Chapter 3, but let's reconsider it in the context of generators.

Your first instinct might be something like:

```
function *foo() {
    var r1 = yield request( "http://some.url.1" );
    var r2 = yield request( "http://some.url.2" );

    var r3 = yield request(
        "http://some.url.3/?v=" + r1 + "," + r2
    );

    console.log( r3 );
}

// use previously defined `run(..)` utility
run( foo );
```

This code will work, but in the specifics of our scenario, it's not optimal. Can you spot why?

Because the r1 and r2 requests can—and for performance reasons, *should*—run concurrently, but in this code they will run sequentially; the "http://some.url.2" URL isn't Ajax fetched until after the "http://some.url.1" request is finished. These two requests are independent, so the better performance approach would likely be to have them run at the same time.

But how exactly would you do that with a generator and yield? We know that yield is only a single pause point in the code, so you can't really do two pauses at the same time.

The most natural and effective answer is to base the async flow on Promises, specifically on their capability to manage state in a time-independent fashion (see "Future Value" on page 52 in Chapter 3).

The simplest approach:

```
function *foo() {
    // make both requests "in parallel"
    var p1 = request( "http://some.url.1" );
    var p2 = request( "http://some.url.2" );

    // wait until both promises resolve
    var r1 = yield p1;
    var r2 = yield p2;

    var r3 = yield request(
        "http://some.url.3/?v=" + r1 + "," + r2
```

```
    );

    console.log( r3 );
}

// use previously defined `run(..)` utility
run( foo );
```

Why is this different from the previous snippet? Look at where the yield is and is not. p1 and p2 are promises for Ajax requests made concurrently (aka "in parallel"). It doesn't matter which one finishes first, because promises will hold onto their resolved state for as long as necessary.

Then we use two subsequent yield statements to wait for and retrieve the resolutions from the promises (into r1 and r2, respectively). If p1 resolves first, the yield p1 resumes first then waits on the yield p2 to resume. If p2 resolves first, it will just patiently hold onto that resolution value until asked, but the yield p1 will hold on first, until p1 resolves.

Either way, both p1 and p2 will run concurrently, and both have to finish, in either order, before the r3 = yield request.. Ajax request will be made.

If that flow control processing model sounds familiar, it's basically the same as what we identified in Chapter 3 as the gate pattern, enabled by the Promise.all([..]) utility. So, we could also express the flow control like this:

```
function *foo() {
    // make both requests "in parallel," and
    // wait until both promises resolve
    var results = yield Promise.all( [
        request( "http://some.url.1" ),
        request( "http://some.url.2" )
    ] );

    var r1 = results[0];
    var r2 = results[1];

    var r3 = yield request(
        "http://some.url.3/?v=" + r1 + "," + r2
    );

    console.log( r3 );
}
```

```
// use previously defined `run(..)` utility
run( foo );
```

 As we discussed in Chapter 3, we can even use ES6 destructuring assignment to simplify the `var r1 = ..` `var r2 = ..` assignments, with `var [r1,r2] = results`.

In other words, all of the concurrency capabilities of Promises are available to us in the generator + Promise approach. So in any place where you need more than sequential this-then-that async flow control steps, Promises are likely your best bet.

Promises, Hidden

As a word of stylistic caution, be careful about how much Promise logic you include *inside your generators*. The whole point of using generators for asynchrony in the way we've described is to create simple, sequential, sync-looking code, and to hide as much of the details of asynchrony away from that code as possible.

For example, this might be a cleaner approach:

```
// note: normal function, not generator
function bar(url1,url2) {
    return Promise.all( [
        request( url1 ),
        request( url2 )
    ] );
}

function *foo() {
    // hide the Promise-based concurrency details
    // inside `bar(..)`
    var results = yield bar(
        "http://some.url.1",
        "http://some.url.2"
    );

    var r1 = results[0];
    var r2 = results[1];

    var r3 = yield request(
        "http://some.url.3/?v=" + r1 + "," + r2
    );

    console.log( r3 );
}
```

```
// use previously defined `run(..)` utility
run( foo );
```

Inside *foo(), it's cleaner and clearer that all we're doing is just asking bar(..) to get us some results, and we'll yield-wait on that to happen. We don't have to care that under the covers a Promise.all([..]) Promise composition will be used to make that happen.

We treat asynchrony, and indeed Promises, as an implementation detail.

Hiding your Promise logic inside a function that you merely call from your generator is especially useful if you're going to do a sophisticated series flow-control. For example:

```
function bar() {
    Promise.all( [
        baz( .. )
        .then( .. ),
        Promise.race( [ .. ] )
    ] )
    .then( .. )
}
```

That kind of logic is sometimes required, and if you dump it directly inside your generator(s), you've defeated most of the reason why you would want to use generators in the first place. We *should* intentionally abstract such details away from our generator code so that they don't clutter up the higher level task expression.

Beyond creating code that is both functional and performant, you should also strive to make code that is as reason-able and maintainable as possible.

Abstraction is not *always* a healthy thing for programming—many times it can increase complexity in exchange for terseness. But in this case, I believe it's much healthier for your generator + Promise async code than the alternatives. As with all such advice, though, pay attention to your specific situations and make proper decisions for you and your team.

Generator Delegation

In the previous section, we showed calling regular functions from inside a generator, and how that remains a useful technique for abstracting away implementation details (like async Promise flow). But the main drawback of using a normal function for this task is that it has to behave by the normal function rules, which means it cannot pause itself with `yield` like a generator can.

It may then occur to you that you might try to call one generator from another generator, using our `run(..)` helper, such as:

```
function *foo() {
    var r2 = yield request( "http://some.url.2" );
    var r3 = yield request( "http://some.url.3/?v=" + r2 );

    return r3;
}

function *bar() {
    var r1 = yield request( "http://some.url.1" );

    // "delegating" to `*foo()` via `run(..)`
    var r3 = yield run( foo );

    console.log( r3 );
}

run( bar );
```

We run `*foo()` inside of `*bar()` by using our `run(..)` utility again. We take advantage here of the fact that the `run(..)` we defined earlier returns a promise which is resolved when its generator is run to completion (or errors out), so if we `yield` out to a `run(..)` instance the promise from another `run(..)` call, it automatically pauses `*bar()` until `*foo()` finishes.

But there's an even better way to integrate calling `*foo()` into `*bar()`, and it's called `yield`-delegation. The special syntax for `yield`-delegation is: `yield * __` (notice the extra `*`). Before we see it work in our previous example, let's look at a simpler scenario:

```
function *foo() {
    console.log( "`*foo()` starting" );
    yield 3;
    yield 4;
    console.log( "`*foo()` finished" );
}
```

```
function *bar() {
    yield 1;
    yield 2;
    yield *foo();    // `yield`-delegation!
    yield 5;
}

var it = bar();

it.next().value;    // 1
it.next().value;    // 2
it.next().value;    // `*foo()` starting
                    // 3
it.next().value;    // 4
it.next().value;    // `*foo()` finished
                    // 5
```

 Similar to a note earlier in this chapter where I explained why I prefer function *foo() .. instead of function* foo() .., I also prefer—differing from most other documentation on the topic—to say yield *foo() instead of yield* foo(). The placement of the * is purely stylistic and up to your best judgment. But I find the consistency of styling attractive.

How does the yield *foo() delegation work?

First, calling foo() creates an *iterator* exactly as we've already seen. Then, yield * delegates/transfers the *iterator* instance control (of the present *bar() generator) over to this other *foo() *iterator*.

So, the first two it.next() calls are controlling *bar(), but when we make the third it.next() call, now *foo() starts up, and now we're controlling *foo() instead of *bar(). That's why it's called delegation—*bar() delegated its iteration control to *foo().

As soon as the it *iterator* control exhausts the entire *foo() *iterator*, it automatically returns to controlling *bar().

So now back to the previous example with the three sequential Ajax requests:

```
function *foo() {
    var r2 = yield request( "http://some.url.2" );
    var r3 = yield request( "http://some.url.3/?v=" + r2 );
```

```
        return r3;
}

function *bar() {
    var r1 = yield request( "http://some.url.1" );

    // "delegating" to `*foo()` via `yield*`
    var r3 = yield *foo();

    console.log( r3 );
}

run( bar );
```

The only difference between this snippet and the version used earlier is the use of yield *foo() instead of the previous yield
run(foo).

 yield * yields iteration control, not generator
control; when you invoke the *foo() generator,
you're now yield-delegating to its *iterator*. But
you can actually yield-delegate to any *iterable*;
yield *[1,2,3] would consume the default
iterator for the [1,2,3] array value.

Why Delegation?

The purpose of yield-delegation is mostly code organization, and
in that way is symmetrical with normal function calling.

Imagine two modules that respectively provide methods foo() and
bar(), where bar() calls foo(). The reason the two are separate is
generally because the proper organization of code for the program
calls for them to be in separate functions. For example, there may be
cases where foo() is called standalone, and other places where
bar() calls foo().

For all these exact same reasons, keeping generators separate aids in
program readability, maintenance, and debuggability. In that
respect, yield * is a syntactic shortcut for manually iterating over
the steps of *foo() while inside of *bar().

Such a manual approach would be especially complex if the steps in
*foo() were asynchronous, which is why you'd probably need to
use that run(..) utility to do it. And as we've shown, yield *foo()

eliminates the need for a subinstance of the `run(..)` utility (like `run(foo)`).

Delegating Messages

You may wonder how this `yield`-delegation works not just with *iterator* control but with the two-way message passing. Carefully follow the flow of messages in and out, through the `yield`-delegation:

```
function *foo() {
    console.log( "inside `*foo()`:", yield "B" );

    console.log( "inside `*foo()`:", yield "C" );

    return "D";
}

function *bar() {
    console.log( "inside `*bar()`:", yield "A" );

    // `yield`-delegation!
    console.log( "inside `*bar()`:", yield *foo() );

    console.log( "inside `*bar()`:", yield "E" );

    return "F";
}

var it = bar();

console.log( "outside:", it.next().value );
// outside: A

console.log( "outside:", it.next( 1 ).value );
// inside `*bar()`: 1
// outside: B

console.log( "outside:", it.next( 2 ).value );
// inside `*foo()`: 2
// outside: C

console.log( "outside:", it.next( 3 ).value );
// inside `*foo()`: 3
// inside `*bar()`: D
// outside: E

console.log( "outside:", it.next( 4 ).value );
// inside `*bar()`: 4
// outside: F
```

Pay particular attention to the processing steps after the it.next(3) call:

1. The 3 value is passed (through the yield-delegation in *bar()) into the waiting yield "C" expression inside of *foo().

2. *foo() then calls return "D", but this value doesn't get returned all the way back to the outside it.next(3) call.

3. Instead, the "D" value is sent as the result of the waiting yield *foo() expression inside of *bar()—this yield-delegation expression has essentially been paused while all of *foo() was exhausted. So "D" ends up inside of *bar() for it to print out.

4. yield "E" is called inside of *bar(), and the "E" value is yielded to the outside as the result of the it.next(3) call.

From the perspective of the external *iterator* (it), it doesn't appear any differently between controlling the initial generator or a delegated one.

In fact, yield-delegation doesn't even have to be directed to another generator; it can just be directed to a non-generator, general *iterable*. For example:

```
function *bar() {
    console.log( "inside `*bar()`:", yield "A" );

    // `yield`-delegation to a non-generator!
    console.log( "inside `*bar()`:", yield *[ "B", "C", "D" ] );

    console.log( "inside `*bar()`:", yield "E" );

    return "F";
}

var it = bar();

console.log( "outside:", it.next().value );
// outside: A

console.log( "outside:", it.next( 1 ).value );
// inside `*bar()`: 1
// outside: B

console.log( "outside:", it.next( 2 ).value );
// outside: C

console.log( "outside:", it.next( 3 ).value );
```

```
// outside: D

console.log( "outside:", it.next( 4 ).value );
// inside `*bar()`: undefined
// outside: E

console.log( "outside:", it.next( 5 ).value );
// inside `*bar()`: 5
// outside: F
```

Notice the differences in where the messages were received/reported between this example and the one previous.

Most strikingly, the default array *iterator* doesn't care about any messages sent in via next(..) calls, so the values 2, 3, and 4 are essentially ignored. Also, because that *iterator* has no explicit return value (unlike the previously used *foo()), the yield * expression gets an undefined when it finishes.

Exceptions Delegated, Too!

In the same way that yield-delegation transparently passes messages through in both directions, errors/exceptions also pass in both directions:

```
function *foo() {
    try {
        yield "B";
    }
    catch (err) {
        console.log( "error caught inside `*foo()`:", err );
    }

    yield "C";

    throw "D";
}

function *bar() {
    yield "A";

    try {
        yield *foo();
    }
    catch (err) {
        console.log( "error caught inside `*bar()`:", err );
    }

    yield "E";
```

```
    yield *baz();

    // note: can't get here!
    yield "G";
}

function *baz() {
    throw "F";
}

var it = bar();

console.log( "outside:", it.next().value );
// outside: A

console.log( "outside:", it.next( 1 ).value );
// outside: B

console.log( "outside:", it.throw( 2 ).value );
// error caught inside `*foo()`: 2
// outside: C

console.log( "outside:", it.next( 3 ).value );
// error caught inside `*bar()`: D
// outside: E

try {
    console.log( "outside:", it.next( 4 ).value );
}
catch (err) {
    console.log( "error caught outside:", err );
}
// error caught outside: F
```

Some things to note from this snippet:

1. When we call it.throw(2), it sends the error message 2 into
   *bar(), which delegates that to *foo(), which then catches it
   and handles it gracefully. Then, the yield "C" sends "C" back
   out as the return value from the it.throw(2) call.

2. The "D" value that's next thrown from inside *foo() propagates
   out to *bar(), which catches it and handles it gracefully. Then
   the yield "E" sends "E" back out as the return value from the
   it.next(3) call.

3. Next, the exception thrown from *baz() isn't caught in *bar()
   —though we did catch it outside—so both *baz() and *bar()
   are set to a completed state. After this snippet, you would not be

able to get the "G" value out with any subsequent next(..) call(s)—they will just return undefined for value.

Delegating Asynchrony

Let's finally get back to our earlier yield-delegation example with the multiple sequential Ajax requests:

```
function *foo() {
    var r2 = yield request( "http://some.url.2" );
    var r3 = yield request( "http://some.url.3/?v=" + r2 );

    return r3;
}

function *bar() {
    var r1 = yield request( "http://some.url.1" );

    var r3 = yield *foo();

    console.log( r3 );
}

run( bar );
```

Instead of calling yield run(foo) inside of *bar(), we just call yield *foo().

In the previous version of this example, the Promise mechanism (controlled by run(..)) was used to transport the value from return r3 in *foo() to the local variable r3 inside *bar(). Now, that value is just returned back directly via the yield * mechanics.

Otherwise, the behavior is pretty much identical.

Delegating Recursion

Of course, yield-delegation can keep following as many delegation steps as you wire up. You could even use yield-delegation for async-capable generator *recursion*—a generator yield-delegating to itself:

```
function *foo(val) {
    if (val > 1) {
        // generator recursion
        val = yield *foo( val - 1 );
    }
```

```
        return yield request( "http://some.url/?v=" + val );
}

function *bar() {
    var r1 = yield *foo( 3 );
    console.log( r1 );
}

run( bar );
```

 Our run(..) utility could have been called with run(foo, 3), because it supports additional parameters being passed along to the initialization of the generator. However, we used a parameter-free *bar() here to highlight the flexibility of yield *.

What processing steps follow from that code? Hang on, this is going to be quite intricate to describe in detail:

1. run(bar) starts up the *bar() generator.

2. foo(3) creates an *iterator* for *foo(..) and passes 3 as its val parameter.

3. Because 3 > 1, foo(2) creates another *iterator* and passes in 2 as its val parameter.

4. Because 2 > 1, foo(1) creates yet another *iterator* and passes in 1 as its val parameter.

5. 1 > 1 is false, so we next call request(..) with the 1 value, and get a promise back for that first Ajax call.

6. That promise is yielded out, which comes back to the *foo(2) generator instance.

7. The yield * passes that promise back out to the *foo(3) generator instance. Another yield * passes the promise out to the *bar() generator instance. And yet again another yield * passes the promise out to the run(..) utility, which will wait on that promise (for the first Ajax request) to proceed.

8. When the promise resolves, its fulfillment message is sent to resume *bar(), which passes through the yield * into the *foo(3) instance, which then passes through the yield * to the

`*foo(2)` generator instance, which then passes through the `yield *` to the normal `yield` that's waiting in the `*foo(3)` generator instance.

9. That first call's Ajax response is now immediately `returned` from the `*foo(3)` generator instance, which sends that value back as the result of the `yield *` expression in the `*foo(2)` instance, and assigned to its local `val` variable.

10. Inside `*foo(2)`, a second Ajax request is made with `request(..)`, whose promise is `yielded` back to the `*foo(1)` instance, and then `yield *` propagates all the way out to `run(..)` (step 7 again). When the promise resolves, the second Ajax response propagates all the way back into the `*foo(2)` generator instance, and is assigned to its local `val` variable.

11. Finally, the third Ajax request is made with `request(..)`, its promise goes out to `run(..)`, and then its resolution value comes all the way back, which is then `returned` so that it comes back to the waiting `yield *` expression in `*bar()`.

Phew! A lot of crazy mental juggling, huh? You might want to read through that a few more times, and then go grab a snack to clear your head!

Generator Concurrency

As we discussed in both Chapter 1 and earlier in this chapter, two simultaneously running "processes" can cooperatively interleave their operations, and many times this can *yield* (pun intended) very powerful asynchrony expressions.

Frankly, our earlier examples of concurrency interleaving of multiple generators showed how to make it really confusing. But we hinted that there's places where this capability is quite useful.

Recall a scenario we looked at in Chapter 1, where two different simultaneous Ajax response handlers needed to coordinate with each other to make sure that the data communication was not a race condition. We slotted the responses into the `res` array like this:

```
function response(data) {
    if (data.url == "http://some.url.1") {
        res[0] = data;
    }
```

```
          else if (data.url == "http://some.url.2") {
              res[1] = data;
          }
      }
```

But how can we use multiple generators concurrently for this scenario?

```
// `request(..)` is a Promise-aware Ajax utility

var res = [];

function *reqData(url) {
    res.push(
        yield request( url )
    );
}
```

 We're going to use two instances of the *reqData(..) generator here, but there's no difference to running a single instance of two different generators; both approaches are reasoned about identically. We'll see two different generators coordinating in just a bit.

Instead of having to manually sort out res[0] and res[1] assignments, we'll use coordinated ordering so that res.push(..) properly slots the values in the expected and predictable order. The expressed logic thus should feel a bit cleaner.

But how will we actually orchestrate this interaction? First, let's just do it manually, with Promises:

```
var it1 = reqData( "http://some.url.1" );
var it2 = reqData( "http://some.url.2" );

var p1 = it1.next();
var p2 = it2.next();

p1
.then( function(data){
    it1.next( data );
    return p2;
} )
.then( function(data){
    it2.next( data );
} );
```

*reqData(..)'s two instances are both started to make their Ajax requests, then paused with yield. Then we choose to resume the first instance when p1 resolves, and then p2's resolution will restart the second instance. In this way, we use Promise orchestration to ensure that res[0] will have the first response and res[1] will have the second response.

But frankly, this is awfully manual, and it doesn't really let the generators orchestrate themselves, which is where the true power can lie. Let's try it a different way:

```js
// `request(..)` is a Promise-aware Ajax utility

var res = [];

function *reqData(url) {
    var data = yield request( url );

    // transfer control
    yield;

    res.push( data );
}

var it1 = reqData( "http://some.url.1" );
var it2 = reqData( "http://some.url.2" );

var p1 = it.next();
var p2 = it.next();

p1.then( function(data){
    it1.next( data );
} );

p2.then( function(data){
    it2.next( data );
} );

Promise.all( [p1,p2] )
.then( function(){
    it1.next();
    it2.next();
} );
```

OK, this is a bit better (though still manual!), because now the two instances of *reqData(..) run truly concurrently, and (at least for the first part) independently.

In the previous snippet, the second instance was not given its data until after the first instance was totally finished. But here, both instances receive their data as soon as their respective responses come back, and then each instance does another yield for control transfer purposes. We then choose what order to resume them in the Promise.all([..]) handler.

What may not be as obvious is that this approach hints at an easier form for a reusable utility, because of the symmetry. We can do even better. Let's imagine using a utility called runAll(..):

```
// `request(..)` is a Promise-aware Ajax utility

var res = [];

runAll(
    function*(){
        var p1 = request( "http://some.url.1" );

        // transfer control
        yield;

        res.push( yield p1 );
    },
    function*(){
        var p2 = request( "http://some.url.2" );

        // transfer control
        yield;

        res.push( yield p2 );
    }
);
```

 We're not including a code listing for run All(..) as it is not only long enough to bog down the text, but is an extension of the logic we've already implemented in run(..) earlier. So, as a good supplementary exercise for the reader, try your hand at evolving the code from run(..) to work like the imagined runAll(..). Also, my *asynquence* library provides a previously mentioned runner(..) utility with this kind of capability already built in, and will be discussed in Appendix A of this book.

Here's how the processing inside runAll(..) would operate:

1. The first generator gets a promise for the first Ajax response from `"http://some.url.1"`, then `yields` control back to the `runAll(..)` utility.

2. The second generator runs and does the same for `"http://some.url.2"`, yielding control back to the `runAll(..)` utility.

3. The first generator resumes, and then `yields` out its promise p1. The `runAll(..)` utility does the same in this case as our previous `run(..)`, in that it waits on that promise to resolve, then resumes the same generator (no control transfer!). When p1 resolves, `runAll(..)` resumes the first generator again with that resolution value, and then `res[0]` is given its value. When the first generator then finishes, that's an implicit transfer of control.

4. The second generator resumes, `yields` out its promise p2, and waits for it to resolve. Once it does, `runAll(..)` resumes the second generator with that value, and `res[1]` is set.

In this running example, we use an outer variable called `res` to store the results of the two different Ajax responses—our concurrency coordination makes that possible.

But it might be quite helpful to further extend `runAll(..)` to provide an inner variable space for the multiple generator instances to *share*, such as an empty object we'll call `data` below. Also, it could take non-Promise values that are `yielded` and hand them off to the next generator.

Consider:

```
// `request(..)` is a Promise-aware Ajax utility

runAll(
    function*(data){
        data.res = [];

        // transfer control (and message pass)
        var url1 = yield "http://some.url.2";

        var p1 = request( url1 ); // "http://some.url.1"

        // transfer control
        yield;

        data.res.push( yield p1 );
```

```
    },
    function*(data){
        // transfer control (and message pass)
        var url2 = yield "http://some.url.1";

        var p2 = request( url2 ); // "http://some.url.2"

        // transfer control
        yield;

        data.res.push( yield p2 );
    }
);
```

In this formulation, the two generators are not just coordinating control transfer, but actually communicating with each other, both through `data.res` and the `yielded` messages that trade `url1` and `url2` values. That's incredibly powerful!

Such realization also serves as a conceptual base for a more sophisticated asynchrony technique called Communicating Sequential Processes (CSP), which is covered in Appendix B of this book.

Thunks

So far, we've made the assumption that `yielding` a Promise from a generator—and having that Promise resume the generator via a helper utility like `run(..)`—was the best possible way to manage asynchrony with generators. To be clear, it is.

But we skipped over another pattern that has some mildly widespread adoption, so in the interest of completeness we'll take a brief look at it.

In general computer science, there's an old pre-JS concept called a *thunk*. Without getting bogged down in the historical nature, a narrow expression of a thunk in JS is a function that—without any parameters—is wired to call another function.

In other words, you wrap a function definition around function call —with any parameters it needs—to defer the execution of that call, and that wrapping function is a thunk. When you later execute the thunk, you end up calling the original function.

For example:

```
function foo(x,y) {
    return x + y;
```

```
    }

    function fooThunk() {
        return foo( 3, 4 );
    }

    // later

    console.log( fooThunk() );   // 7
```

So, a synchronous thunk is pretty straightforward. But what about an async thunk? We can essentially extend the narrow thunk definition to include it receiving a callback.

Consider:

```
    function foo(x,y,cb) {
        setTimeout( function(){
            cb( x + y );
        }, 1000 );
    }

    function fooThunk(cb) {
        foo( 3, 4, cb );
    }

    // later

    fooThunk( function(sum){
        console.log( sum );      // 7
    } );
```

As you can see, fooThunk(..) expects only a cb(..) parameter, as it already has values 3 and 4 (for x and y, respectively) prespecified and ready to pass to foo(..). A thunk is just waiting around patiently for the last piece it needs to do its job: the callback.

You don't want to make thunks manually, though. So, let's invent a utility that does this wrapping for us.

Consider:

```
    function thunkify(fn) {
        var args = [].slice.call( arguments, 1 );
        return function(cb) {
            args.push( cb );
            return fn.apply( null, args );
        };
    }

    var fooThunk = thunkify( foo, 3, 4 );
```

```
// later

fooThunk( function(sum) {
    console.log( sum );      // 7
} );
```

 Here we assume that the original (foo(..))
function signature expects its callback in the last
position, with any other parameters coming
before it. This is a pretty ubiquitous standard for
async JS function standards. You might call it
"callback-last style." If for some reason you had
a need to handle "callback-first style" signatures,
you would just make a utility that used
args.unshift(..) instead of args.push(..).

The preceding formulation of thunkify(..) takes both the foo(..)
function reference, and any parameters it needs, and returns back
the thunk itself (fooThunk(..)). However, that's not the typical
approach you'll find to thunks in JS.

Instead of thunkify(..) making the thunk itself, typically—if not
perplexingly—the thunkify(..) utility would produce a function
that produces thunks.

Uhhhh...yeah.

Consider:

```
function thunkify(fn) {
    return function() {
        var args = [].slice.call( arguments );
        return function(cb) {
            args.push( cb );
            return fn.apply( null, args );
        };
    };
}
```

The main difference here is the extra return function() { .. }
layer. Here's how its usage differs:

```
var whatIsThis = thunkify( foo );

var fooThunk = whatIsThis( 3, 4 );

// later
```

```
fooThunk( function(sum) {
    console.log( sum );     // 7
} );
```

Obviously, the big question this snippet implies is what is whatIs
This properly called? It's not the thunk, it's the thing that will produce thunks from foo(..) calls. It's kind of like a "factory" for
"thunks." There doesn't seem to be any kind of standard agreement
for naming such a thing.

So, my proposal is "thunkory" ("thunk" + "factory"). So, thun
kify(..) produces a thunkory, and a thunkory produces thunks.
That reasoning is symmetric to my proposal for "promisory" in
Chapter 3:

```
var fooThunkory = thunkify( foo );

var fooThunk1 = fooThunkory( 3, 4 );
var fooThunk2 = fooThunkory( 5, 6 );

// later

fooThunk1( function(sum) {
    console.log( sum );     // 7
} );

fooThunk2( function(sum) {
    console.log( sum );     // 11
} );
```

> The running foo(..) example expects a style of
> callback that's not "error-first style." Of course,
> "error-first style" is much more common. If
> foo(..) had some sort of legitimate error-
> producing expectation, we could change it to
> expect and use an error-first callback. None of
> the subsequent thunkify(..) machinery cares
> what style of callback is assumed. The only dif-
> ference in usage would be fooThunk1(func
> tion(err,sum){...

Exposing the thunkory method—instead of how the earlier thun
kify(..) hides this intermediary step—may seem like unnecessary
complication. But in general, it's quite useful to make thunkories at
the beginning of your program to wrap existing API methods, and

then be able to pass around and call those thunkories when you need thunks. The two distinct steps preserve a cleaner separation of capability.

To illustrate:

```
// cleaner:
var fooThunkory = thunkify( foo );

var fooThunk1 = fooThunkory( 3, 4 );
var fooThunk2 = fooThunkory( 5, 6 );

// instead of:
var fooThunk1 = thunkify( foo, 3, 4 );
var fooThunk2 = thunkify( foo, 5, 6 );
```

Regardless of whether you like to deal with the thunkories explicitly, the usage of thunks fooThunk1(..) and fooThunk2(..) remains the same.

s/promise/thunk/

So what's all this thunk stuff have to do with generators?

Comparing thunks to promises generally: they're not directly inter-changable as they're not equivalent in behavior. Promises are vastly more capable and trustable than bare thunks.

But in another sense, they both can be seen as a request for a value, which may be async in its answering.

Recall from Chapter 3 that we defined a utility for promisifying a function, which we called Promise.wrap(..)—we could have called it promisify(..), too! This Promise-wrapping utility doesn't pro-duce Promises; it produces promisories that in turn produce Prom-ises. This is completely symmetric to the thunkories and thunks presently being discussed.

To illustrate the symmetry, let's first alter the running foo(..) example from earlier to assume an "error-first style" callback:

```
function foo(x,y,cb) {
    setTimeout( function(){
        // assume `cb(..)` as "error-first style"
        cb( null, x + y );
    }, 1000 );
}
```

Now, we'll compare using thunkify(..) and promisify(..) (aka Promise.wrap(..) from Chapter 3):

```
// symmetrical: constructing the question asker
var fooThunkory = thunkify( foo );
var fooPromisory = promisify( foo );

// symmetrical: asking the question
var fooThunk = fooThunkory( 3, 4 );
var fooPromise = fooPromisory( 3, 4 );

// get the thunk answer
fooThunk( function(err,sum){
    if (err) {
        console.error( err );
    }
    else {
        console.log( sum );     // 7
    }
} );

// get the promise answer
fooPromise
.then(
    function(sum){
        console.log( sum );     // 7
    },
    function(err){
        console.error( err );
    }
);
```

Both the thunkory and the promisory are essentially asking a question (for a value), and respectively the thunk fooThunk and promise fooPromise represent the future answers to that question. Presented in that light, the symmetry is clear.

With that perspective in mind, we can see that generators which yield Promises for asynchrony could instead yield thunks for asynchrony. All we'd need is a smarter run(..) utility (like from before) that can not only look for and wire up to a yielded Promise but also to provide a callback to a yielded thunk.

Consider:

```
function *foo() {
    var val = yield request( "http://some.url.1" );
    console.log( val );
}
```

```
run( foo );
```

In this example, `request(..)` could either be a promisory that returns a promise, or a thunkory that returns a thunk. From the perspective of what's going on inside the generator code logic, we don't care about that implementation detail, which is quite powerful!

So, `request(..)` could be either:

```
// promisory `request(..)` (see Chapter 3)
var request = Promise.wrap( ajax );

// vs.

// thunkory `request(..)`
var request = thunkify( ajax );
```

Finally, as a thunk-aware patch to our earlier `run(..)` utility, we would need logic like this:

```
// ..
// did we receive a thunk back?
else if (typeof next.value == "function") {
    return new Promise( function(resolve,reject){
        // call the thunk with an error-first callback
        next.value( function(err,msg) {
            if (err) {
                reject( err );
            }
            else {
                resolve( msg );
            }
        } );
    } )
    .then(
        handleNext,
        function handleErr(err) {
            return Promise.resolve(
                it.throw( err )
            )
            .then( handleResult );
        }
    );
}
```

Now, our generators can either call promisories to `yield` Promises, or call thunkories to `yield` thunks, and in either case, `run(..)` would handle that value and use it to wait for the completion to resume the generator.

Symmetry-wise, these two approaches look identical. However, we should point out that's true only from the perspective of Promises or thunks representing the future value continuation of a generator.

From the larger perspective, thunks do not in and of themselves have hardly any of the trustability or composability guarantees that Promises are designed with. Using a thunk as a stand-in for a Promise in this particular generator asynchrony pattern is workable but should be seen as less than ideal when compared to all the benefits that Promises offer (see Chapter 3).

If you have the option, use `yield pr` rather than `yield th`. But there's nothing wrong with having a `run(..)` utility which can handle both value types.

The `runner(..)` utility in my *asynquence* library, which is discussed in Appendix A, handles `yield`s of Promises, thunks and *asynquence* sequences.

Pre-ES6 Generators

You're hopefully convinced now that generators are a very important addition to the async programming toolbox. But it's a new syntax in ES6, which means you can't just polyfill generators like you can Promises (which are just a new API). So what can we do to bring generators to our browser JS if we don't have the luxury of ignoring pre-ES6 browsers?

For all new syntax extensions in ES6, there are tools—the most common term for them is transpilers, for trans-compilers—which can take your ES6 syntax and transform it into equivalent (but obviously uglier!) pre-ES6 code. So, generators can be transpiled into code that will have the same behavior but work in ES5 and below.

But how? The "magic" of `yield` doesn't obviously sound like code that's easy to transpile. We actually hinted at a solution in our earlier discussion of closure-based *iterators*.

Manual Transformation

Before we discuss the transpilers, let's derive how manual transpilation would work in the case of generators. This isn't just an academic exercise, because doing so will actually help further reinforce how they work.

Consider:

```
// `request(..)` is a Promise-aware Ajax utility

function *foo(url) {
    try {
        console.log( "requesting:", url );
        var val = yield request( url );
        console.log( val );
    }
    catch (err) {
        console.log( "Oops:", err );
        return false;
    }
}

var it = foo( "http://some.url.1" );
```

The first thing to observe is that we'll still need a normal `foo()` function that can be called, and it will still need to return an *iterator*. So, let's sketch out the non-generator transformation:

```
function foo(url) {

    // ..

    // make and return an iterator
    return {
        next: function(v) {
            // ..
        },
        throw: function(e) {
            // ..
        }
    };
}

var it = foo( "http://some.url.1" );
```

The next thing to observe is that a generator does its "magic" by suspending its scope/state, but we can emulate that with function closure (see the *Scope & Closures* title of this series). To understand how to write such code, we'll first annotate different parts of our generator with state values:

```
// `request(..)` is a Promise-aware Ajax utility

function *foo(url) {
```

```
// STATE 1

try {
    console.log( "requesting:", url );
    var TMP1 = request( url );

    // STATE 2
    var val = yield TMP1;
    console.log( val );
}
catch (err) {
    // STATE 3
    console.log( "Oops:", err );
    return false;
}
}
```

 For more accurate illustration, we split up the
val = yield request.. statement into two
parts, using the temporary TMP1 variable.
request(..) happens in state 1, and the assignment of its completion value to val happens in
state 2. We'll get rid of that intermediate TMP1
when we convert the code to its non-generator
equivalent.

In other words, 1 is the beginning state, 2 is the state if the
request(..) succeeds, and 3 is the state if the request(..) fails.
You can probably imagine how any extra yield steps would just be
encoded as extra states.

Going back to our transpiled generator, let's define a variable state
in the closure we can use to keep track of the state:

```
function foo(url) {
    // manage generator state
    var state;

    // ..
}
```

Now, let's define an inner function called process(..) inside the
closure which handles each state, using a switch statement:

```
// `request(..)` is a Promise-aware Ajax utility

function foo(url) {
    // manage generator state
```

```
var state;

// generator-wide variable declarations
var val;

function process(v) {
    switch (state) {
        case 1:
            console.log( "requesting:", url );
            return request( url );
        case 2:
            val = v;
            console.log( val );
            return;
        case 3:
            var err = v;
            console.log( "Oops:", err );
            return false;
    }
}

// ..
}
```

Each state in our generator is represented by its own `case` in the switch statement. `process(..)` will be called each time we need to process a new state. We'll come back to how that works in just a moment.

For any generator-wide variable declarations (`val`), we move those to a `var` declaration outside of `process(..)` so they can survive multiple calls to `process(..)`. But the block scoped `err` variable is only needed for the 3 state, so we leave it in place.

In state 1, instead of `yield resolve(..)`, we did `return resolve(..)`. In terminal state 2, there was no explicit `return`, so we just do a `return`; which is the same as `return undefined`. In terminal state 3, there was a `return false`, so we preserve that.

Now we need to define the code in the *iterator* functions so they call `process(..)` appropriately:

```
function foo(url) {
    // manage generator state
    var state;

    // generator-wide variable declarations
    var val;
```

```
function process(v) {
    switch (state) {
        case 1:
            console.log( "requesting:", url );
            return request( url );
        case 2:
            val = v;
            console.log( val );
            return;
        case 3:
            var err = v;
            console.log( "Oops:", err );
            return false;
    }
}

// make and return an iterator
return {
    next: function(v) {
        // initial state
        if (!state) {
            state = 1;
            return {
                done: false,
                value: process()
            };
        }
        // yield resumed successfully
        else if (state == 1) {
            state = 2;
            return {
                done: true,
                value: process( v )
            };
        }
        // generator already completed
        else {
            return {
                done: true,
                value: undefined
            };
        }
    },
    "throw": function(e) {
        // the only explicit error handling is in
        // state 1
        if (state == 1) {
            state = 3;
            return {
                done: true,
                value: process( e )
```

```
            };
        }
        // otherwise, an error won't be handled,
        // so just throw it right back out
        else {
            throw e;
        }
    }
    };
}
```

How does this code work?

1. The first call to the *iterator*'s next() call would move the generator from the unitialized state to state 1, and then call pro cess() to handle that state. The return value from request(..), which is the promise for the Ajax response, is returned back as the value property from the next() call.

2. If the Ajax request succeeds, the second call to next(..) should send in the Ajax response value, which moves our state to 2. process(..) is again called (this time with the passed in Ajax response value), and the value property returned from next(..) will be undefined.

3. However, if the Ajax request fails, throw(..) should be called with the error, which would move the state from 1 to 3 (instead of 2). Again process(..) is called, this time with the error value. That case returns false, which is set as the value property returned from the throw(..) call.

From the outside—that is, interacting only with the *iterator*—this foo(..) normal function works pretty much the same as the *foo(..) generator would have worked. So we've effectively transpiled our ES6 generator to pre-ES6 compatibility!

We could then manually instantiate our generator and control its iterator—calling var it = foo("..") and it.next(..) and such—or better, we could pass it to our previously defined run(..) utility as run(foo,"..").

Automatic Transpilation

The preceding exercise of manually deriving a transformation of our ES6 generator to pre-ES6 equivalent teaches us how generators

---

work conceptually. But that transformation was really intricate and very non-portable to other generators in our code. It would be quite impractical to do this work by hand, and would completely obviate all the benefit of generators.

But luckily, several tools already exist that can automatically convert ES6 generators to things like what we derived in the previous section. Not only do they do the heavy lifting work for us, but they also handle several complications that we glossed over.

One such tool is regenerator (*https://facebook.github.io/regenerator/*), from the smart folks at Facebook.

If we use regenerator to transpile our previous generator, here's the code produced (at the time of this writing):

```
// `request(..)` is a Promise-aware Ajax utility

var foo = regeneratorRuntime.mark(function foo(url) {
    var val;

    return regeneratorRuntime.wrap(function foo$(context$1$0) {
        while (1) switch (context$1$0.prev = context$1$0.next) {
        case 0:
            context$1$0.prev = 0;
            console.log( "requesting:", url );
            context$1$0.next = 4;
            return request( url );
        case 4:
            val = context$1$0.sent;
            console.log( val );
            context$1$0.next = 12;
            break;
        case 8:
            context$1$0.prev = 8;
            context$1$0.t0 = context$1$0.catch(0);
            console.log("Oops:", context$1$0.t0);
            return context$1$0.abrupt("return", false);
        case 12:
        case "end":
            return context$1$0.stop();
        }
    }, foo, this, [[0, 8]]);
});
```

There's some obvious similarities here to our manual derivation, such as the switch / case statements, and we even see val pulled out of the closure just as we did.

Of course, one trade-off is that regenerator's transpilation requires a helper library `regeneratorRuntime` that holds all the reusable logic for managing a general generator/*iterator*. A lot of that boilerplate looks different than our version, but even then, the concepts can be seen, like with `context$1$0.next = 4` keeping track of the next state for the generator.

The main takeaway is that generators are not restricted to only being useful in ES6+ environments. Once you understand the concepts, you can employ them throughout your code, and use tools to transform the code to be compatible with older environments.

This is more work than just using a `Promise` API polyfill for pre-ES6 Promises, but the effort is totally worth it, because generators are so much better at expressing async flow control in a reason-able, sensible, synchronous-looking, sequential fashion.

Once you get hooked on generators, you'll never want to go back to the hell of async spaghetti callbacks!

Review

Generators are a new ES6 function type that does not run-to-completion like normal functions. Instead, the generator can be paused in mid-completion (entirely preserving its state), and it can later be resumed from where it left off.

This pause/resume interchange is cooperative rather than preemptive, which means that the generator has the sole capability to pause itself, using the `yield` keyword, and yet the *iterator* that controls the generator has the sole capability (via `next(..)`) to resume the generator.

The `yield` / `next(..)` duality is not just a control mechanism, it's actually a two-way message passing mechanism. A `yield` `..` expression essentially pauses waiting for a value, and the next `next(..)` call passes a value (or implicit `undefined`) back to that paused `yield` expression.

The key benefit of generators related to async flow control is that the code inside a generator expresses a sequence of steps for the task in a naturally sync/sequential fashion. The trick is that we essentially hide potential asynchrony behind the `yield` keyword—moving the asynchrony to the code where the generator's *iterator* is controlled.

In other words, generators preserve a sequential, synchronous, blocking code pattern for async code, which lets our brains reason about the code much more naturally, addressing one of the two key drawbacks of callback-based async.

CHAPTER 5
Program Performance

This book so far has been all about how to leverage asynchrony patterns more effectively. But we haven't directly addressed why asynchrony really matters to JS. The most obvious explicit reason is *performance*.

For example, if you have two Ajax requests to make, and they're independent, but you need to wait on them both to finish before doing the next task, you have two options for modeling that interaction: serial and concurrent.

You could make the first request and wait to start the second request until the first finishes. Or, as we've seen both with promises and generators, you could make both requests in parallel, and ask the gate to wait on both of them before moving on.

Clearly, the latter is usually going to be more performant than the former. And better performance generally leads to better user experience.

It's even possible that asynchrony (interleaved concurrency) can improve just the perception of performance, even if the overall program still takes the same amount of time to complete. User perception of performance is every bit—if not more!—as important as actual measurable performance.

We want to now move beyond localized asynchrony patterns to talk about some bigger picture performance details at the program level.

You may be wondering about micro-performance issues, like if a++ or ++a is faster. We'll look at those sorts of performance details in Chapter 6.

Web Workers

If you have processing-intensive tasks but you don't want them to run on the main thread (which may slow down the browser/UI), you might have wished that JavaScript could operate in a multi-threaded manner.

In Chapter 1, we talked in detail about how JavaScript is single threaded. And that's still true. But a single thread isn't the only way to organize the execution of your program.

Imagine splitting your program into two pieces, and running one of those pieces on the main UI thread, and running the other piece on an entirely separate thread.

What kinds of concerns would such an architecture bring up?

For one, you'd want to know if running on a separate thread meant that it ran in parallel (on systems with multiple CPUs/cores) such that a long-running process on that second thread would *not* block the main program thread. Otherwise, "virtual threading" wouldn't be of much benefit over what we already have in JS with async concurrency.

And you'd want to know if these two pieces of the program have access to the same shared scope/resources. If they do, then you have all the questions that multithreaded languages (Java, C++, etc.) deal with, such as needing cooperative or preemptive locking (mutexes, etc.). That's a lot of extra work, and shouldn't be undertaken lightly.

Alternatively, you'd want to know how these two pieces could communicate if they couldn't share scope/resources.

All these are great questions to consider as we explore a feature added to the web platform circa HTML5 called Web Workers. This is a feature of the browser (aka host environment) and actually has almost nothing to do with the JS language itself. That is, JavaScript does not *currently* have any features that support threaded execution.

But an environment like your browser can easily provide multiple instances of the JavaScript engine, each on its own thread, and let you run a different program in each thread. Each of those separate threaded pieces of your program is called a (Web) Worker. This type of parallelism is called *task parallelism*, as the emphasis is on splitting up chunks of your program to run in parallel.

From your main JS program (or another Worker), you instantiate a Worker like so:

```
var w1 = new Worker( "http://some.url.1/mycoolworker.js" );
```

The URL should point to the location of a JS file (not an HTML page!) which is intended to be loaded into a Worker. The browser will then spin up a separate thread and let that file run as an independent program in that thread.

 The kind of Worker created with such a URL is called a Dedicated Worker. But instead of providing a URL to an external file, you can also create an Inline Worker by providing a Blob URL (another HTML5 feature); essentially it's an inline file stored in a single (binary) value. However, Blobs are beyond the scope of what we'll discuss here.

Workers do not share any scope or resources with each other or the main program—that would bring all the nightmares of theaded programming to the forefront—but instead have a basic event messaging mechanism connecting them.

The w1 Worker object is an event listener and trigger, which lets you subscribe to events sent by the Worker as well as send events to the Worker.

Here's how to listen for events (actually, the fixed "message" event):

```
w1.addEventListener( "message", function(evt){
    // evt.data
} );
```

And you can send the "message" event to the Worker:

```
w1.postMessage( "something cool to say" );
```

Inside the Worker, the messaging is totally symmetrical:

```
// "mycoolworker.js"

addEventListener( "message", function(evt){
    // evt.data
} );

postMessage( "a really cool reply" );
```

Notice that a dedicated Worker is in a one-to-one relationship with the program that created it. That is, the "message" event doesn't need any disambiguation here, because we're sure that it could only have come from this one-to-one relationship—it came from either the Worker or the main page.

Usually the main page application creates the Workers, but a Worker can instantiate its own child Worker(s)—known as subworkers—as necessary. Sometimes this is useful to delegate such details to a sort of "master" Worker that spawns other Workers to process parts of a task. Unfortunately, at the time of this writing, Chrome still does not support subworkers, while Firefox does.

To kill a Worker immediately from the program that created it, call terminate() on the Worker object (like w1 in the previous snippets). Abruptly terminating a Worker thread does not give it any chance to finish up its work or clean up any resources. It's akin to you closing a browser tab to kill a page.

If you have two or more pages (or multiple tabs with the same page!) in the browser that try to create a Worker from the same file URL, those will actually end up as completely separate Workers. Shortly, we'll discuss a way to share a Worker.

It may seem like a malicious or ignorant JS program could easily perform a denial-of-service attack on a system by spawning hundreds of Workers, seemingly each with their own thread. While it's true that it's somewhat of a guarantee that a Worker will end up on a separate thread, this guarantee is not unlimited. The system is free to decide how many actual threads/CPUs/cores it really wants to create. There's no way to predict or guarantee how many you'll have access to, though many people assume it's at least as many as the number of CPUs/cores available. I think the safest assumption is that there's at least one other thread besides the main UI thread, but that's about it.

Worker Environment

Inside the Worker, you do not have access to any of the main program's resources. That means you cannot access any of its global variables, nor can you access the page's DOM or other resources. Remember: it's a totally separate thread.

You can, however, perform network operations (Ajax, WebSockets) and set timers. Also, the Worker has access to its own copy of several important global variables/features, including navigator, location, JSON, and applicationCache.

You can also load extra JS scripts into your Worker, using importScripts(..):

```
// inside the Worker
importScripts( "foo.js", "bar.js" );
```

These scripts are loaded synchronously, which means the importScripts(..) call will block the rest of the Worker's execution until the file(s) are finished loading and executing.

There have also been some discussions about exposing the `<canvas>` API to Workers, which combined with having canvases be Transferables (see "Data Transfer" on page 192), would allow Workers to perform more sophisticated off-thread graphics processing, which can be useful for high-performance gaming (WebGL) and other similar applications. Although this doesn't exist yet in any browsers, it's likely to happen in the near future.

What are some common uses for Web Workers?

- Processing intensive math calculations
- Sorting large data sets
- Data operations (compression, audio analysis, image pixel manipulations, etc.)
- High-traffic network communications

Data Transfer

You may notice a common characteristic of most of those uses, which is that they require a large amount of information to be transferred across the barrier between threads using the event mechanism, perhaps in both directions.

In the early days of Workers, serializing all data to a string value was the only option. In addition to the speed penalty of the two-way serializations, the other major negative was that the data was being copied, which meant a doubling of memory usage (and the subsequent churn of garbage collection).

Thankfully, we now have a few better options.

If you pass an object, a *structured clone algorithm* (*https://devel oper.mozilla.org/en-US/docs/Web/Guide/API/DOM/The_struc tured_clone_algorithm*) is used to copy/duplicate the object on the other side. This algorithm is fairly sophisticated and can even handle duplicating objects with circular references. The to-string/from-string performance penalty is not paid, but we still have duplication of memory using this approach. There is support for this in IE10 and above, as well as all the other major browsers.

An even better option, especially for larger data sets, is *Transferable Objects* (*http://updates.html5rocks.com/2011/12/Transferable-Objects-Lightning-Fast*). What happens is that the object's ownership is transferred, but the data itself is not moved. Once you transfer away an object to a Worker, it's empty or inaccessible in the the originating location—that eliminates the hazards of threaded programming over a shared scope. Of course, transfer of ownership can go in both directions.

There really isn't much you need to do to opt into a Transferable Object; any data structure that implements the `Transferable` interface (*https://developer.mozilla.org/en-US/docs/Web/API/Transferable*) will automatically be transferred this way (supported in Firefox & Chrome).

For example, typed arrays like `Uint8Array` (see the *ES6 & Beyond* title of this series) are Transferables. This is how you'd send a Transferable Object using `postMessage(..)`:

```
// `foo` is a `Uint8Array` for instance

postMessage( foo.buffer, [ foo.buffer ] );
```

The first parameter is the raw buffer and the second parameter is a list of what to transfer.

Browsers that don't support Transferable Objects simply degrade to structured cloning, which means performance reduction rather than outright feature breakage.

Shared Workers

If your site or app allows for loading multiple tabs of the same page (a common feature), you may very well want to reduce the resource usage of their system by preventing duplicate dedicated Workers; the most common limited resource in this respect is a socket network connection, as browsers limit the number of simultaneous connections to a single host. Of course, limiting multiple connections from a client also eases your server resource requirements.

In this case, creating a single centralized Worker that all the page instances of your site or app can *share* is quite useful.

That's called a `SharedWorker`, which you create like so (support for this is limited to Firefox and Chrome):

```
var w1 = new SharedWorker( "http://some.url.1/mycoolworker.js" );
```

Because a shared Worker can be connected to or from more than
one program instance or page on your site, the Worker needs a way
to know which program a message comes from. This unique identi-
fication is called a *port*—think network socket ports. So the calling
program must use the `port` object of the Worker for communication:

```
w1.port.addEventListener( "message", handleMessages );

// ..

w1.port.postMessage( "something cool" );
```

Also, the port connection must be initialized, as:

```
w1.port.start();
```

Inside the shared Worker, an extra event must be handled:
`"connect"`. This event provides the port `object` for that particular
connection. The most convenient way to keep multiple connections
separate is to use closure (see *Scope & Closures* title of this series)
over the `port`, as shown next, with the event listening and transmit-
ting for that connection defined inside the handler for the `"con
nect"` event:

```
// inside the shared Worker
addEventListener( "connect", function(evt){
    // the assigned port for this connection
    var port = evt.ports[0];

    port.addEventListener( "message", function(evt){
        // ..

        port.postMessage( .. );

        // ..
    } );

    // initialize the port connection
    port.start();
} );
```

Other than that difference, shared and dedicated Workers have the
same capabilities and semantics.

Shared Workers survive the termination of a port connection if other port connections are still alive, whereas dedicated Workers are terminated whenever the connection to their initiating program is terminated.

Polyfilling Web Workers

Web Workers are very attractive performance-wise for running JS programs in parallel. However, you may be in a position where your code needs to run in older browsers that lack support. Because Workers are an API and not a syntax, they can be polyfilled, to an extent.

If a browser doesn't support Workers, there's simply no way to fake multithreading from the performance perspective. Iframes are commonly thought of to provide a parallel environment, but in all modern browsers they actually run on the same thread as the main page, so they're not sufficient for faking parallelism.

As we detailed in Chapter 1, JS's asynchronicity (not parallelism) comes from the event loop queue, so you can force faked Workers to be asynchronous using timers (`setTimeout(..)`, etc.). Then you just need to provide a polyfill for the Worker API. There are some listed on the Modernizr GitHub page (*https://github.com/Modern izr/Modernizr/wiki/HTML5-Cross-Browser-Polyfills#web-workers*), but frankly none of them look great.

I've written a sketch of a polyfill for `Worker` on this gist (*https:// gist.github.com/getify/1b26accb1a09aa53ad25*). It's basic, but it should get the job done for simple `Worker` support, given that the two-way messaging works correctly as well as `"onerror"` handling. You could probably also extend it with more features, such as `termi nate()` or faked Shared Workers, as you see fit.

You can't fake synchronous blocking, so this polyfill just disallows use of `import Scripts(..)`. Another option might have been to parse and transform the Worker's code (once Ajax loaded) to handle rewriting to some asynchronous form of an `importScripts(..)` polyfill, perhaps with a promise-aware interface.

SIMD

Single instruction, multiple data (SIMD) is a form of *data parallelism*, as contrasted to *task parallelism* with Web Workers, because the emphasis is not really on program logic chunks being parallelized, but rather multiple bits of data being processed in parallel.

With SIMD, threads don't provide the parallelism. Instead, modern CPUs provide SIMD capability with "vectors" of numbers—think: type specialized arrays—as well as instructions that can operate in parallel across all the numbers; these are low-level operations leveraging instruction-level parallelism.

The effort to expose SIMD capability to JavaScript is primarily spearheaded by Intel (*https://01.org/node/1495*), namely by Mohammad Haghighat (at the time of this writing), in cooperation with Firefox and Chrome teams. SIMD is on an early standards track with a good chance of making it into a future revision of JavaScript, likely in the ES7 timeframe.

SIMD JavaScript proposes to expose short vector types and APIs to JS code, which on those SIMD-enabled systems would map the operations directly through to the CPU equivalents, with fallback to non-parallelized operation "shims" on non-SIMD systems.

The performance benefits for data-intensive applications (signal analysis, matrix operations on graphics, etc.) with such parallel math processing are quite obvious!

Early proposal forms of the SIMD API at the time of this writing look like this:

```
var v1 = SIMD.float32x4( 3.14159, 21.0, 32.3, 55.55 );
var v2 = SIMD.float32x4( 2.1, 3.2, 4.3, 5.4 );

var v3 = SIMD.int32x4( 10, 101, 1001, 10001 );
var v4 = SIMD.int32x4( 10, 20, 30, 40 );

SIMD.float32x4.mul( v1, v2 );
    // [ 6.597339, 67.2, 138.89, 299.97 ]
SIMD.int32x4.add( v3, v4 );
    // [ 20, 121, 1031, 10041 ]
```

Shown here are two different vector data types, 32-bit floating-point numbers and 32-bit integer numbers. You can see that these vectors are sized exactly to four 32-bit elements, as this matches the SIMD vector sizes (128-bit) available in most modern CPUs. It's also possible we may see an x8 (or larger!) version of these APIs in the future.

Besides mul() and add(), many other operations are likely to be included, such as sub(), div(), abs(), neg(), sqrt(), recipro cal(), reciprocalSqrt() (arithmetic), shuffle() (rearrange vector elements), and(), or(), xor(), not() (logical), equal(), greater Than(), lessThan() (comparison), shiftLeft(), shiftRightLogi cal(), shiftRightArithmetic() (shifts), fromFloat32x4(), and fromInt32x4() (conversions).

 There's an official "prollyfill" (hopeful, expect-ant, future-leaning polyfill) for the SIMD func-tionality available (*https://github.com/ johnmccutchan/ecmascript_simd*), which illus-trates a lot more of the planned SIMD capability than we've illustrated in this section.

asm.js

asm.js (*http://asmjs.org/*) is a label for a highly optimizable subset of the JavaScript language. By carefully avoiding certain mechanisms and patterns that are *hard* to optimize (garbage collection, coercion, etc.), asm.js-styled code can be recognized by the JS engine and given special attention with aggressive low-level optimizations.

Distinct from other program perfomance mechanisms discussed in this chapter, asm.js isn't necessarily something that needs to be adopted into the JS language specification. There *is* an asm.js speci-fication (*http://asmjs.org/spec/latest/*), but it's mostly for tracking an agreed upon set of candidate inferences for optimization rather than a set of requirements of JS engines.

There's not currently any new syntax being proposed. Instead, asm.js suggests ways to recognize existing standard JS syntax that conforms to the rules of asm.js and lets engines implement their own optimizations accordingly.

There's been some disagreement between browser vendors over exactly how asm.js should be activated in a program. Early versions of the asm.js experiment required a "use asm"; pragma (similar to strict mode's "use strict";) to help alert the JS engine to look for asm.js optimization opportunities and hints. Others have asserted that asm.js should just be a set of heuristics that engines automatically recognize without the author having to do anything extra, meaning that existing programs could theoretically benefit from asm.js-style optimizations without doing anything special.

How to Optimize with asm.js

The first thing to understand about asm.js optimizations is around types and coercion (see the *Types & Grammar* title of this series). If the JS engine has to track multiple different types of values in a variable through various operations, so that it can handle coercions between types as necessary, that's a lot of extra work that keeps the program optimization suboptimal.

 We're going to use asm.js-style code here for illustration purposes, but be aware that it's not commonly expected that you'll author such code by hand. asm.js is more intended to be a compilation target from other tools, such as Emscripten (*https://github.com/kripken/emscripten/wiki*). It's of course possible to write your own asm.js code, but that's usually a bad idea because the code is very low level and managing it can be a very time-consuming and error-prone process. Nevertheless, there may be cases where you'd want to hand tweak your code for asm.js optimization purposes.

There are some tricks you can use to hint to an asm.js-aware JS engine what the intended type is for variables/operations, so that it can skip these coercion tracking steps.

For example:

```
var a = 42;

// ..

var b = a;
```

In that program, the b = a assignment leaves the door open for type divergence in variables. However, it could instead be written as:

```
var a = 42;

// ..
```

```
var b = a | 0;
```

Here, we've used the | (binary OR) with value 0, which has no effect on the value other than to make sure it's a 32-bit integer. That code run in a normal JS engine works just fine, but when run in an asm.js-aware JS engine it *can* signal that b should always be treated as a 32-bit integer, so the coercion tracking can be skipped.

Similarly, the addition operation between two variables can be restricted to a more performant integer addition (instead of floating point):

```
(a + b) | 0
```

Again, the asm.js-aware JS engine can see that hint and infer that the + operation should be 32-bit integer addition because the end result of the whole expression would automatically be 32-bit integer conformed anyway.

asm.js Modules

One of the biggest detractors to performance in JS is around memory allocation, garbage collection, and scope access. asm.js suggests one of the ways around these issues is to declare a more formalized asm.js "module"—do not confuse these with ES6 modules; see the *ES6 & Beyond* title of this series.

For an asm.js module, you need to explicitly pass in a tightly conformed namespace—this is referred to in the spec as stdlib, as it should represent standard libraries needed—to import necessary symbols, rather than just using globals via lexical scope. In the base case, the window object is an acceptable stdlib object for asm.js module purposes, but you could and perhaps should construct an even more restricted one.

You also must declare a *heap*—which is just a fancy term for a reserved spot in memory where variables can already be used without asking for more memory or releasing previously used memory—and pass that in, so that the asm.js module won't need to do anything that would cause memory churn; it can just use the pre-reserved space.

A heap is likely a typed ArrayBuffer, such as:

```
var heap = new ArrayBuffer( 0x10000 );  // 64k heap
```

Using that pre-reserved 64k of binary space, an asm.js module can store and retrieve values in that buffer without any memory allocation or garbage collection penalties. For example, the heap buffer could be used inside the module to back an array of 64-bit float values like this:

```
var arr = new Float64Array( heap );
```

OK, so let's make a quick, silly example of an asm.js-styled module to illustrate how these pieces fit together. We'll define a foo(..) that takes a start (x) and end (y) integer for a range, calculates all the inner adjacent multiplications of the values in the range, and then finally averages those values together:

```
function fooASM(stdlib,foreign,heap) {
    "use asm";

    var arr = new stdlib.Int32Array( heap );

    function foo(x,y) {
        x = x | 0;
        y = y | 0;

        var i = 0;
        var p = 0;
        var sum = 0;
        var count = ((y|0) - (x|0)) | 0;

        // calculate all the inner adjacent multiplications
        for (i = x | 0;
            (i | 0) < (y | 0);
            p = (p + 8) | 0, i = (i + 1) | 0
        ) {
            // store result
            arr[ p >> 3 ] = (i * (i + 1)) | 0;
        }

        // calculate average of all intermediate values
        for (i = 0, p = 0;
            (i | 0) < (count | 0);
            p = (p + 8) | 0, i = (i + 1) | 0
        ) {
            sum = (sum + arr[ p >> 3 ]) | 0;
        }

        return +(sum / count);
    }

    return {
        foo: foo
```

```
    };
}

var heap = new ArrayBuffer( 0x1000 );
var foo = fooASM( window, null, heap ).foo;

foo( 10, 20 );      // 233
```

 This asm.js example is hand authored for illustration purposes, so it doesn't represent the same code that would be produced from a compilation tool targeting asm.js. But it does show the typical nature of asm.js code, especially the type hinting and use of the heap buffer for temporary variable storage.

The first call to fooASM(..) is what sets up our asm.js module with its heap allocation. The result is a foo(..) function we can call as many times as necessary. Those foo(..) calls should be specially optimized by an asm.js-aware JS engine. Importantly, the preceding code is completely standard JS and would run just fine (without special optimization) in a non-asm.js engine.

Obviously, the nature of restrictions that make asm.js code so optimizable reduces the possible uses for such code significantly. asm.js won't necessarily be a general optimization set for any given JS program. Instead, it's intended to provide an optimized way of handling specialized tasks such as intensive math operations (e.g., those used in graphics processing for games).

Review

The first four chapters of this book are based on the premise that async coding patterns give you the ability to write more performant code, which is generally a very important improvement. But async behavior only gets you so far, because it's still fundamentally bound to a single event loop thread.

So in this chapter we've covered several program-level mechanisms for improving performance even further.

Web Workers let you run a JS file (aka program) in a separate thread using async events to message between the threads. They're wonderful for offloading long-running or resource-intensive tasks to a different thread, leaving the main UI thread more responsive.

SIMD proposes to map CPU-level parallel math operations to JavaScript APIs for high-performance data-parallel operations, like number processing on large data sets.

Finally, asm.js describes a small subset of JavaScript that avoids the hard-to-optimize parts of JS (like garbage collection and coercion) and lets the JS engine recognize and run such code through aggressive optimizations. asm.js could be hand authored, but that's extremely tedious and error prone, akin to hand authoring assembly language (hence the name). Instead, the main intent is that asm.js would be a good target for cross-compilation from other highly optimized program languages—for example, Emscripten transpiling C/C++ to JavaScript (*https://github.com/kripken/emscripten/wiki*).

While not covered explicitly in this chapter, there are even more radical ideas under very early discussion for JavaScript, including approximations of direct threaded functionality (not just hidden behind data structure APIs). Whether that happens explicitly, or we just see more parallelism creep into JS behind the scenes, the future of more optimized program-level performance in JS looks really promising.

CHAPTER 6

Benchmarking & Tuning

As the first four chapters of this book were all about performance as a coding pattern (asynchrony and concurrency), and Chapter 5 was about performance at the macro program architecture level, this chapter goes after the topic of performance at the micro level, focusing on single expressions/statements.

One of the most common areas of curiosity—indeed, some developers can get quite obsessed about it—is in analyzing and testing various options for how to write a line or chunk of code, and determining which one is faster.

We're going to look at some of these issues, but it's important to understand from the outset that this chapter is *not* about feeding the obsession of micro-performance tuning, like whether some given JS engine can run ++a faster than a++. The more important goal of this chapter is to figure out what kinds of JS performance matter and which ones don't, *and how to tell the difference*.

But even before we get there, we need to explore how to most accurately and reliably test JS performance, because there's tons of misconceptions and myths that have flooded our collective cult knowledge base. We've got to sift through all that junk to find some clarity.

Benchmarking

OK, time to start dispelling some misconceptions. I'd wager the vast majority of JS developers, if asked to benchmark the speed (execution time) of a certain operation, would initially go about it something like this:

```
var start = (new Date()).getTime(); // or `Date.now()`

// do some operation

var end = (new Date()).getTime();

console.log( "Duration:", (end - start) );
```

Raise your hand if that's roughly what came to your mind. Yep, I thought so. There's a lot wrong with this approach, but don't feel bad; we've all been there.

What did that measurement tell you, exactly? Understanding what it does and doesn't say about the execution time of the operation in question is key to learning how to appropriately benchmark performance in JavaScript.

If the duration reported is 0, you may be tempted to believe that it took less than a millisecond. But that's not very accurate. Some platforms don't have single millisecond precision, but instead only update the timer in larger increments. For example, older versions of windows (and thus IE) had only 15ms precision, which means the operation has to take at least that long for anything other than 0 to be reported!

Moreover, whatever duration is reported, the only thing you really know is that the operation took approximately that long on that exact single run. You have near-zero confidence that it will always run at that speed. You have no idea if the engine or system had some sort of interference at that exact moment, and that at other times the operation could run faster.

What if the duration reported is 4? Are you more sure it took about four milliseconds? Nope. It might have taken less time, and there may have been some other delay in getting either start or end timestamps.

More troublingly, you also don't know that the circumstances of this operation test aren't overly optimistic. It's possible that the JS engine figured out a way to optimize your isolated test case, but in a more real program such optimization would be diluted or impossible, such that the operation would run slower than your test.

So...what do we know? Unfortunately, with those realizations stated, we know very little. Something of such low confidence isn't even remotely good enough to build your determinations on. Your benchmark is basically useless. And worse, it's dangerous in that it implies false confidence, not just to you but also to others who don't think critically about the conditions that led to those results.

Repetition

"OK," you now say, "just put a loop around it so the whole test takes longer." If you repeat an operation 100 times, and that whole loop reportedly takes a total of 137ms, then you can just divide by 100 and get an average duration of 1.37ms for each operation, right?

Well, not exactly.

A straight mathematical average by itself is definitely not sufficient for making judgments about performance which you plan to extrapolate to the breadth of your entire application. With a hundred iterations, even a couple of outliers (high or low) can skew the average, and then when you apply that conclusion repeatedly, you even further inflate the skew beyond credulity.

Instead of just running for a fixed number of iterations, you can instead choose to run the loop of tests until a certain amount of time has passed. That might be more reliable, but how do you decide how long to run? You might guess that it should be some multiple of how long your operation should take to run once. Wrong.

Actually, the length of time to repeat across should be based on the accuracy of the timer you're using, specifically to minimize the chances of inaccuracy. The less precise your timer, the longer you need to run to make sure you've minimized the error percentage. A 15ms timer is pretty bad for accurate benchmarking; to minimize its uncertainty (aka error rate) to less than 1%, you need to run your each cycle of test iterations for 750ms. A 1ms timer needs a cycle to run for only 50ms to get the same confidence.

But then, that's just a single sample. To be sure you're factoring out the skew, you'll want lots of samples to average across. You'll also want to understand something about just how slow the worst sample is, how fast the best sample is, how far apart those best and worse cases were, and so on. You'll want to know not just a number that tells you how fast something ran, but also to have some quantifiable measure of how trustable that number is.

Also, you probably want to combine these different techniques (as well as others), so that you get the best balance of all the possible approaches.

That's all the bare minimum just to get started. If you've been approaching performance benchmarking in a less serious manner than what I just glossed over, well...*you don't know: proper benchmarking.*

Benchmark.js

Any relevant and reliable benchmark should be based on statistically sound practices. I am not going to write a chapter on statistics here, so I'll hand wave around some terms: standard deviation, variance, margin of error. If you don't know what those terms really mean—I took a stats class back in college and I'm still a little fuzzy on them— you are not actually qualified to write your own benchmarking logic.

Luckily, smart folks like John-David Dalton and Mathias Bynens do understand these concepts, and wrote a statistically sound benchmarking tool called Benchmark.js (*http://benchmarkjs.com/*). So I can end the suspense by simply saying: "just use that tool."

I won't repeat their whole documentation for how Benchmark.js works; they have fantastic API docs (*http://benchmarkjs.com/docs*) you should read. Also there are some great writeups on more of the details and methodology here (*http://calendar.perfplanet.com/2010/ bulletproof-javascript-benchmarks*) and here (*http:// monsur.hossa.in/2012/12/11/benchmarkjs.html*).

But just for quick illustration purposes, here's how you could use Benchmark.js to run a quick performance test:

```
function foo() {
    // operation(s) to test
}

var bench = new Benchmark(
    "foo test",              // test name
    foo,                     // function to test (just contents)
    {
        // ..                // optional extra options (see docs)
    }
```

```
);

bench.hz;                // number of operations per second
bench.stats.moe;         // margin of error
bench.stats.variance;    // variance across samples
// ..
```

There's *lots* more to learn about using Benchmark.js besides this glance I'm including here. But the point is that it's handling all of the complexities of setting up a fair, reliable, and valid performance benchmark for a given piece of JavaScript code. If you're going to try to test and benchmark your code, this library is the first place you should turn.

We're showing here the usage to test a single operation like X, but it's fairly common that you want to compare X to Y. This is easy to do by simply setting up two different tests in a *suite* (a Benchmark.js organizational feature). Then, you run them head-to-head, and compare the statistics to conclude whether X or Y was faster.

Benchmark.js can of course be used to test JavaScript in a browser (see "jsPerf.com" on page 211 later in this chapter), but it can also run in nonbrowser environments (Node.js, etc.).

One largely untapped potential use-case for Benchmark.js is to use it in your Dev or QA environments to run automated performance regression tests against critical path parts of your application's Java-Script. Similar to how you might run unit test suites before deployment, you can also compare the performance against previous benchmarks to monitor if you are improving or degrading application performance.

Setup/Teardown

In the previous code snippet, we glossed over the "extra options" { .. } object. But there are two options we should discuss: `setup` and `teardown`.

These two options let you define functions to be called before and after your test case runs.

It's incredibly important to understand that your `setup` and `tear down` code *does not run for each test iteration*. The best way to think about it is that there's an outer loop (repeating cycles), and an inner loop (repeating test iterations). `setup` and `teardown` are run at the beginning and end of each *outer* loop (aka cycle) iteration, but not inside the inner loop.

Why does this matter? Let's imagine you have a test case that looks like this:

```
a = a + "w";
b = a.charAt( 1 );
```

Then, you set up your test setup as follows:

```
var a = "x";
```

Your temptation is probably to believe that a is starting out as "x" for each test iteration.

But it's not! It's starting a at "x" for each test cycle, and then your repeated + "w" concatenations will be making a larger and larger a value, even though you're only ever accessing the character "w" at the 1 position.

Where this most commonly bites you is when you make side effect changes to something like the DOM, like appending a child element. You may think your parent element is set as empty each time, but it's actually getting lots of elements added, and that can significantly sway the results of your tests.

Context Is King

Don't forget to check the context of a particular performance benchmark, especially a comparison between X and Y tasks. Just because your test reveals that X is faster than Y doesn't mean that the conclusion "X is faster than Y" is actually relevant.

For example, let's say a performance test reveals that X runs 10,000,000 operations per second, and Y runs at 8,000,000 operations per second. You could claim that Y is 20% slower than X, and you'd be mathematically correct, but your assertion doesn't hold as much water as you'd think.

Let's think about the results more critically: 10,000,000 operations per second is 10,000 operations per millisecond, and 10 operations per microsecond. In other words, a single operation takes 0.1 microseconds, or 100 nanoseconds. It's hard to fathom just how small 100ns is, but for comparison, it's often cited that the human eye isn't generally capable of distinguishing anything less than 100ms, which is one million times slower than the 100ns speed of the X operation.

Even recent scientific studies showing that maybe the brain can process as quick as 13ms (about 8x faster than previously asserted) would mean that X is still running 125,000 times faster than the human brain can perceive a distinct thing happening. *X is going really, really fast.*

But more importantly, let's talk about the difference between X and Y, the 2,000,000 operations per second difference. If X takes 100ns, and Y takes 80ns, the difference is 20ns, which in the best case is still one 650-thousandth of the interval the human brain can perceive.

What's my point? None of this performance difference matters, at all!

But wait, what if this operation is going to happen a whole bunch of times in a row? Then the difference could add up, right?

OK, so what we're asking then is, how likely is it that operation X is going to be run over and over again, one right after the other, and that this has to happen 650,000 times just to get a sliver of a hope the human brain could perceive it. More likely, it'd have to happen 5,000,000 to 10,000,000 times together in a tight loop to even approach relevance.

While the computer scientist in you might protest that this is possible, the louder voice of realism in you should sanity check just how likely or unlikely that really is. Even if it is relevant in rare occasions, it's irrelevant in most situations.

The vast majority of your benchmark results on tiny operations— like the ++x vs x++ myth—are just totally bogus for supporting the conclusion that X should be favored over Y on a performance basis.

Engine Optimizations

You simply cannot reliably extrapolate that if X was 10 microseconds faster than Y in your isolated test, that means X is always faster than Y and should always be used. That's not how performance works. It's vastly more complicated.

For example, let's imagine (purely hypothetical) that you test some microperformance behavior such as comparing:

```
var twelve = "12";
var foo = "foo";

// test 1
var X1 = parseInt( twelve );
var X2 = parseInt( foo );

// test 2
var Y1 = Number( twelve );
var Y2 = Number( foo );
```

If you understand what `parseInt(..)` does compared to `Number(..)`, you might intuit that `parseInt(..)` potentially has more work to do, especially in the `foo` case. Or you might intuit that they should have the same amount of work to do in the `foo` case, as both should be able to stop at the first character, `f`.

Which intuition is correct? I honestly don't know. But I'll make the case it doesn't matter what your intuition is. What might the results be when you test it? Again, I'm making up a pure hypothetical here; I haven't actually tried testing this, nor do I care to.

Let's pretend the test comes back that X and Y are statistically identical. Have you then confirmed your intuition about the `f` character thing? Nope.

It's possible in our hypothetical that the engine might recognize that the variables `twelve` and `foo` are being used in only one place in each test, and so it might decide to inline those values. Then it may realize that `Number( "12" )` can just be replaced by `12`. And maybe it comes to the same conclusion with `parseInt(..)`, or maybe not.

Or an engine's dead-code removal heuristic could kick in, and it could realize that variables X and Y aren't being used, so declaring them is irrelevant, so it doesn't end up doing anything at all in either test.

And all that's just made with the mindset of assumptions about a single test run. Modern engines are fantastically more complicated than what we're intuiting here. They do all sorts of tricks, like tracing and tracking how a piece of code behaves over a short period of time, or with a particularly constrained set of inputs.

What if the engine optimizes a certain way because of the fixed input, but in your real program you give more varied input and the optimization decisions shake out differently (or not at all!)? Or what if the engine kicks in optimizations because it sees the code being run tens of thousands of times by the benchmarking utility, but in your real program it will only run a hundred times in near proximity, and under those conditions the engine determines the optimizations are not worth it?

And all those optimizations we just hypothesized about might happen in our constrained test but maybe the engine wouldn't do them in a more complex program (for various reasons). Or it could be reversed—the engine might not optimize such trivial code but may be more inclined to optimize it more aggressively when the system is already more taxed by a more sophisticated program.

The point I'm trying to make is that you really don't know for sure exactly what's going on under the covers. All the guesses and hypothesis you can muster don't amount to anything concrete for making such decisions.

Does that mean you can't really do any useful testing? Definitely not!

What this boils down to is that testing *not real* code gives you *not real* results. If possible and practical, you should test actual real, nontrivial snippets of your code, and under as best of real conditions as you can actually hope to. Only then will the results you get have a chance to approximate reality.

Microbenchmarks like ++x vs x++ are so incredibly likely to be bogus, we might as well just flatly assume them as such.

jsPerf.com

While Benchmark.js is useful for testing the performance of your code in whatever JS environment you're running, it cannot be stressed enough that you need to compile test results from lots of different environments (desktop browsers, mobile devices, etc.) if you want to have any hope of reliable test conclusions.

For example, Chrome on a high-end desktop machine is not likely to perform anywhere near the same as Chrome mobile on a smartphone. And a smartphone with a full battery charge is not likely to perform anywhere near the same as a smartphone with 2% battery life left, when the device is starting to power down the radio and processor.

If you want to make assertions like "X is faster than Y" in any reasonable sense across more than just a single environment, you'll need to actually test as many of those real-world environments as possible. Just because Chrome executes some X operation faster than Y doesn't mean that all browsers do. And of course you also probably will want to cross-reference the results of multiple browser test runs with the demographics of your users.

There's an awesome website for this purpose called jsPerf (*http://jsperf.com*). It uses the Benchmark.js library we talked about earlier to run statistically accurate and reliable tests, and makes the test on an openly available URL that you can pass around to others.

Each time a test is run, the results are collected and persisted with the test, and the cumulative test results are graphed on the page for anyone to see.

When creating a test on the site, you start out with two test cases to fill in, but you can add as many as you need. You also have the ability to set up `setup` code that is run at the beginning of each test cycle and `teardown` code run at the end of each cycle.

 A trick for doing just one test case (if you're benchmarking a single approach instead of a head-to-head) is to fill in the second test input boxes with placeholder text on first creation, then edit the test and leave the second test blank, which will delete it. You can always add more test cases later.

You can define the initial page setup (importing libraries, defining utility helper functions, declaring variables, etc.). There are also options for defining setup and teardown behavior if needed—consult "Setup/Teardown" on page 207.

Sanity Check

jsPerf is a fantastic resource, but there's an awful lot of tests published that, when you analyze them, are quite flawed or bogus, for a variety of reasons as outlined so far in this chapter.

Consider:

```
// Case 1
var x = [];
```

```
for (var i=0; i<10; i++) {
    x[i] = "x";
}

// Case 2
var x = [];
for (var i=0; i<10; i++) {
    x[x.length] = "x";
}

// Case 3
var x = [];
for (var i=0; i<10; i++) {
    x.push( "x" );
}
```

Some observations to ponder about this test scenario:

- It's extremely common for devs to put their own loops into test cases, and they forget that Benchmark.js already does all the repetition you need. There's a really strong chance that the for loops in these cases are totally unnecessary noise.

- The declaring and initializing of x is included in each test case, possibly unnecessarily. Recall from earlier that if x = [] were in the setup code, it wouldn't actually be run before each test iteration, but instead once at the beginning of each cycle. That means x would continue growing quite large, not just the size 10 implied by the for loops.

  So is the intent to make sure the tests are constrained only to how the JS engine behaves with very small arrays (size 10)? That *could* be the intent, but if it is, you have to consider if that's not focusing far too much on nuanced internal implementation details.

  On the other hand, does the intent of the test embrace the context that the arrays will actually be growing quite large? Is the JS engines' behavior with larger arrays relevant and accurate when compared with the intended real-world usage?

- Is the intent to find out how much x.length or x.push(..) add to the performance of the operation to append to the x array? OK, that might be a valid thing to test. But then again, push(..) is a function call, so of course it's going to be slower than [..] access. Arguably, cases 1 and 2 are fairer than case 3.

Here's another example that illustrates a common apples-to-oranges flaw:

```
// Case 1
var x = ["John","Albert","Sue","Frank","Bob"];
x.sort();

// Case 2
var x = ["John","Albert","Sue","Frank","Bob"];
x.sort( function mySort(a,b){
    if (a < b) return -1;
    if (a > b) return 1;
    return 0;
} );
```

Here, the obvious intent is to find out how much slower the custom mySort(..) comparator is than the built-in default comparator. But by specifying the function mySort(..) as inline function expression, you've created an unfair/bogus test. Here, the second case is not only testing a custom user JS function, but it's also testing creating a new function expression for each iteration.

Would it surprise you to find out that if you run a similar test but update it to isolate only for creating an inline function expression versus using a pre-declared function, the inline function expression creation can be from 2% to 20% slower!?

Unless your intent with this test is to consider the inline function expression creation cost, a better/fairer test would put mySort(..)'s declaration in the page setup—don't put it in the test setup as that's unnecessary redeclaration for each cycle—and simply reference it by name in the test case: x.sort(mySort).

Building on the previous example, another pitfall is in opaquely avoiding or adding extra work to one test case that creates an apples-to-oranges scenario:

```
// Case 1
var x = [12,-14,0,3,18,0,2.9];
x.sort();

// Case 2
var x = [12,-14,0,3,18,0,2.9];
x.sort( function mySort(a,b){
    return a - b;
} );
```

Setting aside the previously mentioned inline function expression pitfall, the second case's mySort(..) works in this case because you have provided it numbers, but would have of course failed with strings. The first case doesn't throw an error, but it actually behaves differently and has a different outcome! It should be obvious, but a different outcome between two test cases almost certainly invalidates the entire test!

But beyond the different outcomes, in this case, the built-in sort(..)'s comparator is actually doing extra work that mySort() does not, in that the built-in one coerces the compared values to strings and does lexicographic comparison. The first snippet results in [-14, 0, 0, 12, 18, 2.9, 3] while the second snippet results (likely more accurately based on intent) in [-14, 0, 0, 2.9, 3, 12, 18].

So that test is unfair because it's not actually doing the same task between the cases. Any results you get are bogus.

These same pitfalls can even be much more subtle:

```
// Case 1
var x = false;
var y = x ? 1 : 2;

// Case 2
var x;
var y = x ? 1 : 2;
```

Here, the intent might be to test the performance impact of the coercion to a Boolean that the ? : operator will do if the x expression is not already a Boolean (see the *Types & Grammar* title of this book series). So, you're apparently OK with the fact that there is extra work to do the coercion in the second case.

The subtle problem? You're setting x's value in the first case and not setting it in the other, so you're actually doing work in the first case that you're not doing in the second. To eliminate any potential (albeit minor) skew, try:

```
// Case 1
var x = false;
var y = x ? 1 : 2;

// Case 2
var x = undefined;
var y = x ? 1 : 2;
```

Now there's an assignment in both cases, so the thing you want to test—the coercion of x or not—has likely been more accurately isolated and tested.

Writing Good Tests

Let me see if I can articulate the bigger point I'm trying to make here.

Good test authoring requires careful analytical thinking about what differences exist between two test cases and whether the differences between them are *intentional* or *unintentional*.

Intentional differences are of course normal and OK, but it's too easy to create unintentional differences that skew your results. You have to be really, really careful to avoid that skew. Moreover, you may intend a difference but it may not be obvious to other readers of your test what your intent was, so they may doubt (or trust!) your test incorrectly. How do you fix that?

Write better, clearer tests. But also, take the time to document (using the jsPerf.com "Description" field and/or code comments) exactly what the intent of your test is, even to the nuanced detail. Call out the intentional differences, which will help others and your future self to better identify unintentional differences that could be skewing the test results.

Isolate things which aren't relevant to your test by pre-declaring them in the page or test setup settings so they're outside the timed parts of the test.

Instead of trying to narrow in on a tiny snippet of your real code and benchmarking just that piece out of context, tests and benchmarks are better when they include a larger (while still relevant) context. Those tests also tend to run slower, which means any differences you spot are more relevant in context.

Microperformance

OK, until now we've been dancing around various microperformance issues and generally looking disfavorably upon obsessing about them. I want to take just a moment to address them directly.

The first thing you need to get more comfortable with when thinking about performance benchmarking your code is that the code you write is not always the code the engine actually runs. We briefly looked at that topic back in Chapter 1 when we discussed statement reordering by the compiler, but here we're going to suggest the compiler can sometimes decide to run different code than you wrote, not just in different orders but different in substance.

Let's consider this piece of code:

```
var foo = 41;

(function(){
    (function(){
        (function(baz){
            var bar = foo + baz;
            // ..
        })(1);
    })();
})();
```

You may think about the foo reference in the innermost function as needing to do a three-level scope lookup. We covered in the *Scope & Closures* title of this series how lexical scope works, and the fact that the compiler generally caches such lookups so that referencing foo from different scopes doesn't really cost anything extra.

But there's something deeper to consider. What if the compiler realizes that foo isn't referenced anywhere else but that one location, and it further notices that the value never is anything except the 41 as shown?

Isn't it quite possible and acceptable that the JS compiler could decide to just remove the foo variable entirely, and *inline* the value, such as this:

```
(function(){
    (function(){
        (function(baz){
            var bar = 41 + baz;
            // ..
        })(1);
    })();
})();
```

Of course, the compiler could probably also do a similar analysis and rewrite with the `baz` variable here, too.

When you begin to think about your JS code as being a hint or suggestion to the engine of what to do, rather than a literal requirement, you realize that a lot of the obsession over discrete syntactic minutia is most likely unfounded.

Another example:

```
function factorial(n) {
    if (n < 2) return 1;
    return n * factorial( n - 1 );
}

factorial( 5 );      // 120
```

Ah, the good ol' fashioned factorial algorithm! You might assume that the JS engine will run that code mostly as is. And to be honest, it might—I'm not really sure.

But as an anecdote, the same code expressed in C and compiled with advanced optimizations would result in the compiler realizing that the call `factorial(5)` can just be replaced with the constant value `120`, eliminating the function and call entirely!

Moreover, some engines have a practice called *unrolling recursion*, where it can realize that the recursion you've expressed can actually be done more easily (i.e., optimally) with a loop. It's possible the preceding code could be rewritten by a JS engine to run as:

```
function factorial(n) {
    if (n < 2) return 1;

    var res = 1;
    for (var i=n; i>1; i--) {
        res *= i;
    }
    return res;
}

factorial( 5 );      // 120
```

Now, let's imagine that in the earlier snippet you had been worried about whether n * factorial(n-1) or n *= factorial(--n) runs faster. Maybe you even did a performance benchmark to try to figure out which was better. But you miss the fact that in the bigger context, the engine may not run either line of code because it may unroll the recursion!

Speaking of --, --n versus n-- is often cited as one of those places where you can optimize by choosing the --n version, because theoretically it requires less effort down at the assembly level of processing.

That sort of obsession is basically nonsense in modern JavaScript. That's the kind of thing you should be letting the engine take care of. You should write the code that makes the most sense. Compare these three for loops:

```
// Option 1
for (var i=0; i<10; i++) {
    console.log( i );
}

// Option 2
for (var i=0; i<10; ++i) {
    console.log( i );
}

// Option 3
for (var i=-1; ++i<10; ) {
    console.log( i );
}
```

Even if you have some theory where the second or third option is more performant than the first option by a tiny bit, which is dubious at best, the third loop is more confusing because you have to start with -1 for i to account for the fact that ++i pre-increment is used. And the difference between the first and second options is really quite irrelevant.

It's entirely possible that a JS engine may see a place where i++ is used and realize that it can safely replace it with the ++i equivalent, which means your time spent deciding which one to pick was completely wasted and the outcome moot.

Here's another common example of silly microperformance obsession:

```
var x = [ .. ];

// Option 1
for (var i=0; i < x.length; i++) {
    // ..
}

// Option 2
for (var i=0, len = x.length; i < len; i++) {
    // ..
}
```

The theory here goes that you should cache the length of the x array in the variable `len`, because ostensibly it doesn't change, to avoid paying the price of `x.length` being consulted for each iteration of the loop.

If you run performance benchmarks around `x.length` usage compared to caching it in a `len` variable, you'll find that while the theory sounds nice, in practice any measured differences are statistically completely irrelevant.

In fact, in some engines like v8, it can be shown (*http://mrale.ph/blog/2014/12/24/array-length-caching.html*) that you could make things slightly worse by pre-caching the length instead of letting the engine figure it out for you. Don't try to outsmart your JavaScript engine; you'll probably lose when it comes to performance optimizations.

Not All Engines Are Alike

The different JS engines in various browsers can all be "spec compliant" while having radically different ways of handling code. The JS specification doesn't require anything performance related—well, except for ES6's "tail call optimization," covered in "Tail Call Optimization (TCO)" on page 225.

The engines are free to decide that one operation will receive its attention to optimize, perhaps trading off for lesser performance on another operation. It can be very tenuous to find an approach for an operation that always runs faster in all browsers.

There's a movement among some in the JS dev community, especially those who work with Node.js, to analyze the specific internal implementation details of the v8 JavaScript engine and make decisions about writing JS code that is tailored to take best advantage of how v8 works. You can actually achieve a surprisingly high degree of performance optimization with such endeavors, so the payoff for the effort can be quite high.

Some commonly cited examples for v8 (*https://github.com/petkaan tonov/bluebird/wiki/Optimization-killers*) are as follows:

- Don't pass the `arguments` variable from one function to any other function, as such leakage slows down the function implementation.

- Isolate a `try..catch` in its own function. Browsers struggle with optimizing any function with a `try..catch` in it, so moving that construct to its own function means you contain the de-optimization harm while letting the surrounding code be optimizable.

But rather than focus on those tips specifically, let's sanity check the v8-only optimization approach in a general sense.

Are you genuinely writing code that needs to run in only one JS engine? Even if your code is entirely intended for Node.js *right now*, is the assumption that v8 will *always* be the used JS engine reliable? Is it possible that someday, a few years from now, there will be another server-side JS platform besides Node.js that you choose to run your code on? What if what you optimized for before is now a much slower way of doing that operation on the new engine?

Or what if your code always stays running on v8 from here on out, but v8 decides at some point to change the way some set of operations works such that what used to be fast is now slow, and vice versa?

These scenarios aren't just theoretical, either. It used to be that it was faster to put multiple string values into an array and then call `join("")` on the array to concatenate the values than to just use + concatenation directly with the values. The historical reason for this is nuanced, but it has to do with internal implementation details about how string values were stored and managed in memory.

As a result, best practice advice at the time disseminated across the industry suggesting developers always use the array `join(..)` approach. And many followed.

Except, somewhere along the way, the JS engines changed approaches for internally managing strings, and specifically put in optimizations for + concatenation. They didn't slow down join(..) per se, but they put more effort into helping + usage, as it was still quite a bit more widespread.

 The practice of standardizing or optimizing some particular approach based mostly on its existing widespread usage is often called (metaphorically) "paving the cowpath."

Once that new approach to handling strings and concatenation took hold, unfortunately all the code out in the wild that was using array join(..) to concatenate strings was then suboptimal.

Another example: at one time, the Opera browser differed from other browsers in how it handled the boxing/unboxing of primitive wrapper objects (see the *Types & Grammar* title of this series). As such, their advice to developers was to use a String object instead of the primitive string value if properties like length or methods like charAt(..) needed to be accessed. This advice may have been correct for Opera at the time, but it was literally completely opposite for other major contemporary browsers, as they had optimizations specifically for the string primitives and not their object wrapper counterparts.

I think these various gotchas are at least possible, if not likely, for code even today. So I'm very cautious about making wide-ranging performance optimizations in my JS code based purely on engine implementation details, *especially if those details are only true of a single engine.*

The reverse is also something to be wary of: you shouldn't necessarily change a piece of code to work around one engine's difficulty with running a piece of code in an acceptably performant way.

Historically, IE has been the brunt of many such frustrations, given that there have been plenty of scenarios in older IE versions where it struggled with some performance aspect that other major browsers of the time seemed not to have much trouble with. The string concatenation discussion we just had was actually a real concern back in the IE6 and IE7 days, when it was possible to get better performance out of join(..) than +.

But it's troublesome to suggest that just one browser's trouble with performance is justification for using a code approach that quite possibly could be suboptimal in all other browsers. Even if the browser in question has a large market share for your site's audience, it may be more practical to write the proper code and rely on the browser to update itself with better optimizations eventually.

"There is nothing more permanent than a temporary hack." Chances are, the code you write now to work around some performance bug will probably outlive the performance bug in the browser itself.

In the days when a browser only updated once every five years, that was a tougher call to make. But as it stands now, browsers across the board are updated at a much more rapid interval (though obviously the mobile world still lags), and they're all competing to optimize web features better and better.

If you run across a case where a browser *does* have a performance wart that others don't suffer from, make sure to report the issue to its developers through whatever means you have available. Most browsers have open public bug trackers suitable for this purpose.

I'd suggest working around a performance issue in a browser only if it is a really drastic show-stopper, not just an annoyance or frustration. And I'd be very careful to check that the performance hack didn't have noticeable negative side effects in another browser.

Big Picture

Instead of worrying about all these microperformance nuances, we should instead be looking at big-picture types of optimizations.

How do you know what's big picture or not? You have to first understand if your code is running on a critical path. If it's not on a critical path, chances are your optimizations are not worth much.

Ever heard the admonition, "that's premature optimization!"? It comes from a famous quote from Donald Knuth: "premature optimization is the root of all evil." Many developers cite this quote to suggest that most optimizations are "premature" and are thus a waste of effort. The truth is, as usual, more nuanced.

Here is Knuth's quote, in context (*http://web.archive.org/web/20130731202547/http://pplab.snu.ac.kr/courses/adv_pl05/papers/p261-knuth.pdf*) (emphasis added):

> Programmers waste enormous amounts of time thinking about, or worrying about, the speed of *noncritical* parts of their programs, and these attempts at efficiency actually have a strong negative impact when debugging and maintenance are considered. We should forget about small efficiencies, say about 97% of the time: premature optimization is the root of all evil. Yet we should not pass up our opportunities in that *critical* 3%.
>
> —Computing Surveys 6
(December 1974)

I believe it's a fair paraphrasing to say that Knuth *meant*: "noncritical path optimization is the root of all evil." So the key is to figure out if your code is on a critical path—if it is, you should optimize it!

I'd even go so far as to say this: no amount of time spent optimizing critical paths is wasted, no matter how little is saved; but no amount of optimization on noncritical paths is justified, no matter how much is saved.

If your code is on a critical path, such as a "hot" piece of code that's going to be run over and over again, or in UX critical places where users will notice, like an animation loop or CSS style updates, then you should spare no effort in trying to employ relevant, measurably significant optimizations.

For example, consider a critical path animation loop that needs to coerce a string value to a number. There are of course multiple ways to do that (see the *Types & Grammar* title of this series), but which one, if any, is the fastest?

```
var x = "42";   // need number `42`

// Option 1: let implicit coercion automatically happen
var y = x / 2;

// Option 2: use `parseInt(..)`
var y = parseInt( x, 0 ) / 2;

// Option 3: use `Number(..)`
var y = Number( x ) / 2;

// Option 4: use `+` unary operator
var y = +x / 2;
```

```
// Option 5: use `|` unary operator
var y = (x | 0) / 2;
```

 I will leave it as an exercise to the reader to set up a test if you're interested in examining the minute differences in performance among these options.

When considering these different options, as they say, "One of these things is not like the others." `parseInt(..)` does the job, but it also does a lot more—it parses the string rather than just coercing. You can probably guess, correctly, that `parseInt(..)` is a slower option, and you should probably avoid it.

Of course, if x can ever be a value that *needs parsing*, such as "42px" (like from a CSS style lookup), then `parseInt(..)` really is the only suitable option!

`Number(..)` is also a function call. From a behavioral perspective, it's identical to the + unary operator option, but it may in fact be a little slower, requiring more machinery to execute the function. Of course, it's also possible that the JS engine recognizes this behavioral symmetry and just handles the inlining of `Number(..)`'s behavior (aka +x) for you!

But remember, obsessing about +x versus x | 0 is in most cases a waste of effort. This is a microperformance issue, and one that you shouldn't let dictate/degrade the readability of your program.

While performance is very important in critical paths of your program, it's not the only factor. Among several options that are roughly similar in performance, readability should be another important concern.

Tail Call Optimization (TCO)

As we briefly mentioned earlier, ES6 includes a specific requirement that ventures into the world of performance. It's related to a specific form of optimization that can occur with function calls: *tail call optimization*.

Briefly, a tail call is a function call that appears at the "tail" of another function, such that after the call finishes, there's nothing left to do (except perhaps return its result value).

For example, here's a nonrecursive setup with tail calls:

```
function foo(x) {
    return x;
}

function bar(y) {
    return foo( y + 1 );    // tail call
}

function baz() {
    return 1 + bar( 40 );   // not tail call
}

baz();                                  // 42
```

foo(y+1) is a tail call in bar(..) because after foo(..) finishes, bar(..) is also finished and just needs to return the result of the foo(..) call. However, bar(40) is *not* a tail call because after it completes, its result value must be added to 1 before baz() can return it.

Without getting into too much nitty-gritty detail, calling a new function requires an extra amount of reserved memory to manage the call stack, called a *stack frame*. So the preceding snippet would generally require a stack frame for each of baz(), bar(..), and foo(..) all at the same time.

However, if a TCO-capable engine can realize that the foo(y+1) call is in *tail position* meaning bar(..) is basically complete, then when calling foo(..), it doesn't need to create a new stack frame, but can instead reuse the existing stack frame from bar(..). That's not only faster, but it also uses less memory.

That sort of optimization isn't a big deal in a simple snippet, but it becomes a much bigger deal when dealing with recursion, especially if the recursion could have resulted in hundreds or thousands of stack frames. With TCO, the engine can perform all those calls with a single stack frame!

Recursion is a hairy topic in JS because without TCO, engines have had to implement arbitrary (and different!) limits to how deep they will let the recursion stack get before they stop it, to prevent running out of memory. With TCO, recursive functions with *tail position* calls can essentially run unbounded, because there's never any extra usage of memory!

Consider that recursive `factorial(..)` from before, but rewritten to make it TCO-friendly:

```
function factorial(n) {
    function fact(n,res) {
        if (n < 2) return res;

        return fact( n - 1, n * res );
    }

    return fact( n, 1 );
}

factorial( 5 );     // 120
```

This version of `factorial(..)` is still recursive, but it's also optimizable with TCO, because both inner `fact(..)` calls are in tail position.

 It's important to note that TCO applies only if there's actually a tail call. If you write recursive functions without tail calls, the performance will still fall back to normal stack frame allocation, and the engines' limits on such recursive call stacks will still apply. Many recursive functions can be rewritten as we just showed with `facto rial(..)`, but it takes careful attention to detail.

One reason that ES6 requires engines to implement TCO rather than leaving it up to their discretion is because the *lack of TCO* actually tends to reduce the chances that certain algorithms will be implemented in JS using recursion, for fear of the call stack limits.

If the lack of TCO in the engine would just gracefully degrade to slower performance in all cases, it wouldn't have been something that ES6 needed to *require*. But because the lack of TCO can actually make certain programs impractical, it's more an important feature of the language than just a hidden implementation detail.

ES6 guarantees that from now on, JS developers will be able to rely on this optimization across all ES6+ compliant browsers. That's a win for JS performance!

Review

Effectively benchmarking performance of a piece of code, especially to compare it to another option for that same code to see which approach is faster, requires careful attention to detail.

Rather than rolling your own statistically valid benchmarking logic, just use the Benchmark.js library, which does that for you. But be careful about how you author tests, because it's far too easy to construct a test that seems valid but that's actually flawed—even tiny differences can skew the results to be completely unreliable.

It's important to get as many test results from as many different environments as possible to eliminate hardware/device bias. jsPerf.com is a fantastic website for crowdsourcing performance benchmark test runs.

Many common performance tests unfortunately obsess about irrelevant microperformance details like x++ versus ++x. Writing good tests means understanding how to focus on big picture concerns, like optimizing on a critical path, and avoiding falling into traps like different JS engines' implementation details.

Tail call optimization (TCO) is a required optimization as of ES6 that will make some recursive patterns practical in JS where they would have been impossible otherwise. TCO allows a function call in the tail position of another function to execute without needing any extra resources, which means the engine no longer needs to place arbitrary restrictions on call stack depth for recursive algorithms.

asynquence Library

Chapters 1 and 2 went into quite a bit of detail about typical asynchronous programming patterns and how they're commonly solved with callbacks. But we also saw why callbacks are fatally limited in capability, which led us to Chapters 3 and 4, with Promises and generators offering a much more solid, trustable, and reason-able base to build your asynchrony on.

I referenced my own asynchronous library *asynquence* (*http://github.com/getify/asynquence*)—"async" + "sequence" = "asynquence"—several times in this book, and I want to now briefly explain how it works and why its unique design is important and helpful.

In Appendix B, we'll explore some advanced async patterns, but you'll probably want a library to make those palatable enough to be useful. We'll use *asynquence* to express those patterns, so you'll want to spend a little time here getting to know the library first.

asynquence is obviously not the only option for good async coding; certainly there are many great libraries in this space. But *asynquence* provides a unique perspective by combining the best of all these patterns into a single library, and moreover is built on a single basic abstraction: the (async) sequence.

My premise is that sophisticated JS programs often need bits and pieces of various different asynchronous patterns woven together, and this is usually left entirely up to each developer to figure out. Instead of having to bring in two or more different async libraries that focus on different aspects of asynchrony, *asynquence* unifies them into variated sequence steps, with just one core library to learn and deploy.

I believe the value is strong enough with *asynquence* to make async flow control programming with Promise-style semantics super easy to accomplish, so that's why we'll exclusively focus on that library here.

To begin, I'll explain the design principles behind *asynquence*, and then we'll illustrate how its API works with code examples.

Sequences and Abstraction Design

Understanding *asynquence* begins with understanding a fundamental abstraction: any series of steps for a task, whether they separately are synchronous or asynchronous, can be collectively thought of as a *sequence*. In other words, a sequence is a container that represents a task, and is comprised of individual (potentially async) steps to complete that task.

Each step in the sequence is controlled under the covers by a Promise (see Chapter 3). That is, every step you add to a sequence implicitly creates a Promise that is wired to the previous end of the sequence. Because of the semantics of Promises, every single step advancement in a sequence is asynchronous, even if you synchronously complete the step.

Moreover, a sequence will always proceed linearly from step to step, meaning that step 2 always comes after step 1 finishes, and so on.

Of course, a new sequence can be forked off an existing sequence, meaning the fork only occurs once the main sequence reaches that point in the flow. Sequences can also be combined in various ways, including having one sequence subsumed by another sequence at a particular point in the flow.

A sequence is kind of like a Promise chain. However, with Promise chains, there is no "handle" to grab that references the entire chain. Whichever Promise you have a reference to only represents the current step in the chain plus any other steps hanging off it. Essentially, you cannot hold a reference to a Promise chain unless you hold a reference to the first Promise in the chain.

There are many cases where it turns out to be quite useful to have a handle that references the entire sequence collectively. The most important of those cases is with sequence abort/cancel. As we covered extensively in Chapter 3, Promises themselves should never be able to be canceled, as this violates a fundamental design imperative: external immutability.

But sequences have no such immutability design principle, mostly because sequences are not passed around as future-value containers that need immutable value semantics. So sequences are the proper level of abstraction to handle abort/cancel behavior. *asynquence* sequences can be abort()ed at any time, and the sequence will stop at that point and not go for any reason.

There's plenty more reasons to prefer a sequence abstraction on top of Promise chains for flow control purposes.

First, Promise chaining is a rather manual process—one that can get pretty tedious once you start creating and chaining Promises across a wide swath of your programs—and this tedium can act counterproductively to dissuade the developer from using Promises in places where they are quite appropriate.

Abstractions are meant to reduce boilerplate and tedium, so the sequence abstraction is a good solution to this problem. With Promises, your focus is on the individual step, and there's little assumption that you will keep the chain going. With sequences, the opposite approach is taken, assuming the sequence will keep having more steps added indefinitely.

This abstraction complexity reduction is especially powerful when you start thinking about higher-order Promise patterns (beyond race([..]) and all([..]).

For example, in the middle of a sequence, you may want to express a step that is conceptually like a try..catch in that the step will always result in success, either the intended main success resolution or a positive nonerror signal for the caught error. Or, you might want to express a step that is like a retry/until loop, where it keeps trying the same step over and over until success occurs.

These sorts of abstractions are quite nontrivial to express using only Promise primitives, and doing so in the middle of an existing Promise chain is not pretty. But if you abstract your thinking to a sequence, and consider a step as a wrapper around a Promise, that step wrapper can hide such details, freeing you to think about the flow control in the most sensible way without being bothered by the details.

Second, and perhaps more importantly, thinking of async flow control in terms of steps in a sequence allows you to abstract out the details of what types of asynchronicity are involved with each individual step. Under the covers, a Promise will always control the step, but above the covers, that step can look either like a continuation callback (the simple default), or like a real Promise, or as a run-to-completion generator, or... Hopefully, you get the picture.

Third, sequences can more easily be twisted to adapt to different modes of thinking, such as event-, stream-, or reactive-based coding. *asynquence* provides a pattern I call *reactive sequences* (which we'll cover later) as a variation on the *reactive observable* ideas in RxJS (Reactive Extensions), which lets a repeatable event fire off a new sequence instance each time. Promises are one-shot-only, so it's quite awkward to express repetitious asynchrony with Promises alone.

Another alternate mode of thinking inverts the resolution/control capability in a pattern I call *iterable sequences*. Instead of each individual step internally controlling its own completion (and thus advancement of the sequence), the sequence is inverted so the advancement control is through an external iterator, and each step in the iterable sequence just responds to the next(..) iterator control.

We'll explore all of these different variations as we go throughout the rest of this appendix, so don't worry if we ran over those bits far too quickly just now.

The takeaway is that sequences are a more powerful and sensible abstraction for complex asynchrony than just Promises (Promise chains) or just generators, and *asynquence* is designed to express that abstraction with just the right level of sugar to make async programming more understandable and more enjoyable.

asynquence API

To start off, the way you create a sequence (an *asynquence* instance) is with the ASQ(..) function. An ASQ() call with no parameters creates an empty initial sequence, whereas passing one or more values or functions to ASQ(..) sets up the sequence with each argument representing the initial steps of the sequence.

For the purposes of all code examples here, I will use the *asynquence* top-level identifier in global browser usage: ASQ. If you include and use *asynquence* through a module system (browser or server), you can, of course, define whichever symbol you prefer, and *asynquence* won't care!

Many of the API methods discussed here are built into the core of *asynquence*, but others are provided through including the optional "contrib" plug-ins package. See the documentation for *asynquence* (*http://github.com/getify/asynquence*) for whether a method is built in or defined via plug-in.

Steps

If a function represents a normal step in the sequence, that function is invoked with the first parameter being the continuation callback, and any subsequent parameters being any messages passed on from the previous step. The step will not complete until the continuation callback is called. Once it's called, any arguments you pass to it will be sent along as messages to the next step in the sequence.

To add an additional normal step to the sequence, call then(..) (which has essentially the exact same semantics as the ASQ(..) call):

```
ASQ(
    // step 1
    function(done){
        setTimeout( function(){
            done( "Hello" );
        }, 100 );
    },
    // step 2
    function(done,greeting) {
        setTimeout( function(){
            done( greeting + " World" );
        }, 100 );
    }
)
// step 3
.then( function(done,msg){
    setTimeout( function(){
        done( msg.toUpperCase() );
```

```
    }, 100 );
} )
// step 4
.then( function(done,msg){
    console.log( msg );          // HELLO WORLD
} );
```

 Though the name then(..) is identical to the native Promises API, this then(..) is different. You can pass as few or as many functions or values to then(..) as you'd like, and each is taken as a separate step. There's no two-callback fulfilled/rejected semantics involved.

Unlike with Promises, where to chain one Promise to the next you have to create and return that Promise from a then(..) fulfillment handler, with *asynquence*, all you need to do is call the continuation callback—I always call it done() but you can name it whatever suits you—and optionally pass it completion messages as arguments.

Each step defined by then(..) is assumed to be asynchronous. If you have a step that's synchronous, you can either just call done(..) right away, or you can use the simpler val(..) step helper:

```
// step 1 (sync)
ASQ( function(done){
    done( "Hello" );      // manually synchronous
} )
// step 2 (sync)
.val( function(greeting){
    return greeting + " World";
} )
// step 3 (async)
.then( function(done,msg){
    setTimeout( function(){
        done( msg.toUpperCase() );
    }, 100 );
} )
// step 4 (sync)
.val( function(msg){
    console.log( msg );
} );
```

As you can see, val(..)-invoked steps don't receive a continuation callback, as that part is assumed for you—and the parameter list is less cluttered as a result! To send a message along to the next step, you simply use return.

Think of val(..) as representing a synchronous "value-only" step, which is useful for synchronous value operations, logging, and the like.

Errors

One important difference with *asynquence* compared to Promises is with error handling.

With Promises, each individual Promise (step) in a chain can have its own independent error, and each subsequent step has the ability to handle the error (or not). The main reason for this semantic comes (again) from the focus on individual Promises rather than on the chain (sequence) as a whole.

I believe that most of the time, an error in one part of a sequence is generally not recoverable, so the subsequent steps in the sequence are moot and should be skipped. So, by default, an error at any step of a sequence throws the entire sequence into error mode, and the rest of the normal steps are ignored.

If you *do* need to have a step where its error is recoverable, there are several different API methods that can accommodate, such as try(..) (previously mentioned as a kind of try..catch step) or until(..) (a retry loop that keeps attempting the step until it succeeds or you manually break() the loop). *asynquence* even has pThen(..) and pCatch(..) methods, which work identically to how normal Promise then(..) and catch(..) work (see Chapter 3), so you can do localized mid-sequence error handling if you so choose.

The point is, you have both options, but the more common one in my experience is the default. With Promises, to get a chain of steps to ignore all steps once an error occurs, you have to take care not to register a rejection handler at any step; otherwise, that error gets swallowed as handled, and the sequence may continue (perhaps unexpectedly). This kind of desired behavior is a bit awkward to properly and reliably handle.

To register a sequence error notification handler, *asynquence* provides an or(..) sequence method, which also has an alias of onerror(..). You can call this method anywhere in the sequence, and you can register as many handlers as you'd like. That makes it easy for multiple different consumers to listen in on a sequence to know if it failed or not; it's kind of like an error event handler in that respect.

Just like with Promises, all JS exceptions become sequence errors, or you can programmatically signal a sequence error:

```
var sq = ASQ( function(done){
    setTimeout( function(){
        // signal an error for the sequence
        done.fail( "Oops" );
    }, 100 );
} )
.then( function(done){
    // will never get here
} )
.or( function(err){
    console.log( err );         // Oops
} )
.then( function(done){
    // won't get here either
} );

// later

sq.or( function(err){
    console.log( err );         // Oops
} );
```

Another really important difference with error handling in *asynquence* compared to native Promises is the default behavior of unhandled exceptions. As we discussed at length in Chapter 3, a rejected Promise without a registered rejection handler will just silently hold (aka swallow) the error; you have to remember to always end a chain with a final catch(..).

In *asynquence*, the assumption is reversed.

If an error occurs on a sequence, and it *at that moment* has no error handlers registered, the error is reported to the console. In other words, unhandled rejections are by default always reported so as not to be swallowed and missed.

As soon as you register an error handler against a sequence, it opts that sequence out of such reporting, to prevent duplicate noise.

There may, in fact, be cases where you want to create a sequence that may go into the error state before you have a chance to register the handler. This isn't common, but it can happen from time to time.

In those cases, you can also *opt a sequence instance out* of error reporting by calling `defer()` on the sequence. You should only opt out of error reporting if you are sure that you're going to eventually handle such errors:

```
var sq1 = ASQ( function(done){
    doesnt.Exist();          // will throw exception to console
} );

var sq2 = ASQ( function(done){
    doesnt.Exist();          // will throw only a sequence error
} )
// opt-out of error reporting
.defer();

setTimeout( function(){
    sq1.or( function(err){
        console.log( err ); // ReferenceError
    } );

    sq2.or( function(err){
        console.log( err ); // ReferenceError
    } );
}, 100 );

// ReferenceError (from sq1)
```

This is better error handling behavior than Promises themselves have, because it's the pit of success, not the pit of failure (see Chapter 3).

 If a sequence is piped into (aka subsumed by) another sequence—see "Combining Sequences" on page 244 for a complete description—then the source sequence is opted out of error reporting, but now the target sequence's error reporting or lack thereof must be considered.

Parallel Steps

Not all steps in your sequences will have just a single (async) task to perform; some will need to perform multiple steps in parallel (concurrently). A step in a sequence in which multiple substeps are processing concurrently is called a `gate(..)`—there's an `all(..)` alias if you prefer—and is directly symmetric to native `Promise.all([..])`.

If all the steps in the gate(..) complete successfully, all success messages will be passed to the next sequence step. If any of them generate errors, the whole sequence immediately goes into an error state.

Consider:

```
ASQ( function(done){
    setTimeout( done, 100 );
} )
.gate(
    function(done){
        setTimeout( function(){
            done( "Hello" );
        }, 100 );
    },
    function(done){
        setTimeout( function(){
            done( "World", "!" );
        }, 100 );
    }
)
.val( function(msg1,msg2){
    console.log( msg1 );     // Hello
    console.log( msg2 );     // [ "World", "!" ]
} );
```

For illustration, let's compare that example to native Promises:

```
new Promise( function(resolve,reject){
    setTimeout( resolve, 100 );
} )
.then( function(){
    return Promise.all( [
        new Promise( function(resolve,reject){
            setTimeout( function(){
                resolve( "Hello" );
            }, 100 );
        } ),
        new Promise( function(resolve,reject){
            setTimeout( function(){
                // note: we need a [ ] array here
                resolve( [ "World", "!" ] );
            }, 100 );
        } )
    ] );
} )
.then( function(msgs){
    console.log( msgs[0] ); // Hello
    console.log( msgs[1] ); // [ "World", "!" ]
} );
```

Yuck. Promises require a lot more boilerplate overhead to express the same asynchronous flow control. That's a great illustration of why the *asynquence* API and abstraction make dealing with Promise steps a lot nicer. The improvement only goes higher the more complex your asynchrony is.

Step Variations

There are several variations in the contrib plug-ins on *asynquence*'s gate(..) step type that can be quite helpful:

- any(..) is like gate(..), except just one segment has to eventually succeed to proceed on the main sequence.

- first(..) is like any(..), except as soon as any segment succeeds, the main sequence proceeds (ignoring subsequent results from other segments).

- race(..) (symmetric with Promise.race([..])) is like first(..), except the main sequence proceeds as soon as any segment completes (either success or failure).

- last(..) is like any(..), except only the latest segment to complete successfully sends its message(s) along to the main sequence.

- none(..) is the inverse of gate(..): the main sequence proceeds only if all the segments fail (with all segment error message(s) transposed as success message(s) and vice versa).

Let's first define some helpers to make illustration cleaner:

```
function success1(done) {
    setTimeout( function(){
        done( 1 );
    }, 100 );
}

function success2(done) {
    setTimeout( function(){
        done( 2 );
    }, 100 );
}

function failure3(done) {
    setTimeout( function(){
        done.fail( 3 );
    }, 100 );
```

```
    }

    function output(msg) {
        console.log( msg );
    }
```

Now, let's demonstrate these `gate(..)` step variations:

```
ASQ().race(
    failure3,
    success1
)
.or( output );      // 3


ASQ().any(
    success1,
    failure3,
    success2
)
.val( function(){
    var args = [].slice.call( arguments );
    console.log(
        args        // [ 1, undefined, 2 ]
    );
} );


ASQ().first(
    failure3,
    success1,
    success2
)
.val( output );     // 1


ASQ().last(
    failure3,
    success1,
    success2
)
.val( output );     // 2

ASQ().none(
    failure3
)
.val( output )      // 3
.none(
    failure3
    success1
)
.or( output );      // 1
```

Another step variation is map(..), which lets you asynchronously map elements of an array to different values, and the step doesn't proceed until all the mappings are complete. map(..) is very similar to gate(..), except it gets the initial values from an array instead of from separately specified functions, and also because you define a single function callback to operate on each value:

```
function double(x,done) {
    setTimeout( function(){
        done( x * 2 );
    }, 100 );
}

ASQ().map( [1,2,3], double )
.val( output );                    // [2,4,6]
```

Also, map(..) can receive either of its parameters (the array or the callback) from messages passed from the previous step:

```
function plusOne(x,done) {
    setTimeout( function(){
        done( x + 1 );
    }, 100 );
}

ASQ( [1,2,3] )
.map( double )                     // message `[1,2,3]` comes in
.map( plusOne )                    // message `[2,4,6]` comes in
.val( output );                    // [3,5,7]
```

Another variation is waterfall(..), which is kind of like a mixture between gate(..)'s message collection behavior but then(..)'s sequential processing.

Step 1 is first executed, then the success message from step 1 is given to step 2, and then both success messages go to step 3, and then all three success messages go to step 4, and so on, such that the messages sort of collect and cascade down the "waterfall."

Consider:

```
function double(done) {
    var args = [].slice.call( arguments, 1 );
    console.log( args );

    setTimeout( function(){
        done( args[args.length - 1] * 2 );
    }, 100 );
}
```

```
ASQ( 3 )
.waterfall(
    double,                  // [ 3 ]
    double,                  // [ 6 ]
    double,                  // [ 6, 12 ]
    double                   // [ 6, 12, 24 ]
)
.val( function(){
    var args = [].slice.call( arguments );
    console.log( args );     // [ 6, 12, 24, 48 ]
} );
```

If at any point in the "waterfall" an error occurs, the whole sequence immediately goes into an error state.

Error Tolerance

Sometimes you want to manage errors at the step level and not let them necessarily send the whole sequence into the error state. *asynquence* offers two step variations for that purpose.

try(..) attempts a step, and if it succeeds, the sequence proceeds as normal, but if the step fails, the failure is turned into a success message formated as { catch: .. } with the error message(s) filled in:

```
ASQ()
.try( success1 )
.val( output )          // 1
.try( failure3 )
.val( output )          // { catch: 3 }
.or( function(err){
    // never gets here
} );
```

You could instead set up a retry loop using until(..), which tries the step and if it fails, retries the step again on the next event loop tick, and so on.

This retry loop can continue indefinitely, but if you want to break out of the loop, you can call the break() flag on the completion trigger, which sends the main sequence into an error state:

```
var count = 0;

ASQ( 3 )
.until( double )
.val( output )              // 6
.until( function(done){
    count++;
```

```
            setTimeout( function(){
                if (count < 5) {
                    done.fail();
                }
                else {
                    // break out of the `until(..)` retry loop
                    done.break( "Oops" );
                }
            }, 100 );
        } )
        .or( output );                      // Oops
```

Promise-Style Steps

If you would prefer to have, inline in your sequence, Promise-style semantics like Promises' then(..) and catch(..) (see Chapter 3), you can use the pThen and pCatch plug-ins:

```
ASQ( 21 )
.pThen( function(msg){
    return msg * 2;
} )
.pThen( output )                    // 42
.pThen( function(){
    // throw an exception
    doesnt.Exist();
} )
.pCatch( function(err){
    // caught the exception (rejection)
    console.log( err );         // ReferenceError
} )
.val( function(){
    // main sequence is back in a
    // success state because previous
    // exception was caught by
    // `pCatch(..)`
} );
```

pThen(..) and pCatch(..) are designed to run in the sequence, but behave as if it was a normal Promise chain. As such, you can resolve genuine Promises or *asynquence* sequences from the fulfillment handler passed to pThen(..) (see Chapter 3).

Forking Sequences

One feature that can be quite useful about Promises is that you can attach multiple then(..) handler registrations to the same promise, effectively forking the flow-control at that promise:

```
var p = Promise.resolve( 21 );

// fork 1 (from `p`)
p.then( function(msg){
    return msg * 2;
} )
.then( function(msg){
    console.log( msg );      // 42
} )

// fork 2 (from `p`)
p.then( function(msg){
    console.log( msg );      // 21
} );
```

The same forking is easy in *asynquence* with fork():

```
var sq = ASQ(..).then(..).then(..);

var sq2 = sq.fork();

// fork 1
sq.then(..)..;

// fork 2
sq2.then(..)..;
```

Combining Sequences

If you want to do the reverse of fork()ing, you can combine two sequences by subsuming one into another, using the seq(..) instance method:

```
var sq = ASQ( function(done){
    setTimeout( function(){
        done( "Hello World" );
    }, 200 );
} );

ASQ( function(done){
    setTimeout( done, 100 );
} )
// subsume `sq` sequence into this sequence
.seq( sq )
.val( function(msg){
    console.log( msg );      // Hello World
} )
```

seq(..) can accept either a sequence itself, as shown here, or a function. If it accepts a function, it's expected that the function will return a sequence when called, so the preceding code could have been done with:

```
// ..
.seq( function(){
    return sq;
} )
// ..
```

Also, that step could instead have been accomplished with a pipe(..):

```
// ..
.then( function(done){
    // pipe `sq` into the `done` continuation callback
    sq.pipe( done );
} )
// ..
```

When a sequence is subsumed, both its success message stream and its error stream are piped in.

 As mentioned in an earlier note, piping (manually with pipe(..) or automatically with seq(..)) opts the source sequence out of error-reporting, but doesn't affect the error reporting status of the target sequence.

Value and Error Sequences

If any step of a sequence is just a normal value, that value is mapped to that step's completion message:

```
var sq = ASQ( 42 );

sq.val( function(msg){
    console.log( msg );      // 42
} );
```

If you want to make a sequence that's automatically errored:

```
var sq = ASQ.failed( "Oops" );

ASQ()
.seq( sq )
.val( function(msg){
    // won't get here
} )
.or( function(err){
```

```
        console.log( err );      // Oops
    } );
```

You also may want to automatically create a delayed-value or a delayed-error sequence. Using the `after` and `failAfter` contrib plug-ins, this is easy:

```
    var sq1 = ASQ.after( 100, "Hello", "World" );
    var sq2 = ASQ.failAfter( 100, "Oops" );

    sq1.val( function(msg1,msg2){
        console.log( msg1, msg2 );      // Hello World
    } );

    sq2.or( function(err){
        console.log( err );             // Oops
    } );
```

You can also insert a delay in the middle of a sequence using `after(..)`:

```
    ASQ( 42 )
    // insert a delay into the sequence
    .after( 100 )
    .val( function(msg){
        console.log( msg );     // 42
    } );
```

Promises and Callbacks

I think *asynquence* sequences provide a lot of value on top of native Promises, and for the most part you'll find it more pleasant and more powerful to work at that level of abstration. However, integrating *asynquence* with other non-*asynquence* code will be a reality.

You can easily subsume a promise (e.g., a thenable—see Chapter 3) into a sequence using the `promise(..)` instance method:

```
    var p = Promise.resolve( 42 );

    ASQ()
    .promise( p )           // could also: function(){ return p; }
    .val( function(msg){
        console.log( msg ); // 42
    } );
```

And to go the opposite direction and fork/vend a promise from a sequence at a certain step, use the `toPromise` contrib plug-in:

```
var sq = ASQ.after( 100, "Hello World" );

sq.toPromise()
// this is a standard promise chain now
.then( function(msg){
    return msg.toUpperCase();
} )
.then( function(msg){
    console.log( msg );      // HELLO WORLD
} );
```

To adapt *asynquence* to systems using callbacks, there are several helper facilities. To automatically generate an "error-first style" callback from your sequence to wire into a callback-oriented utility, use errfcb:

```
var sq = ASQ( function(done){
    // note: expecting "error-first style" callback
    someAsyncFuncWithCB( 1, 2, done.errfcb )
} )
.val( function(msg){
    // ..
} )
.or( function(err){
    // ..
} );

// note: expecting "error-first style" callback
anotherAsyncFuncWithCB( 1, 2, sq.errfcb() );
```

You also may want to create a sequence-wrapped version of a utility —compare to "promisory" in Chapter 3 and "thunkory" in Chapter 4—and *asynquence* provides ASQ.wrap(..) for that purpose:

```
var coolUtility = ASQ.wrap( someAsyncFuncWithCB );

coolUtility( 1, 2 )
.val( function(msg){
    // ..
} )
.or( function(err){
    // ..
} );
```

 For the sake of clarity (and for fun!), let's coin yet another term, for a sequence-producing function that comes from ASQ.wrap(..), like coolUtility here. I propose "sequory" ("sequence" + "factory").

Iterable Sequences

The normal paradigm for a sequence is that each step is responsible for completing itself, which is what advances the sequence. Promises work the same way.

The unfortunate part is that sometimes you need external control over a Promise/step, which leads to awkward *capability extraction*.

Consider this Promises example:

```
var domready = new Promise( function(resolve,reject){
    // don't want to put this here, because
    // it belongs logically in another part
    // of the code
    document.addEventListener( "DOMContentLoaded", resolve );
} );

// ..

domready.then( function(){
    // DOM is ready!
} );
```

The capability extraction anti-pattern with Promises looks like this:

```
var ready;

var domready = new Promise( function(resolve,reject){
    // extract the `resolve()` capability
    ready = resolve;
} );

// ..

domready.then( function(){
    // DOM is ready!
} );

// ..

document.addEventListener( "DOMContentLoaded", ready );
```

 This anti-pattern has an awkward code smell, in my opinion, but some developers like it, for reasons I can't grasp.

asynquence offers an inverted sequence type I call iterable sequences, which externalizes the control capability (it's quite useful in use cases like the domready):

```
// note: `domready` here is an iterator that
// controls the sequence
var domready = ASQ.iterable();

// ..

domready.val( function(){
    // DOM is ready
} );

// ..

document.addEventListener( "DOMContentLoaded", domready.next );
```

There's more to iterable sequences than what we see in this scenario. We'll come back to them in Appendix B.

Running Generators

In Chapter 4 we derived a utility called run(..), which can run generators to completion, listening for yielded Promises and using them to asynchronously resume the generator. *asynquence* has just such a utility built in, called runner(..).

Let's first set up some helpers for illustration:

```
function doublePr(x) {
    return new Promise( function(resolve,reject){
        setTimeout( function(){
            resolve( x * 2 );
        }, 100 );
    } );
}

function doubleSeq(x) {
    return ASQ( function(done){
        setTimeout( function(){
            done( x * 2 )
        }, 100 );
    } );
}
```

Now we can use `runner(..)` as a step in the middle of a sequence:

```
ASQ( 10, 11 )
.runner( function*(token){
    var x = token.messages[0] + token.messages[1];

    // yield a real promise
    x = yield doublePr( x );

    // yield a sequence
    x = yield doubleSeq( x );

    return x;
} )
.val( function(msg){
    console.log( msg );         // 84
} );
```

Wrapped Generators

You can also create a self-packaged generator—that is, a normal function that runs your specified generator and returns a sequence for its completion—by `ASQ.wrap(..)`ing it:

```
var foo = ASQ.wrap( function*(token){
    var x = token.messages[0] + token.messages[1];

    // yield a real promise
    x = yield doublePr( x );

    // yield a sequence
    x = yield doubleSeq( x );

    return x;
}, { gen: true } );

// ..

foo( 8, 9 )
.val( function(msg){
    console.log( msg );         // 68
} );
```

There's a lot more awesome that `runner(..)` is capable of, but we'll come back to that in Appendix B.

Review

asynquence is a simple abstraction—a sequence is a series of (async) steps—on top of Promises, aimed at making working with various asynchronous patterns much easier, without compromising capability.

There are other goodies in the *asynquence* core API and its contrib plug-ins beyond what we saw in this appendix, but we'll leave checking out the rest of the capabilities as an exercise for the reader.

You've now seen the essence and spirit of *asynquence*. The key takeaway is that a sequence is comprised of steps, and those steps can be any of dozens of different variations on Promises, or they can be a generator-run, or... The choice is up to you; you have the freedom to weave together whatever async flow control logic is appropriate for your tasks. No more library switching to catch different async patterns.

If these *asynquence* snippets have made sense to you, you're now pretty well up to speed on the library; it doesn't take that much to learn, actually!

If you're still a little fuzzy on how it works (or why!), you'll want to spend a little more time examining the previous examples and playing around with *asynquence* before going on to Appendix B, where we will push *asynquence* into several more advanced and powerful async patterns.

Advanced Async Patterns

Appendix A introduced the *asynquence* library for sequence-oriented async flow control, primarily based on Promises and generators.

Now we'll explore other advanced asynchronous patterns built on top of that existing understanding and functionality, and see how *asynquence* makes those sophisticated async techniques easy to mix and match in our programs without needing lots of separate libraries.

Iterable Sequences

We introduced *asynquence*'s iterable sequences in the previous appendix, but we want to revisit them in more detail.

To refresh, recall:

```
var domready = ASQ.iterable();

// ..

domready.val( function(){
    // DOM is ready
} );

// ..

document.addEventListener( "DOMContentLoaded", domready.next );
```

Now, let's define a sequence of multiple steps as an iterable sequence:

```
var steps = ASQ.iterable();

steps
.then( function STEP1(x){
    return x * 2;
} )
.steps( function STEP2(x){
    return x + 3;
} )
.steps( function STEP3(x){
    return x * 4;
} );

steps.next( 8 ).value;   // 16
steps.next( 16 ).value;  // 19
steps.next( 19 ).value;  // 76
steps.next().done;       // true
```

As you can see, an iterable sequence is a standard-compliant iterator (see Chapter 4). So, it can be iterated with an ES6 for..of loop, just like a generator (or any other iterable) can:

```
var steps = ASQ.iterable();

steps
.then( function STEP1(){ return 2; } )
.then( function STEP2(){ return 4; } )
.then( function STEP3(){ return 6; } )
.then( function STEP4(){ return 8; } )
.then( function STEP5(){ return 10; } );

for (var v of steps) {
    console.log( v );
}
// 2 4 6 8 10
```

Beyond the event triggering example shown in Appendix A, iterable sequences are interesting because in essence they can be seen as a stand-in for generators or Promise chains, but with even more flexibility.

Consider a multiple Ajax request example—we've seen the same scenario in Chapters 3 and 4, both as a Promise chain and as a generator, respectively—expressed as an iterable sequence:

```
// sequence-aware ajax
var request = ASQ.wrap( ajax );
```

```
ASQ( "http://some.url.1" )
.runner(
    ASQ.iterable()

    .then( function STEP1(token){
        var url = token.messages[0];
        return request( url );
    } )

    .then( function STEP2(resp){
        return ASQ().gate(
            request( "http://some.url.2/?v=" + resp ),
            request( "http://some.url.3/?v=" + resp )
        );
    } )

    .then( function STEP3(r1,r2){ return r1 + r2; } )
)
.val( function(msg){
    console.log( msg );
} );
```

The iterable sequence expresses a sequential series of (sync or async) steps that looks awfully similar to a Promise chain—in other words, it's much cleaner looking than just plain nested callbacks, but not quite as nice as the yield-based sequential syntax of generators.

But we pass the iterable sequence into ASQ#runner(..), which runs it to completion as it would a generator. The fact that an iterable sequence behaves essentially the same as a generator is notable for a couple of reasons.

First, iterable sequences are kind of a pre-ES6 equivalent to a certain subset of ES6 generators, which means you can either author them directly (to run anywhere), or you can author ES6 generators and transpile/convert them to iterable sequences (or Promise chains for that matter!).

Thinking of an async-run-to-completion generator as just syntactic sugar for a Promise chain is an important recognition of their iso-morphic relationship.

Before we move on, we should note that the previous snippet could have been expressed in *asynquence* as:

```
ASQ( "http://some.url.1" )
.seq( /*STEP 1*/ request )
.seq( function STEP2(resp){
    return ASQ().gate(
```

```
            request( "http://some.url.2/?v=" + resp ),
            request( "http://some.url.3/?v=" + resp )
        );
    } )
    .val( function STEP3(r1,r2){ return r1 + r2; } )
    .val( function(msg){
        console.log( msg );
    } );
```

Moreover, step 2 could have even been expressed as:

```
.gate(
    function STEP2a(done,resp) {
        request( "http://some.url.2/?v=" + resp )
        .pipe( done );
    },
    function STEP2b(done,resp) {
        request( "http://some.url.3/?v=" + resp )
        .pipe( done );
    }
)
```

So, why would we go to the trouble of expressing our flow control as an iterable sequence in a ASQ#runner(..) step, when it seems like a simpler/flatter *asynquence* chain does the job well?

Because the iterable sequence form has an important trick up its sleeve that gives us more capability. Read on.

Extending Iterable Sequences

Generators, normal *asynquence* sequences, and Promise chains are all *eagerly evaluated*—whatever flow control is expressed initially *is* the fixed flow that will be followed.

However, iterable sequences are *lazily evaluated*, which means that during execution of the iterable sequence, you can extend the sequence with more steps if desired.

 You can only append to the end of an iterable sequence, not inject into the middle of the sequence.

Let's first look at a simpler (synchronous) example of that capability to get familiar with it:

```
function double(x) {
    x *= 2;

    // should we keep extending?
    if (x < 500) {
        isq.then( double );
    }

    return x;
}

// setup single-step iterable sequence
var isq = ASQ.iterable().then( double );

for (var v = 10, ret;
    (ret = isq.next( v )) && !ret.done;
) {
    v = ret.value;
    console.log( v );
}
```

The iterable sequence starts out with only one defined step (isq.then(double)), but the sequence keeps extending itself under certain conditions (x < 500). Both *asynquence* sequences and Promise chains technically *can* do something similar, but we'll see in a little bit why their capability is insufficient.

Though this example is rather trivial and could otherwise be expressed with a while loop in a generator, we'll consider more sophisticated cases.

For instance, you could examine the response from an Ajax request and if it indicates that more data is needed, conditionally insert more steps into the iterable sequence to make the additional request(s). Or you could conditionally add a value-formatting step to the end of your Ajax handling.

Consider:

```
var steps = ASQ.iterable()

.then( function STEP1(token){
    var url = token.messages[0].url;

    // was an additional formatting step provided?
    if (token.messages[0].format) {
        steps.then( token.messages[0].format );
    }

    return request( url );
```

```
    } )

    .then( function STEP2(resp){
        // add another Ajax request to the sequence?
        if (/x1/.test( resp )) {
            steps.then( function STEP5(text){
                return request(
                    "http://some.url.4/?v=" + text
                );
            } );
        }

        return ASQ().gate(
            request( "http://some.url.2/?v=" + resp ),
            request( "http://some.url.3/?v=" + resp )
        );
    } )

    .then( function STEP3(r1,r2){ return r1 + r2; } );
```

You can see two different places where we conditionally extend
steps with steps.then(..). And to run this steps iterable
sequence, we just wire it into our main program flow with an *asynquence* sequence (called main here) using ASQ#runner(..):

```
var main = ASQ( {
    url: "http://some.url.1",
    format: function STEP4(text){
        return text.toUpperCase();
    }
} )
.runner( steps )
.val( function(msg){
    console.log( msg );
} );
```

Can the flexibility (conditional behavior) of the steps iterable
sequence be expressed with a generator? Kind of, but we have to
rearrange the logic in a slightly awkward way:

```
function *steps(token) {
    // STEP 1
    var resp = yield request( token.messages[0].url );

    // STEP 2
    var rvals = yield ASQ().gate(
        request( "http://some.url.2/?v=" + resp ),
        request( "http://some.url.3/?v=" + resp )
    );

    // STEP 3
```

```
    var text = rvals[0] + rvals[1];

    // STEP 4
    // was an additional formatting step provided?
    if (token.messages[0].format) {
        text = yield token.messages[0].format( text );
    }

    // STEP 5
    // need another Ajax request added to the sequence?
    if (/foobar/.test( resp )) {
        text = yield request(
            "http://some.url.4/?v=" + text
        );
    }

    return text;
}

// note: `*steps()` can be run by the same `ASQ` sequence
// as `steps` was previously
```

Setting aside the already identified benefits of the sequential, synchronous-looking syntax of generators (see Chapter 4), the steps logic had to be reordered in the *steps() generator form, to fake the dynamicism of the extendable iterable sequence steps.

What about expressing the functionality with Promises or sequences, though? You *can* do something like this:

```
var steps = something( .. )
.then( .. )
.then( function(..){
    // ..

    // extending the chain, right?
    steps = steps.then( .. );

    // ..
})
.then( .. );
```

The problem is subtle but important to grasp. So, consider trying to wire up our steps Promise chain into our main program flow—this time expressed with Promises instead of *asynquence*:

```
var main = Promise.resolve( {
    url: "http://some.url.1",
    format: function STEP4(text){
        return text.toUpperCase();
    }
```

```
} )
.then( function(..){
    return steps;           // hint!
} )
.val( function(msg){
    console.log( msg );
} );
```

Can you spot the problem now? Look closely!

There's a race condition for sequence steps ordering. When you `return` `steps`, at that moment `steps` *might* be the originally defined Promise chain, or it might now point to the extended Promise chain via the `steps = steps.then(..)` call, depending on what order things happen.

Here are the two possible outcomes:

- If `steps` is still the original Promise chain, once it's later "extended" by `steps = steps.then(..)`, that extended promise on the end of the chain is *not* considered by the `main` flow, as it's already tapped the `steps` chain. This is the unfortunately limiting *eager evaluation*.

- If `steps` is already the extended Promise chain, it works as we expect in that the extended promise is what `main` taps.

Other than the obvious fact that a race condition is intolerable, the first case is the concern; it illustrates *eager evaluation* of the Promise chain. By contrast, we easily extended the iterable sequence without such issues, because iterable sequences are *lazily evaluated*.

The more dynamic you need your flow control, the more iterable sequences will shine.

 Check out more information and examples of iterable sequences on the *asynquence* site (*https://github.com/getify/asynquence/blob/ master/README.md#iterable-sequences*).

Event Reactive

It should be obvious from (at least!) Chapter 3 that Promises are a very powerful tool in your async toolbox. But one thing that's clearly lacking is in their capability to handle streams of events, as a

Promise can only be resolved once. And frankly, this exact same weakness is true of plain *asynquence* sequences as well.

Consider a scenario where you want to fire off a series of steps every time a certain event is fired. A single Promise or sequence cannot represent all occurrences of that event. So, you have to create a whole new Promise chain (or sequence) for *each* event occurrence, such as:

```
listener.on( "foobar", function(data){

    // create a new event handling promise chain
    new Promise( function(resolve,reject){
        // ..
    } )
    .then( .. )
    .then( .. );

} );
```

The base functionality we need is present in this approach, but it's far from a desirable way to express our intended logic. There are two separate capabilities conflated in this paradigm: the event listening, and responding to the event; separation of concerns would implore us to separate out these capabilities.

The carefully observant reader will see this problem as somewhat symmetrical to the problems we detailed with callbacks in Chapter 2; it's kind of an inversion of control problem.

Imagine uninverting this paradigm, like so:

```
var observable = listener.on( "foobar" );

// later
observable
.then( .. )
.then( .. );

// elsewhere
observable
.then( .. )
.then( .. );
```

The `observable` value is not exactly a Promise, but you can *observe* it much like you can observe a Promise, so it's closely related. In fact, it can be observed many times, and it will send out notifications every time its event ("foobar") occurs.

This pattern I've just illustrated is a *massive simplification* of the concepts and motivations behind reactive programming (RP), which has been implemented/expounded upon by several great projects and languages. A variation on RP is functional reactive programming (FRP), which refers to applying functional programming techniques (immutability, referential integrity, etc.) to streams of data. "Reactive" refers to spreading this functionality out over time in response to events. The interested reader should consider studying "Reactive Observables" in the fantastic "Reactive Extensions" library ("RxJS" for JavaScript) by Microsoft (*http://reactive-extensions.github.io/RxJS/*); it's much more sophisticated and powerful than I've just shown. Also, Andre Staltz has an excellent write-up (*https://gist.github.com/staltz/868e7e9bc2a7b8c1f754*) that pragmatically lays out RP in concrete examples.

ES7 Observables

At the time of this writing, there's an early ES7 proposal for a new data type called "Observable" (*https://github.com/jhusain/asyncgenerator#introducing-observable*), which in spirit is similar to what we've laid out here, but is definitely more sophisticated.

The notion of this kind of Observable is that the way you "subscribe" to the events from a stream is to pass in a generator—actually the iterator is the interested party—whose next(..) method will be called for each event.

You could imagine it sort of like this:

```
// `someEventStream` is a stream of events, like from
// mouse clicks, and the like.

var observer = new Observer( someEventStream, function*(){
    while (var evt = yield) {
        console.log( evt );
    }
} );
```

The generator you pass in will yield pause the while loop waiting for the next event. The iterator attached to the generator instance will have its next(..) called each time someEventStream has a new

---

event published, and so that event data will resume your generator/iterator with the `evt` data.

In the subscription to events functionality here, it's the iterator part that matters, not the generator. So conceptually you could pass in practically any iterable, including `ASQ.iterable()` iterable sequences.

Interestingly, there are also proposed adapters to make it easy to construct Observables from certain types of streams, such as `fromEvent(..)` for DOM events. If you look at a suggested implementation of `fromEvent(..)` in the earlier linked ES7 proposal, it looks an awful lot like the `ASQ.react(..)` we'll see in the next section.

Of course, these are all early proposals, so what shakes out may very well look/behave differently than shown here. But it's exciting to see the early alignments of concepts across different libraries and language proposals!

Reactive Sequences

With that crazy brief summary of Observables (and F/RP) as our inspiration and motivation, I will now illustrate an adaptation of a small subset of "Reactive Observables," which I call "Reactive Sequences."

First, let's start with how to create an Observable, using an *asynquence* plug-in utility called `react(..)`:

```
var observable = ASQ.react( function setup(next){
    listener.on( "foobar", next );
} );
```

Now, let's see how to define a sequence that "reacts"—in F/RP, this is typically called "subscribing"—to that `observable`:

```
observable
.seq( .. )
.then( .. )
.val( .. );
```

So, you just define the sequence by chaining off the Observable. That's easy, huh?

In F/RP, the stream of events typically channels through a set of functional transforms, like `scan(..)`, `map(..)`, `reduce(..)`, and so on. With reactive sequences, each event channels through a new instance of the sequence. Let's look at a more concrete example:

```
ASQ.react( function setup(next){
    document.getElementById( "mybtn" )
    .addEventListener( "click", next, false );
} )
.seq( function(evt){
    var btnID = evt.target.id;
    return request(
        "http://some.url.1/?id=" + btnID
    );
} )
.val( function(text){
    console.log( text );
} );
```

The "reactive" portion of the reactive sequence comes from assigning one or more event handlers to invoke the event trigger (calling next(..)).

The "sequence" portion of the reactive sequence is exactly like the sequences we've already explored: each step can be whatever asynchronous technique makes sense, from continuation callback to Promise to generator.

Once you set up a reactive sequence, it will continue to initiate instances of the sequence as long as the events keep firing. If you want to stop a reactive sequence, you can call stop().

If a reactive sequence is stop()ped, you likely want the event handler(s) to be unregistered as well; you can register a teardown handler for this purpose:

```
var sq = ASQ.react( function setup(next,registerTeardown){
    var btn = document.getElementById( "mybtn" );

    btn.addEventListener( "click", next, false );

    // will be called once `sq.stop()` is called
    registerTeardown( function(){
        btn.removeEventListener( "click", next, false );
    } );
} )
.seq( .. )
.then( .. )
.val( .. );

// later
sq.stop();
```

The this binding reference inside the setup(..) handler is the same sq reactive sequence, so you can use the this reference to add to the reactive sequence definition, call methods like stop(), and so on.

Here's an example from the Node.js world, using reactive sequences to handle incoming HTTP requests:

```
var server = http.createServer();
server.listen(8000);

// reactive observer
var request = ASQ.react( function setup(next,registerTeardown){
    server.addListener( "request", next );
    server.addListener( "close", this.stop );

    registerTeardown( function(){
        server.removeListener( "request", next );
        server.removeListener( "close", request.stop );
    } );
});

// respond to requests
request
.seq( pullFromDatabase )
.val( function(data,res){
    res.end( data );
} );

// node teardown
process.on( "SIGINT", request.stop );
```

The next(..) trigger can also adapt to node streams easily, using onStream(..) and unStream(..):

```
ASQ.react( function setup(next){
    var fstream = fs.createReadStream( "/some/file" );

    // pipe the stream's "data" event to `next(..)`
    next.onStream( fstream );

    // listen for the end of the stream
    fstream.on( "end", function(){
        next.unStream( fstream );
    } );
} )
.seq( .. )
.then( .. )
.val( .. );
```

You can also use sequence combinations to compose multiple reactive sequence streams:

```
var sq1 = ASQ.react( .. ).seq( .. ).then( .. );
var sq2 = ASQ.react( .. ).seq( .. ).then( .. );

var sq3 = ASQ.react(..)
.gate(
    sq1,
    sq2
)
.then( .. );
```

The main takeaway is that `ASQ.react(..)` is a lightweight adaptation of F/RP concepts, enabling the wiring of an event stream to a sequence, hence the term "reactive sequence." Reactive sequences are generally capable enough for basic reactive uses.

 Here's an example of using `ASQ.react(..)` in managing UI state (*http://jsbin.com/rozipaki/6/ edit?js,output*), and another example of handling HTTP request/response streams with `ASQ.react(..)` (*https://gist.github.com/getify/ bba5ec0de9d6047b720e*).

Generator Coroutine

Hopefully Chapter 4 helped you get pretty familiar with ES6 generators. In particular, we want to revisit the "Generator Concurrency" discussion, and push it even further.

We imagined a `runAll(..)` utility that could take two or more generators and run them concurrently, letting them cooperatively `yield` control from one to the next, with optional message passing.

In addition to being able to run a single generator to completion, the `ASQ#runner(..)` we discussed in Appendix A is a similar implementation of the concepts of `runAll(..)`, which can run multiple generators concurrently to completion.

So let's see how we can implement the concurrent Ajax scenario from Chapter 4:

```
ASQ(
    "http://some.url.2"
)
.runner(
```

```
function*(token){
    // transfer control
    yield token;

    var url1 = token.messages[0]; // "http://some.url.1"

    // clear out messages to start fresh
    token.messages = [];

    var p1 = request( url1 );

    // transfer control
    yield token;

    token.messages.push( yield p1 );
},
function*(token){
    var url2 = token.messages[0]; // "http://some.url.2"

    // message pass and transfer control
    token.messages[0] = "http://some.url.1";
    yield token;

    var p2 = request( url2 );

    // transfer control
    yield token;

    token.messages.push( yield p2 );

    // pass along results to next sequence step
    return token.messages;
}
)
.val( function(res){
    // `res[0]` comes from "http://some.url.1"
    // `res[1]` comes from "http://some.url.2"
} );
```

The main differences between ASQ#runner(..) and runAll(..) are
as follows:

- Each generator (coroutine) is provided an argument we call
  token, which is the special value to yield when you want to
  explicitly transfer control to the next coroutine.

- token.messages is an array that holds any messages passed in
  from the previous sequence step. It's also a data structure that
  you can use to share messages between coroutines.

- yielding a Promise (or sequence) value does not transfer control, but instead pauses the coroutine processing until that value is ready.

- The last `returned` or `yielded` value from the coroutine processing run will be forward passed to the next step in the sequence.

It's also easy to layer helpers on top of the base `ASQ#runner(..)` functionality to suit different uses.

State Machines

One example that may be familiar to many programmers is state machines. You can, with the help of a simple cosmetic utility, create an easy-to-express state machine processor.

Let's imagine such a utility. We'll call it `state(..)`, and will pass it two arguments: a state value and a generator that handles that state. `state(..)` will do the dirty work of creating and returning an adapter generator to pass to `ASQ#runner(..)`.

Consider:

```
function state(val,handler) {
    // make a coroutine handler for this state
    return function*(token) {
        // state transition handler
        function transition(to) {
            token.messages[0] = to;
        }

        // set initial state (if none set yet)
        if (token.messages.length < 1) {
            token.messages[0] = val;
        }

        // keep going until final state (false) is reached
        while (token.messages[0] !== false) {
            // current state matches this handler?
            if (token.messages[0] === val) {
                // delegate to state handler
                yield *handler( transition );
            }

            // transfer control to another state handler?
            if (token.messages[0] !== false) {
                yield token;
            }
        }
    }
}
```

```
    };
}
```

If you look closely, you'll see that `state(..)` returns back a genera-tor that accepts a `token`, and then it sets up a `while` loop that will run until the state machine reaches its final state (which we arbitrar-ily pick as the `false` value); that's exactly the kind of generator we want to pass to `ASQ#runner(..)`!

We also arbitrarily reserve the `token.messages[0]` slot as the place where the current state of our state machine will be tracked, which means we can even seed the initial state as the value passed in from the previous step in the sequence.

How do we use the `state(..)` helper along with `ASQ#runner(..)`?

```
var prevState;

ASQ(
    /* optional: initial state value */
    2
)
// run our state machine
// transitions: 2 -> 3 -> 1 -> 3 -> false
.runner(
    // state `1` handler
    state( 1, function *stateOne(transition){
        console.log( "in state 1" );

        prevState = 1;
        yield transition( 3 );  // goto state `3`
    } ),

    // state `2` handler
    state( 2, function *stateTwo(transition){
        console.log( "in state 2" );

        prevState = 2;
        yield transition( 3 );  // goto state `3`
    } ),

    // state `3` handler
    state( 3, function *stateThree(transition){
        console.log( "in state 3" );

        if (prevState === 2) {
            prevState = 3;
            yield transition( 1 ); // goto state `1`
        }
        // all done!
```

```
        else {
            yield "That's all folks!";

            prevState = 3;
            yield transition( false ); // terminal state
        }
    } )
)
// state machine complete, so move on
.val( function(msg){
    console.log( msg ); // That's all folks!
} );
```

It's important to note that the *stateOne(..), *stateTwo(..), and
*stateThree(..) generators themselves are reinvoked each time
that state is entered, and they finish when you transition(..) to
another value. While not shown here, of course these state generator
handlers can be asynchronously paused by yielding Promises/
sequences/thunks.

The underneath hidden generators produced by the state(..)
helper and actually passed to ASQ#runner(..) are the ones that continue to run concurrently for the length of the state machine, and
each of them handles cooperatively yielding control to the next,
and so on.

 See this "ping pong" example (*http://jsbin.com/
qutabu/1/edit?js,output*) for more illustration of
using cooperative concurrency with generators
driven by ASQ#runner(..).

Communicating Sequential Processes (CSP)

Communicating Sequential Processes (CSP) was first described by
C. A. R. Hoare in a 1978 academic paper (*http://dl.acm.org/cita
tion.cfm?doid=359576.359585*), and later covered in a 1985 book of
the same name (*http://www.usingcsp.com/*). CSP describes a formal
method for concurrent "processes" to interact (communicate) during processing.

You may recall that we examined concurrent "processes" back in
Chapter 1, so our exploration of CSP here will build upon that
understanding.

Like most great concepts in computer science, CSP is heavily steeped in academic formalism, expressed as a process algebra. However, I suspect symbolic algebra theorems won't make much practical difference to the reader, so we will want to find some other way of wrapping our brains around CSP.

I will leave much of the formal description and proof of CSP to Hoare's work, and the many other fantastic writings since. Instead, we will try to just briefly explain the idea of CSP in as unacademic and hopefully intuitively understandable a way as possible.

Message Passing

The core principle in CSP is that all communication/interaction between otherwise independent processes must be through formal message passing. Perhaps counter to your expectations, CSP message passing is described as a synchronous action, where the sender process and the receiver process have to mutually be ready for the message to be passed.

How could such synchronous messaging possibly be related to asynchronous programming in JavaScript?

The concreteness of relationship comes from the nature of how ES6 generators are used to produce synchronous-looking actions that under the covers can indeed either be synchronous or (more likely) asynchronous.

In other words, two or more concurrently running generators can appear to synchronously message each other while preserving the fundamental asynchrony of the system because each generator's code is paused (blocked), waiting on resumption of an asynchronous action.

How does this work?

Imagine a generator ("process") called "A" that wants to send a message to generator "B." First, "A" yields the message (thus pausing "A") to be sent to "B." When "B" is ready and takes the message, "A" is then resumed (unblocked).

Symmetrically, imagine a generator "A" that wants a message *from* "B." "A" yields its request (thus pausing "A") for the message from "B," and once "B" sends a message, "A" takes the message and is resumed.

One of the more popular expressions of this CSP message passing theory comes from ClojureScript's *core.async* library, and also from the *go* language. These takes on CSP embody the described communication semantics in a conduit that is opened between processes called a *channel*.

 The term *channel* is used in part because there are modes in which more than one value can be sent at once into the buffer of the channel; this is similar to what you may think of as a stream. We won't go into depth about it here, but it can be a very powerful technique for managing streams of data.

In the simplest notion of CSP, a channel that we create between "A" and "B" would have a method called `take(..)` for blocking to receive a value, and a method called `put(..)` for blocking to send a value.

This might look like:

```
var ch = channel();

function *foo() {
    var msg = yield take( ch );

    console.log( msg );
}

function *bar() {
    yield put( ch, "Hello World" );

    console.log( "message sent" );
}

run( foo );
run( bar );
// Hello World
// "message sent"
```

Compare this structured, synchronous(-looking) message passing interaction to the informal and unstructured message sharing that `ASQ#runner(..)` provides through the `token.messages` array and cooperative `yield`ing. In essence, `yield put(..)` is a single operation that both sends the value and pauses execution to transfer control, whereas in earlier examples we did those as separate steps.

Moreover, CSP stresses that you don't really explicitly transfer control, but rather design your concurrent routines to block expecting either a value received from the channel, or to block expecting to try to send a message on the channel. The blocking around receiving or sending messages is how you coordinate sequencing of behavior between the coroutines.

 Fair warning: this pattern is very powerful but it's also a little mind twisting to get used to at first. You will want to practice this a bit to get used to this new way of thinking about coordinating your concurrency.

There are several great libraries that have implemented this flavor of CSP in JavaScript, most notably js-csp (*https://github.com/ubolon ton/js-csp*), which James Long (*http://twitter.com/jlongster*) forked (*https://github.com/jlongster/js-csp*) and has written extensively about (*http://jlongster.com/Taming-the-Asynchronous-Beast-with-CSP-in-JavaScript*). Also, it cannot be stressed enough how amazing the many writings of David Nolen (*http://twitter.com/swannodette*) are on the topic of adapting ClojureScript's go-style core.async CSP into JS generators (*http://swannodette.github.io/2013/08/24/es6-generators-and-csp/*).

asynquence CSP emulation

Because we've been discussing async patterns here in the context of my *asynquence* library, you might be interested to see that we can fairly easily add an emulation layer on top of ASQ#runner(..) generator handling as a nearly perfect porting of the CSP API and behavior. This emulation layer ships as an optional part of the "asynquence-contrib" package alongside *asynquence*.

Very similar to the state(..) helper from earlier, ASQ.csp.go(..) takes a generator—in go/core.async terms, it's known as a goroutine —and adapts it to use with ASQ#runner(..) by returning a new generator.

Instead of being passed a token, your goroutine receives an initially created channel (ch) that all goroutines in this run will share. You can create more channels (which is often quite helpful!) with ASQ.csp.chan(..).

In CSP, we model all asynchrony in terms of blocking on channel messages, rather than blocking waiting for a Promise/sequence/thunk to complete.

So, instead of yielding the Promise returned from request(..), request(..) should return a channel that you take(..) a value from. In other words, a single-value channel is roughly equivalent in this context/usage to a Promise/sequence.

Let's first make a channel-aware version of request(..):

```
function request(url) {
    var ch = ASQ.csp.channel();
    ajax( url ).then( function(content){
        // `putAsync(..)` is a version of `put(..)` that
        // can be used outside of a generator. It returns
        // a promise for the operation's completion. We
        // don't use that promise here, but we could if
        // we needed to be notified when the value had
        // been `take(..)`n.
        ASQ.csp.putAsync( ch, content );
    } );
    return ch;
}
```

From Chapter 3, "promisory" is a Promise-producing utility, "thunkory" from Chapter 4 is a thunk-producing utility, and finally, in Appendix A we invented "sequory" for a sequence-producing utility.

Naturally, we need to coin a symmetric term here for a channel-producing utility. So let's unsurprisingly call it a "chanory" ("channel" + "factory"). As an exercise for the reader, try your hand at defining a channelify(..) utility similar to Promise.wrap(..)/promisify(..) (Chapter 3), thunkify(..) (Chapter 4), and ASQ.wrap(..) (Appendix A).

Now consider the concurrent Ajax example using *asynquence*-flavored CSP:

```
ASQ()
.runner(
    ASQ.csp.go( function*(ch){
        yield ASQ.csp.put( ch, "http://some.url.2" );

        var url1 = yield ASQ.csp.take( ch );
        // "http://some.url.1"

        var res1 = yield ASQ.csp.take( request( url1 ) );
```

```
            yield ASQ.csp.put( ch, res1 );
        } ),
        ASQ.csp.go( function*(ch){
            var url2 = yield ASQ.csp.take( ch );
            // "http://some.url.2"

            yield ASQ.csp.put( ch, "http://some.url.1" );

            var res2 = yield ASQ.csp.take( request( url2 ) );
            var res1 = yield ASQ.csp.take( ch );

            // pass along results to next sequence step
            ch.buffer_size = 2;
            ASQ.csp.put( ch, res1 );
            ASQ.csp.put( ch, res2 );
        } )
    )
    .val( function(res1,res2){
        // `res1` comes from "http://some.url.1"
        // `res2` comes from "http://some.url.2"
    } );
```

The message passing that trades the URL strings between the two goroutines is pretty straightforward. The first goroutine makes an Ajax request to the first URL, and that response is put onto the ch channel. The second goroutine makes an Ajax request to the second URL, then gets the first response res1 off the ch channel. At that point, both responses res1 and res2 are completed and ready.

If there are any remaining values in the ch channel at the end of the goroutine run, they will be passed along to the next step in the sequence. So, to pass out message(s) from the final goroutine, put(..) them into ch. As shown, to avoid the blocking of those final put(..)s, we switch ch into buffering mode by setting its buffer_size to 2 (default: 0).

 See many more examples of using *asynquence-*flavored CSP on this gist (*https://gist.github.com/getify/e0d04f1f5aa24b1947ae*).

Review

Promises and generators provide the foundational building blocks upon which we can build much more sophisticated and capable asynchrony.

asynquence has utilities for implementing iterable sequences, reactive sequences ("Observables"), concurrent coroutines, and even CSP goroutines.

Those patterns, combined with the continuation-callback and Promise capabilities, give *asynquence* a powerful mix of different asynchronous functionalities, all integrated in one clean async flow control abstraction: the sequence.

Acknowledgments

I have many people to thank for making this book title and the overall series happen.

First, I must thank my wife Christen Simpson, and my two kids Ethan and Emily, for putting up with Dad always pecking away at the computer. Even when not writing books, my obsession with JavaScript glues my eyes to the screen far more than it should. That time I borrow from my family is the reason these books can so deeply and completely explain JavaScript to you, the reader. I owe my family everything.

I'd like to thank my editors at O'Reilly, namely Simon St.Laurent and Brian MacDonald, as well as the rest of the editorial and marketing staff. They are fantastic to work with, and have been especially accommodating during this experiment into open source book writing, editing, and production.

Thank you to the many folks who have participated in making this book series better by providing editorial suggestions and corrections, including Shelley Powers, Tim Ferro, Evan Borden, Forrest L. Norvell, Jennifer Davis, Jesse Harlin, Kris Kowal, Rick Waldron, Jordan Harband, and many others. A big thank you to Jake Archibald for writing the foreword for this title.

Thank you to the countless folks in the community, including members of the TC39 committee, who have shared so much knowledge with the rest of us, and especially tolerated my incessant questions and explorations with patience and detailed answers. John-David

Dalton, Juriy "kangax" Zaytsev, Mathias Bynens, Axel Rauschmayer, Nicholas Zakas, Angus Croll, Reginald Braithwaite, Dave Herman, Brendan Eich, Allen Wirfs-Brock, Bradley Meck, Domenic Denicola, David Walsh, Tim Disney, Peter van der Zee, Andrea Giammarchi, Kit Cambridge, Eric Elliott, and so many others, I can't even scratch the surface.

The *You Don't Know JS* series was born on Kickstarter, so I also wish to thank all of my (nearly) 500 generous backers, without whom this series could not have happened:

Jan Szpila, nokiko, Murali Krishnamoorthy, Ryan Joy, Craig Patchett, pdqtrader, Dale Fukami, ray hatfield, R0drigo Perez [Mx], Dan Petitt, Jack Franklin, Andrew Berry, Brian Grinstead, Rob Sutherland, Sergi Meseguer, Phillip Gourley, Mark Watson, Jeff Carouth, Alfredo Sumaran, Martin Sachse, Marcio Barrios, Dan, AimelyneM, Matt Sullivan, Delnatte Pierre-Antoine, Jake Smith, Eugen Tudorancea, Iris, David Trinh, simonstl, Ray Daly, Uros Gruber, Justin Myers, Shai Zonis, Mom & Dad, Devin Clark, Dennis Palmer, Brian Panahi Johnson, Josh Marshall, Marshall, Dennis Kerr, Matt Steele, Erik Slagter, Sacah, Justin Rainbow, Christian Nilsson, Delapouite, D.Pereira, Nicolas Hoizey, George V. Reilly, Dan Reeves, Bruno Laturner, Chad Jennings, Shane King, Jeremiah Lee Cohick, od3n, Stan Yamane, Marko Vucinic, Jim B, Stephen Collins, Ægir Þorsteinsson, Eric Pederson, Owain, Nathan Smith, Jeanetteurphy, Alexandre ELISÉ, Chris Peterson, Rik Watson, Luke Matthews, Justin Lowery, Morten Nielsen, Vernon Kesner, Chetan Shenoy, Paul Tregoing, Marc Grabanski, Dion Almaer, Andrew Sullivan, Keith Elsass, Tom Burke, Brian Ashenfelter, David Stuart, Karl Swedberg, Graeme, Brandon Hays, John Christopher, Gior, manoj reddy, Chad Smith, Jared Harbour, Minoru TODA, Chris Wigley, Daniel Mee, Mike, Handyface, Alex Jahraus, Carl Furrow, Rob Foulkrod, Max Shishkin, Leigh Penny Jr., Robert Ferguson, Mike van Hoenselaar, Hasse Schougaard, rajan venkataguru, Jeff Adams, Trae Robbins, Rolf Langenhuijzen, Jorge Antunes, Alex Koloskov, Hugh Greenish, Tim Jones, Jose Ochoa, Michael Brennan-White, Naga Harish Muvva, Barkóczi Dávid, Kitt Hodsden, Paul McGraw, Sascha Goldhofer, Andrew Metcalf, Markus Krogh, Michael Mathews, Matt Jared, Juanfran, Georgie Kirschner, Kenny Lee, Ted Zhang, Amit Pahwa, Inbal Sinai, Dan Raine, Schabse Laks, Michael Tervoort, Alexandre Abreu, Alan Joseph Williams, NicolasD, Cindy Wong, Reg Braithwaite, LocalPCGuy, Jon Friskics, Chris Merriman, John Pena, Jacob Katz, Sue Lockwood, Magnus Johansson, Jeremy Crapsey, Grzegorz Pawłowski, nico nuzzaci, Christine Wilks, Hans Bergren, charles montgomery, Ariel בב׳ל-רב Fogel, Ivan Kolev, Daniel Campos, Hugh Wood,

Christian Bradford, Frédéric Harper, Ionuț Dan Popa, Jeff Trimble, Rupert Wood, Trey Carrico, Pancho Lopez, Joël kuijten, Tom A Marra, Jeff Jewiss, Jacob Rios, Paolo Di Stefano, Soledad Penades, Chris Gerber, Andrey Dolganov, Wil Moore III, Thomas Martineau, Kareem, Ben Thouret, Udi Nir, Morgan Laupies, jory carson-burson, Nathan L Smith, Eric Damon Walters, Derry Lozano-Hoyland, Geoffrey Wiseman, mkeehner, KatieK, Scott MacFarlane, Brian LaShomb, Adrien Mas, christopher ross, Ian Littman, Dan Atkinson, Elliot Jobe, Nick Dozier, Peter Wooley, John Hoover, dan, Martin A. Jackson, Héctor Fernando Hurtado, andy ennamorato, Paul Seltmann, Melissa Gore, Dave Pollard, Jack Smith, Philip Da Silva, Guy Israeli, @megalithic, Damian Crawford, Felix Gliesche, April Carter Grant, Heidi, jim tierney, Andrea Giammarchi, Nico Vignola, Don Jones, Chris Hartjes, Alex Howes, john gibbon, David J. Groom, BBox, Yu *Dilys* Sun, Nate Steiner, Brandon Satrom, Brian Wyant, Wesley Hales, Ian Pouncey, Timothy Kevin Oxley, George Terezakis, sanjay raj, Jordan Harband, Marko McLion, Wolfgang Kaufmann, Pascal Peuckert, Dave Nugent, Markus Liebelt, Welling Guzman, Nick Cooley, Daniel Mesquita, Robert Syvarth, Chris Coyier, Rémy Bach, Adam Dougal, Alistair Duggin, David Loidolt, Ed Richer, Brian Chenault, GoldFire Studios, Carles Andrés, Carlos Cabo, Yuya Saito, roberto ricardo, Barnett Klane, Mike Moore, Kevin Marx, Justin Love, Joe Taylor, Paul Dijou, Michael Kohler, Rob Cassie, Mike Tierney, Cody Leroy Lindley, tofuji, Shimon Schwartz, Raymond, Luc De Brouwer, David Hayes, Rhys Brett-Bowen, Dmitry, Aziz Khoury, Dean, Scott Tolinski - Level Up, Clement Boirie, Djordje Lukic, Anton Kotenko, Rafael Corral, Philip Hurwitz, Jonathan Pidgeon, Jason Campbell, Joseph C., SwiftOne, Jan Hohner, Derick Bailey, getify, Daniel Cousineau, Chris Charlton, Eric Turner, David Turner, Joël Galeran, Dharma Vagabond, adam, Dirk van Bergen, dave ♥♫★ furf, Vedran Zakanj, Ryan McAllen, Natalie Patrice Tucker, Eric J. Bivona, Adam Spooner, Aaron Cavano, Kelly Packer, Eric J, Martin Drenovac, Emilis, Michael Pelikan, Scott F. Walter, Josh Freeman, Brandon Hudgeons, vijay chennupati, Bill Glennon, Robin R., Troy Forster, otaku_coder, Brad, Scott, Frederick Ostrander, Adam Brill, Seb Flippence, Michael Anderson, Jacob, Adam Randlett, Standard, Joshua Clanton, Sebastian Kouba, Chris Deck, SwordFire, Hannes Papenberg, Richard Woeber, hnzz, Rob Crowther, Jedidiah Broadbent, Sergey Chernyshev, Jay-Ar Jamon, Ben Combee, luciano bonachela, Mark Tomlinson, Kit Cambridge, Michael Melgares, Jacob Adams, Adrian Bruinhout, Bev Wieber, Scott Puleo, Thomas Herzog, April Leone, Daniel Mizieliński, Kees van Ginkel, Jon Abrams, Erwin Heiser, Avi Laviad, David newell, Jean-Francois Turcot, Niko Roberts, Erik Dana, Charles Neill, Aaron Holmes, Grzegorz Ziółkowski, Nathan Youngman, Timothy, Jacob Mather, Michael Allan, Mohit Seth, Ryan Ewing, Benjamin Van Treese,

Marcelo Santos, Denis Wolf, Phil Keys, Chris Yung, Timo Tijhof, Martin Lekvall, Agendine, Greg Whitworth, Helen Humphrey, Dougal Campbell, Johannes Harth, Bruno Girin, Brian Hough, Darren Newton, Craig McPheat, Olivier Tille, Dennis Roethig, Mathias Bynens, Brendan Stromberger, sundeep, John Meyer, Ron Male, John F Croston III, gigante, Carl Bergenhem, B.J. May, Rebekah Tyler, Ted Foxberry, Jordan Reese, Terry Suitor, afeliz, Tom Kiefer, Darragh Duffy, Kevin Vanderbeken, Andy Pearson, Simon Mac Donald, Abid Din, Chris Joel, Tomas Theunissen, David Dick, Paul Grock, Brandon Wood, John Weis, dgrebb, Nick Jenkins, Chuck Lane, Johnny Megahan, marzsman, Tatu Tamminen, Geoffrey Knauth, Alexander Tarmolov, Jeremy Tymes, Chad Auld, Sean Parmelee, Rob Staenke, Dan Bender, Yannick derwa, Joshua Jones, Geert Plaisier, Tom LeZotte, Christen Simpson, Stefan Bruvik, Justin Falcone, Carlos Santana, Michael Weiss, Pablo Villoslada, Peter deHaan, Dimitris Iliopoulos, seyDoggy, Adam Jordens, Noah Kantrowitz, Amol M, Matthew Winnard, Dirk Ginader, Phinam Bui, David Rapson, Andrew Baxter, Florian Bougel, Michael George, Alban Escalier, Daniel Sellers, Sasha Rudan, John Green, Robert Kowalski, David I. Teixeira (@ditma), Charles Carpenter, Justin Yost, Sam S, Denis Ciccale, Kevin Sheurs, Yannick Croissant, Pau Fracés, Stephen McGowan, Shawn Searcy, Chris Ruppel, Kevin Lamping, Jessica Campbell, Christopher Schmitt, Sablons, Jonathan Reisdorf, Bunni Gek, Teddy Huff, Michael Mullany, Michael Fürstenberg, Carl Henderson, Rick Yoesting, Scott Nichols, Hernán Ciudad, Andrew Maier, Mike Stapp, Jesse Shawl, Sérgio Lopes, jsulak, Shawn Price, Joel Clermont, Chris Ridmann, Sean Timm, Jason Finch, Aiden Montgomery, Elijah Manor, Derek Gathright, Jesse Harlin, Dillon Curry, Courtney Myers, Diego Cadenas, Arne de Bree, João Paulo Dubas, James Taylor, Philipp Kraeutli, Mihai Păun, Sam Gharegozlou, joshjs, Matt Murchison, Eric Windham, Timo Behrmann, Andrew Hall, joshua price, Théophile Villard

This series is being produced in an open source fashion, including editing and production. We owe GitHub a debt of gratitude for making that sort of thing possible for the community!

Thank you again to all the countless folks I didn't name but who I nonetheless owe thanks. May this series be "owned" by all of us and serve to contribute to increasing awareness and understanding of the JavaScript language, to the benefit of all current and future community contributors.

About the Author

Kyle Simpson is an Open Web evangelist from Austin, TX, who's passionate about all things JavaScript. He's an author, workshop trainer, tech speaker, and OSS contributor/leader.

Colophon

The cover font for *Async & Performance* is Interstate. The text font is Adobe Minion Pro; the heading font is Adobe Myriad Condensed; and the code font is Dalton Maag's Ubuntu Mono.

Have it your way.

Get even more for your money.

Join the O'Reilly Community, and register the O'Reilly books you own. It's free, and you'll get:

- $4.99 ebook upgrade offer
- 40% upgrade offer on O'Reilly print books
- Membership discounts on books and events
- Free lifetime updates to ebooks and videos
- Multiple ebook formats, DRM FREE
- Participation in the O'Reilly community
- Newsletters
- Account management
- 100% Satisfaction Guarantee

Signing up is easy:

1. Go to: oreilly.com/go/register
2. Create an O'Reilly login.
3. Provide your address.
4. Register your books.

Note: English-language books only

To order books online:
oreilly.com/store

For questions about products or an order:
orders@oreilly.com

To sign up to get topic-specific email announcements and/or news about upcoming books, conferences, special offers, and new technologies:
elists@oreilly.com

For technical questions about book content:
booktech@oreilly.com

To submit new book proposals to our editors:
proposals@oreilly.com

O'Reilly books are available in multiple DRM-free ebook formats. For more information:
oreilly.com/ebooks

84299642R00166

Made in the USA
San Bernardino, CA
06 August 2018